For Lisa and the three little pigs

"How well Your Majesty's new clothes look. Aren't they becoming!" He heard on all sides, "That pattern, so perfect! Those colors, so suitable! It is a magnificent outfit."

-From Jean Hersholt's translation of
Hans Christian Anderson's
The Emperor's New Clothes

Table of Contents

Preface: How I Got Here

August 29, 2020:

Humor is survival. If you can make people laugh, or even if you laugh easily at the jokes of others, you have a weapon at your disposal more powerful than anything you can purchase. Those who have not simply survived tragedy but flourished in its aftermath understand. My father would always say in challenging times, *if you can't laugh, you'd have to cry*. Yet even in my family, where a macabre sense of humor was more of a feature than a flaw, I knew there were boundaries. We didn't joke about the Holocaust. Death of a family member, yeah; a joke about Hitler, sure; but we all implicitly understood the death of millions demands reverence. That's it, I guess. I was going to list all the sacred cows for which humor was off-limits, but it was only just this one momentous cataclysm. Family, religion, politics, sex, death, illness? It was all fair game. I suppose every family casts off social norms of one kind or another.

Six years ago, my family and I were huddled around my father's deathbed. We had made a heartbreaking decision to cease all medical intervention. Age and disease had turned a once vibrant and inspirational man into a shell of what once was. I considered what remained—gray, wrinkled flesh that could not feel and a pallid, impassive face with eyes no longer capable of expression, even if they could have opened. The hospital's equipment was only prolonging pain. You have to understand, my father was the first love of my life. My parents divorced early in my youth, and dad was the fun one. I loved him for all the reasons you love a parent, but he was much more than that—a renaissance man whose goodness and genius left a legacy spanning decades and continents. My family and I loved this man intensely, and I would argue that few humans deserved to be loved as much as he did.

It was incredibly painful to be in the room as his ventilator was turned off. I didn't know what would follow. I don't think any of us did. COPD had ravaged his respiratory system, and a hospital infection had been his final undoing. With the ventilator off, his body took shallow weakened breaths for a minute or two, and then there were no breaths at all. But his heart continued beating. We listened to the EKG monitor, every beep an act of defiance against his body's inability to take in oxygen. My family's eyes shifted from my father's face to each other's, to the yellow squiggles and numbers of the hospital monitor's display. We all wept quietly, expecting his heart to succumb quickly.

Beep— beep—went the EKG audio.

This painful scene endured. His heart slowed but refused to yield. Emotionally, I began to have misgivings. If he had this much life left in him, surely his doctors must have made a mistake. Intellectually, I knew better. His kidneys and liver were shot, he'd been in a coma for days, and his brain function was gone.

We waited for what seemed an agonizing span of time. But it didn't end. Ten minutes, and then eleven, then twelve, and perhaps even more, I don't remember. His heartbeat became irregular, but still it continued, on and on, until finally, it stopped.

I felt this tiny release. At least this part was over. The sound of sniffs and sobs, intensified, though not so loud we didn't hear.

Beep, went the EKG.

Beep.

I looked up at a device I understood well. It was working perfectly.

Beep.

My father's heart was beating again, though I knew immediately the answer to that aching question.

This was no resurrection—only a physiological reflex, an additional prolonging to one of the most painful moments of my life. My eyes traveled from my father, again to the monitor, which conveyed his body's obstinacy and then to my family's faces. They displayed a combination of shock, confusion and anguish. And then through our tears, there was a nervous giggle which might have been my own. Then another, and then a guffaw of sorts, until I could look around the room and see only smiles.

This is how sacred humor is to my family. For what it's worth, my father had been an entertainer in his younger years, and he placed great value in humor. This had been his final macabre, *dad* joke to the family. His heart beat again for perhaps an additional minute of defiance before its final curtain. Humor is survival. If you're lucky, you understand.

I'm not a terribly religious man, but in reflection, some time after the loss of my dad, I realized his death had taught me something important. Life has a stubbornness, an inviolability, and a sanctity beyond what most of us realize. It neither yields emotionally or physically without great resistance, but when it does, the loss is more palpable than simply having one less human on this planet. Death has immense meaning. Every loss is always more than just a number.

Today we have this new moment in history, the pandemic. I giggled at my own father's deathbed, but I can find no humor in this global tragedy. As of this writing, over 180,000 Americans have died. Worldwide, it won't be long before we reach one million. For *every single* casualty, there is untold grief and pain and loss. Holocaust is a horribly overused term. This is not *the* Holocaust, but it certainly is *a* holocaust.

As of this writing, over half of the world's COVID-19 deaths can be found in four countries: Mexico, India, Brazil, and America. Of these four, America leads the pack. By far. India was destined to experience catastrophe from the pandemic's inception. They simply have too many people in too tight a space. Similarly, Mexico suffers from population density and poverty issues that offer fertile ground to contagious disease, and of course, they border a highly infected country. Brazil is another story. They have substantial poverty, but also substantial resources. They could be doing better, but their president has chosen a deadlier path for his people. The USA, though? American COVID-19 mortality has not been an act of God. Any person with respect for science should be horrified by the American leadership failures of 2020.

As a military pilot, I went to war in the skies over Iraq to defend my country and my fellow citizens, but the great thing about patriotism is that you don't have to take up arms to love your country or even to protect and defend it. Especially here in America. At least for now. Perhaps especially now. Democracy only asks of us that we care.

I'm of a view that Americans don't understand death very well. Some would call this snobbery. Perhaps it is, but if there is any reason to look down upon another, it would be this. Consider that for the last two decades, we have insinuated ourselves into a war story that is well over two thousand years in the making. Now that we've written our own chapters in that book, what have we learned? The next time the news covers the bombing of some Mid-East village, look into the eyes of that person who lost their home and their loved ones, and try to find peace in their eyes. Those who believe that war leads to peace because peace tends to follow war should pray for enlightenment. Loss of life always incurs a cost that must be reconciled. Just ask the mother, father, sister, brother, spouse, or child of anyone killed by another.

I wonder how many people who've judged others and preached about the sanctity of life within the context of abortion—how many of these people have at some time refused to wear a mask to prevent the spread of COVID-19? I know of one person with certainty: our president. If there is any sanctity in life, there must be sanctity in all life. Too few people seem to understand this.

This pandemic isn't in my view a holocaust purely because of the loss of life. Using that criteria, one could label heart disease or cancer or numerous other deadly tragedies a holocaust. No, COVID-19 is a holocaust because so many of us, particularly in America, but certainly elsewhere, have made conscious decisions that the lives of others aren't worth minimal inconvenience and minor discomfort.

What do you do once you realize something so important is badly broken?

A New Reality

Leadership is the answer to how we got here. I bet you can already picture the faces of those who'd disagree—friends, relatives—that jerk on Facebook you haven't gotten around to deleting because you're still hoping she will enlighten you with something or anything relevant. She might quarrel for hours, but we all know that on any day in history up until 2020, any one of us could have made the same exact statement unchallenged. It's always all about leadership.

I used to think that maxim about a captain going down with his ship was stupid. Then I became an airline captain, and I got it. Leaders extend an unspoken covenant to those in their care. There should be consequences when leaders break that covenant. For anyone with a normal psychological profile, the solemn nature of strangers trusting you with their lives cannot be escaped.

Not every leader sees it exactly so. There is, as with many things, a continuum. History has had its fair share of captains that have not gone down with their ships and even a few that have been among the first to abandon their posts. Consider the man at the helm of American leadership and how far he has stretched that continuum. Do you feel betrayed every time you turn on the news?

Donald Trump is an addict. It's shocking, I know, but any time spent easing you into this reality would be wasted. It's only in the context of understanding addiction that the man begins to make any sense. We are fortunate for recent books explaining who the man is and what he does. Honest illumination is the perfect remedy to gas-lighting. But 'why?' is always the most important question to be answered. It's only when we add context to information that we can view anything with a human perspective.

Businesses hire consultants with backgrounds like mine to identify problems and find solutions— often to answer *why*? At first, I didn't believe a consultant model could apply so readily to our nation. Turns out it can. This book though? You may already be wondering if it's going to go according to plan. Who said anything about a plan?

You and I have a journey ahead of us, and I think you should know a few things about me before things get too.... Well, too much of whatever it is we have ahead of us. I've never written a book establishing the American president as an addict, but then again, neither has anyone else. I have done a lot of other things with expertise and success. I spent 11 years as a pilot and officer in the US Air Force, commanding strike force packages of up to 100 aircrew and building and then running the quality improvement program for a squadron of over 500. I was an adjunct business professor in Daniel Webster College's MBA program. I have an engineering degree from MIT and an MBA from RPI. I founded three businesses and can list among my inventions a new kind of helicopter, a new kind of high-performance personal submarine that I test piloted myself, an underwater/outer space life support system, and several novel recreational simulators. I've fought in Operation Desert Storm, and I am currently a 737 captain at a major US airline.

If you have been by chance one of my hundreds of thousands of passengers, you'd have been informed regarding what was happening and what was going to happen your entire flight. On those unavoidable occasions when I've arrived hours late, I'm used to seeing my passengers deplane with sincere gratitude and smiles. I think most of us appreciate the truth and loathe bullshit. That's the only way I know how to fly. I'll do everything I can to get us to our destination with your gratitude and maybe even a few grins, because if you can't laugh....

We are all in this together. The distressed state of our nation drives my sense of urgency. The president is an addict, and we all need to understand the problem because addiction, chemical or otherwise, can be an incredibly destructive disease. One needs only to turn on the news to understand. But Trump's addiction, though fascinating, is a fraction of the story. If that's all you're here for, simply skip ahead. Or find a recovering addict or alcoholic and ask them if Donald Trump is an addict. They may give you a puzzled look for a moment, but there's a good chance they'll eventually say something like, "You know.... He sure acts like one." Addicts know addicts.

Big things need to be done, and big things need to be fixed. Most of us know this, can feel it in our bones, except that odd vocal minority who can look at the lives lost, jobs gone, the destruction of our economy, and even see the fabric of our society tearing, and conclude that our government is doing a brilliant job. The other sixty-something percent of us realize we are on a rudderless ship.

If *you* discovered why…if you knew *how we got here*, what would you do? How would you get the word out? Every day, the noise around us grows, and it feels as though we are heard less and less. Imagine Paul Revere without a horse. That's me, typing.

In the military, you can get charged with a difficult or even impossible mission – I.e., charge that hill or take out an enemy air defense battery—and maybe do it by dawn the following day, in the face of overwhelming odds. If you're fortunate, you build a plan so good, everyone has confidence in it. If your plan's not so good, guess what? It's still the plan. Your single *alternative* is to begin the mission with an expectation that you will execute your plan with exceptionalism, or you will fail. Combat is no place for those given to self-doubt.

I have a mission to share what I know. Whether you realize it or not, you joined the mission as soon as you began reading. You're about to scrutinize bold claims. Some are verifiable, while others are based upon conclusions drawn from available facts. From the repudiation of science to the president's denials of criminal behavior, my overarching goal is exposing the truth. All I ask in turn is that you hold me to account, and where I have erred, I welcome you to write and let me know.

Let's start with something simple before we move on to the sexy stuff. If you hate math, bear with me.

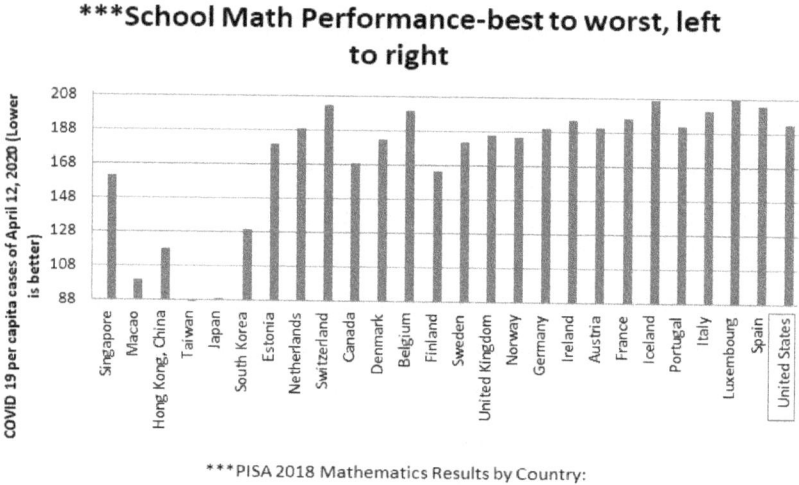

***School Math Performance-best to worst, left to right

***PISA 2018 Mathematics Results by Country:

Figure 1

Figure 1 shows that there is a significant correlation of .70 between a country's handling of the COVID-19 pandemic and their schoolkids' standardized math scores. That's an incredible though seemingly random statistic, but I didn't discover it by compiling a bunch of data and then searching for correlation. This was the first dataset I examined. Like so many things happening with this pandemic, they're simple to understand if you just do the math. It turns out the countries that have done the math are figuring things out better than those that haven't. That's what this chart shows. We'll discuss this more in "Epidemiology 101."

If your eyes glazed over—relax. That's all the math for now. Feel free to skip any science, charts, and math that follow. There's no test at the end of this book. There is plenty of important information, even if you choose to ramdump the technical stuff.

* * * * *

Since mid-April 2020, the president has tried to defend his leadership skills vis-à-vis the coronavirus pandemic by highlighting as his crowning achievement, his decision to shut down travel between the US and China. The thing is: it wasn't his decision.

In the last week of January 2020, pilots and flight attendants flying to China were becoming concerned about a rapidly spreading virus. Pilots manage risk. It's the most important responsibility we have. Most people are not aware, but we frequently take off with one or more known problems with the aircraft. There are a whole host of deficiencies that the FAA permits. They can be anything from a passenger seat not leaning back properly, to a broken coffee maker, to dents in an engine nacelle. A problem may be safe under some conditions, but that doesn't mean it's safe in all conditions. The captain of that aircraft is the final authority on whether the flight can be safely conducted. We are the airlines' risk management experts.

When the dangers of COVID-19 became apparent, the APA, the union for the pilots of American Airlines, requested that the airline quit flying to China as soon as possible. American Airlines management was aware of the problem, but they realized the vast majority of stakeholders would not want to cease service. There were contracts that would have to be adjusted or violated, diplomatic issues, and a long list of other hassles that would have to be addressed. American Airlines management settled on what they believed to be a reasonable compromise—to cease all flights the second week of February.

That wasn't good enough for its pilots. On January 30, 2020, the pilots of American Airlines took their management to court and won an emergency order to cease all flights to China immediately. In less than 24 hours, United and Delta decided upon the same. All of a sudden, nearly the entire market of US air carriers that once flew to China would no longer be doing so.

President Trump could have continued to permit Chinese airlines to transport infected passengers to the US, in spite of the US carriers' unwillingness to do so. However, he must have realized, the weakness in that position. Trump's only politically palatable action was to *officially* shut down air traffic with China. As it turns out, this inartfully executed order was followed by tens of thousands of people continuing to fly from China to the US. Trump did nothing brave, clever, or demonstrative of any meaningful foresight.

In the first ten weeks of 2020, this supposed China travel ban was the only visible step the president had made to fight the pandemic. If he had made this decision based upon science, why were no other travel bans imposed once it became clear the virus had spread to other countries?

These details are publicly available. Why the media never made an issue of it or corrected Trump's many claims of "shutting it down" is an example of how the media is as much a lapdog as a watchdog of our politicians.

* * * * *

Why does Donald Trump do these things? If you're from New York, you've been subjected to his exploits for nearly five decades. Few New Yorkers took the man seriously, even Election Day, 2016. Then everything changed. Since he's taken office, on almost a daily basis, Donald Trump does something that makes reasonable people do that confused turn of the head thing that dogs do when faced with something beyond their realm of understanding. Far too many of our president's actions appear to be those of a person who is not well…mentally and/or cognitively. Psychologists and pundits have put forth theories to support diagnoses such as narcissistic personality disorder, sociopath/antisocial personality disorder, or dementia/major neurocognitive disorder. Trump almost certainly meets the criteria for both of the first two diagnoses, and one could build a weak argument for early dementia, but none of these perspectives alone fully explain his personality.

If you have addicts or alcoholics in your life as I have had, and you have studied the disease of addiction, and you pay close attention to the president, you may notice the same thing I did. The president behaves like an addict. The science of addiction is an ever-evolving area of study. The Diagnostic and Statistical Manual of Mental Disorders (DSM 5), which is *The Manual* for psychological disorders, only partly addresses addiction. The sanctioned definition of addiction, by design, puts psychologists in a box with respect to offering diagnoses that can be listed on insurance, medical, and legal paperwork. Professionals are frequently constrained in seeing beyond classical definitions. As this is not a discussion among clinicians, we need not be encumbered by classical definitions which prove insufficient in explaining the extremely rare life circumstance of Donald Trump.

There is a reason why Trump's behavior is highly predictable in some respects then suddenly unpredictable, and rarely seems rational. Anyone close to someone with a serious addiction will immediately recognize this destructive pattern of behavior. Donald Trump lives his life too much like an addict to not be an addict. To quote Bill Maher, "I don't know if for a fact, I just know it's true."

After you read about the nature of Trump's addiction, you'll find a small bonus. There's a trail of clues about the addiction problems of another Trump family member, but you'll never guess who.

* * * * *

We wouldn't be here today if tens of millions of people weren't buying what the president is selling. Many of us are bewildered by how these supporters keep coming back for more...in spite of reality. We have come to agree with Trump's frightful, hyperbolic claim that he could shoot someone on Fifth Avenue in New York and not lose a single supporter. In response, two important questions should come to mind. 1) Why? and 2) What would have to change for Trump to lose such loyal support?

The reason why is tragically simple. Trump's supporters act the way they do because Donald Trump validates their view of the world. He says that the world is a dangerous place because foreigners are stealing jobs and people who believe in other religions are coming to destroy Christianity. Supporters are scared of these boogeymen, and Trump's xenophobia actually makes people feel safer because he's the one person with any power who's willing to even address their irrational concerns. His promise to "make America great again" is, as many understand, a dog whistle expressing discontent with progressive societal changes in matters such as constitutional freedoms, LGBTQ rights, and racial justice. Trump validates bigoted and irrational fears regarding social change in a way that only the most extreme contemporary politicians (such as Iowa Congressman Steve King and Louisiana politician David Duke) previously dared even consider. What's worse, his perceived business successes brought credibility to his repulsive worldview.

To label it simply a problem of bigotry would be a disservice to our understanding and our ability to effect change. People feel powerless when the world starts changing around them in unexpected and undesirable ways. Powerlessness is a strong motivator—so strong that often all it takes to gain someone's trust, affection, and loyalty is to offer sincerity and understanding of their fears and concerns. Donald Trump has been doing this since well before his escalator descent. Trump supporters should certainly not be considered monolithic, but some generalities hold water.

Punditry has often referenced Trump's economic platform of returning lost jobs as being instrumental to his support. Certainly, this was the case for some at one time. However, the president has done little to restore jobs in dying industries. Trump spoke endlessly on the campaign trail about bringing back manufacturing jobs, but these jobs grew no faster under Trump than they did in the Obama years. None of the coal jobs he promised to deliver, more to tease liberals than anything else, ever materialized. Since COVID-19, total manufacturing and coal employment are both below their levels on the day Trump took office.

If the support was only about these jobs, the bloom would have fallen off the rose long ago. The reason for the continued loyalty is that Trump genuinely believes that we should mine and burn coal. He believes that no level of water pollution is too much if it costs manufacturing jobs. It doesn't matter what he delivers. Never mind that he does not understand and can do next to nothing to alter environmental, economic, and political realities. Having higher-paying "green" jobs replace dangerous coal mining jobs is a construct that doesn't fit the worldview of a Trump supporter.

Trump's disdain and disregard for *experts* justifies the notion that *elites* don't know nearly as much as they think they do and destroy far more than they fix. It is easier to point a finger and blame someone than comprehend that the world is always changing and leaving those who cannot change behind.

The president's regressive worldview matches that of his supporters. No matter the size or impact of his failures, no matter the destruction to our economy, our health, or even our standing in the world, Trump continues to validate his supporters' worldview. Trump is the Jerry Maguire of Washington politics. *He had them at hello.*

This is why his supporters ignore the reality of the world around them. Though conservative media (and social media) buttresses the validity of their audience's worldview, Trump would still have plenty of support without them, because his supporters are no more interested in a progressive worldview than liberals would be interested in (primetime) Fox's worldview. It doesn't matter what the 'truth' is. It has always been about how people feel when they are validated.

For Trump's support to end, he would have to do or say something to convince his voters that he no longer shares their views. This is why he struggles to tell his supporters to wear masks. It's why he has to continue appearing to destroy Obamacare. It's why he has never tried to *grow his tent*. Politicians have typically made outreach efforts to build coalitions. Trump can lie twice a minute, but he doesn't have the luxury of being duplicitous with respect to that corrupted worldview. Aside from judicial appointments that every other Republican would be making in his stead, Trump offers little to nothing beyond validation. As soon as that is gone, his support would drop out the bottom.

He does have one trick that he keeps returning to. He knows everyone loves a winner, so he inflates everything about himself and his presidency. Everything. For those too disinterested to do a speck of investigation, who always take the president at his word, he can win their votes by simply claiming how wonderful a job he is doing despite all evidence to the contrary.

Trump stands upon the shoulders of numerous Republican branding campaigns of the past. Even with some Fox News commentators disputing Trump's claims, the Democratic Party's alternative "brand" has been so badly tarnished by conservative media that right-leaning swing voters will continue to support Trump in surprising numbers (or at least fail to vote against him) because they don't know any better.

As Trump will not do anything to attack the worldview of his base, is there anything that Democrats can do to mitigate his unprecedented level of loyalty? Before COVID-19, I would say that it would have been difficult to peel meaningful numbers of loyal supporters away. Within the context of current events, it might be enough for Joe Biden to make people feel heard and at least in that way validated, even if he doesn't share their worldview. This is one of Biden's core strengths, and he has already shown that he can win Trump voters. We will find out soon if this will be enough.

An Old Challenge

There's a well-known Chinese curse, *"May you live in interesting times."* For better or worse, I've been living an *interesting* life. We can start with my 20-year-old triplets—two boys and a girl. In the interest of their privacy, I'll call them Mary, John, and Jim. Each one of them has put me through hell, as I am certain I came nowhere close to doing to my own parents. Somehow though, each one of my kids brings me great joy. They are the center of my world, and I love them all to pieces.

It didn't start out that way. My kids were born shy of 27 weeks gestation, each weighing two pounds. Fundamentally, they were all born healthy, which is to say that if they avoided any adverse events in the NICU (neonatal intensive care unit), once we got them home, they would have been like any other healthy babies.

NICU care requires frequent blood draws to test and assess their fragile condition to sufficient detail. As the blood is removed, it somehow has to get replaced. Two-pound babies don't produce a lot of surplus blood. They require donated blood transfusions. Jim and John both had my blood type, so I donated what the hospital would take, but it wasn't enough. They needed additional blood from the blood bank. Six weeks after birth, John had a blood transfusion reaction that went catastrophically wrong. None of the gifted doctors in the entire NICU knew what had happened, why blood had clot throughout John's tiny body. We would eventually learn that he had dead tissue in his brain, lungs, and digestive tract. All the doctors could tell us at that time was that John was dying.

Tiny preemies require breathing support, to various degrees. Our three were initially typical, spending the first few weeks of their lives on ventilators. Then they graduated to tiny nasal cannulas for about a week, before finally being able to breathe on their own. These milestones are big moments that only happen with a lot of work. The NICU staff must consistently adjust the equipment to push the kids to breathe more and more on their own. It's a delicate balance. Push them too hard, and they desat—they don't get enough oxygen and risk brain damage. Don't push hard enough, and they will stay on the vent for too long, ultimately doing damage to their young, fragile lungs.

My wife Lisa and I spent days, weeks, and months in the NICU. As a military pilot, I already knew a fair amount about things like blood oxygen levels and hypoxia. All the lights and controls of the ventilators and the other medical equipment appealed to my pilot-engineer mind. Learning everything I could about our kids' conditions and the medicine involved was my coping mechanism.

When John got sick and no one understood why, it had been a nightmare, and not even where our panic began. Days before, Jim developed necrotic bowel which had required surgery. No explanation— just a part of the rollercoaster world of the NICU.

A day after John's hemolytic reaction, Mary "crashed," medical lingo in her case, for respiratory distress. Within a few days, all three were back on ventilators and each of them had infections of unknown origins. The doctors had no answers for us. It was terrifying.

The one common link between the three was breast milk. Mom's milk is the healthiest nutrition possible, especially for a preemie, and it offers a small sense of control to mothers who otherwise have to depend upon strangers to care for their newborns. Our three were still too small to suckle—they received their nutrition through a feeding tube, which meant Mom would have to pump the milk and store it first. Lisa had been pumping for over six weeks and had amassed a respectable amount of nutrition.

Breastmilk has to be kept reasonably sterile when stored. It had been my job to clean the bottles and freeze the breastmilk before delivering it to the NICU. I do a lot of things reasonably well, but keeping things sterile has never been one of them.

"Could it be the breastmilk making the kids sick?" I asked the physicians.

"Maybe. We don't know," they replied.

I said, "Let me donate more blood." John had crashed during a blood transfusion from an anonymous donor, and the doctors believed the transfusion had set off his condition, but they had no idea why. I figured he'd be better off with my blood for future transfusions.

But no. "We don't think that's a good idea. His immune system may have become over-sensitized. He might overreact to antigens in your blood since his immune system has been exposed to it before. It's best to go with a new donor with each future unit he receives."

We asked, "If the breastmilk is the problem, should we throw out what we have?"

The doctors said, "We don't think it's the breastmilk. But yeah, it would probably be wise to throw it out."

So that was that. The most tangible thing we as parents had done for our three kids, and yes ladies, my role in this particular feat was not really worthy of mention, except perhaps in its failings. The demoralization of throwing away several gallons of breast milk was, if you will excuse the phrase, a drop in the bucket compared to the abject fear of having three children simultaneously at death's door. And then what would happen if they did survive? Would we be raising three handicapped kids?

I was determined to figure out what was happening, and I was fortunate to have at my disposal several resources that most people do not. My best friend was a gifted ER physician and diagnostician who suffered with us while patiently answering hundreds of my questions. He was also at a loss to explain why all three of our kids had turned suddenly ill, but he was giving me a great and rapid medical education.

I am also fortunate to have a cousin who was has been a senior scientist at several pharmaceutical companies. His specialty is more closely related to immunology, but he knew many of the smartest scientists throughout every biological discipline. He put me in touch with a series of experts.

Frequently parents of chronically sick children and those with sick spouses get a thorough medical education— not enough to be a medical professional, but if this applies to you, then you understand. You become an expert in meds, symptoms, treatment options, et al. I have a mind for these things, so I quickly learned and became conversant in the lingo, the Latin, the big words, and the technology.

By some point in this crazy roller-coaster ride, in my phone consultations with new physicians or scientists, I was consistently asked, "Didn't you say you're the parent?"

"I am," I'd answer.

"And you're also a physician?"

The first time I heard this, it was kind of flattering. "No, I'm the dad," I'd say.

So they'd answer, "Okay, I didn't understand. You sound more like the attending physician. Are you in healthcare?"

"No, I'm a pilot."

There was nothing ingenious about what I was doing. Doctors speak a language all their own, as do many professionals. I've been to Brazil dozens of times and can barely speak a lick of Portuguese, but technical lingo of assorted varieties comes naturally to me, and I had learned enough to demonstrate fluency.

I spent an hour or more on the phone each day, speaking with specialists who would fax me information or refer me to various documents and/or other specialists. Of course, John wasn't our only problem-child, but his siblings were getting better even as John's condition further deteriorated. The doctors would eventually place him on an oscillating ventilator – basically last-ditch equipment. The oscillations/vibrations attempt to, for lack of a better word, pound oxygen into blood at a frequency of about three thumps per second. Imagine that on your three-pound newborn. His body swelled as his kidneys weakened, unable to rid himself of fluids. He became yellow with jaundice as his liver struggled to filter toxins from his blood, but the ventilator did the one thing it absolutely needed to do, oxygenating his blood enough to keep him alive. Were that machine to have turned off or failed for even a minute, he would have been rapidly subjected to additional brain damage and then death. I imagine the machine had an excellent battery back-up system. I don't wonder why medical equipment is so expensive. Meanwhile, clocks seemed to turn backwards as specialist after specialist was at a loss to identify the problem.

After 10 days of research, my cousin connected me with an expert in Seattle in NICU blood transfusions. A thorough conversation with this medical scientist revealed a certain diagnosis: John had suffered an extremely rare blood transfusion reaction that only occurs with premature babies with necrotizing enterocolitis who receive blood from a donor with a rare antigen in their blood. Bad luck as rare as a lightning strike. Today, NICU's screen for this rare antigen, uncommon as it is. Sometimes I wonder if John's case contributed to that change.

I was terrified at the time - more scared than any other time in my life, which I suppose is saying something. But crises have a way of bringing my mind into focus. The worse things get, the more my thoughts become clinical, all left hemisphere. Many people, even some professional therapists, would label this kind of emotional shutdown as dysfunction, and perhaps it is. But there's another name for it, too— compartmentalization. Merriam-Webster defines the medical definition of compartmentalization as, "isolation or splitting off of part of the personality or mind with lack of communication and consistency between the parts."

25

I can tell you that for those in life and death professions, this is how most of those minds work, and no one should want it any other way. Imagine Sully's outcome if he'd been a deer in headlights after both his engines quit. Does anyone want to schedule a hip replacement with a surgeon in the midst of an existential crisis? How about a lawyer paralyzed by self-doubt over losing a death penalty case? The professionals that you rely on are all living the same imperfect lives as everyone else, with financial woes, spousal problems, and yeah, sometimes really sick kids.

Compartmentalization is the self-defense mechanism that helps the mind handle the cognitive dissonance of personal fear and or anxiety in the face of life or ego threatening challenges. It's different from suppression, which is an unhealthy effort to ignore negative thoughts or feelings entirely. Compartmentalization is more like sealing away fearful, anxiety-provoking feelings in a box to be opened at a later time, when it is presumably safe to do so.

Managing life and death requires a mastery of emotional response not too dissimilar to what is needed in the face of extreme leadership challenges. Many supporters viewed President Obama's calm demeanor to be his greatest strength—*no drama Obama*. Contrast that with what we have today, a man whose emotions are always on display. No wonder Trump couldn't run a casino—no poker face. He has a tell for almost every occasion. I.e., it's so obvious to anyone paying attention that he ALWAYS points blame at someone else for whatever crimes or misdemeanors he's been up to. Imagine how easy it has been for foreign leaders to know exactly what Trump is thinking. Dictators like Kim and Putin have been able to manipulate him like a game of international Twister. *The Art of the Deal*? Yeah, right.

It took me ten days of dedicated research to figure out what had happened to John. Imagine how much longer it might have been if every scientist I contacted had to filter their comments and thoughts so as to not agitate, frighten, or enrage a terrified parent. My son was dying. I didn't have the luxury of displaying emotions. Fortunately, I had a decade of experience in compartmentalization, one more reason why I appeared to medical professionals as one of their own, able to immediately get down to business.

I passed John's diagnosis to the NICU physicians, who were able to proceed more aggressively once they fully understood what had happened. The clotted blood had killed off some of his bowel, which was becoming septic. They knew about the dead bowel from his x-rays, and they knew it needed to be removed, but they had been hoping he would stabilize first. John wasn't going to give them that luxury. With a firm diagnosis though, the possibility of a deadly surprise when they opened him up was low enough to proceed. I remember asking how dangerous it would be to operate on John's tiny anatomy with that oscillating ventilator firing three times a second. I don't remember the answer. I can only guess it did not bring me comfort.

My memory also fails me with respect to Lisa and my time in the waiting room during John's lengthy surgery or Jim's earlier surgery for that matter. That seems pretty odd to me now as an experienced parent, but I understand psychology well enough to know that at the time, I hadn't yet gained the reference for what was happening context. It would have been like hearing ancient Greek and then trying to remember those words weeks or months later (assuming you're not already fluent in ancient Greek).

I remember well, in the NICU, getting to hold each of my tiny kids for the first time. I remember some of the other moments that fall under the "win" column. The value in remembering most of the losses is questionable. I certainly remember that John's surgery was a success, at least from a technical viewpoint. We would learn soon enough, the damage to his brain from that errant transfusion was irreversible.

Jim and Mary made it through the NICU with no further complications and are now perfectly healthy college juniors. John was to grow up, consistently defying the odds. He became an amazing young man, though not without distinct physical and intellectual disabilities. And some truly bad luck that will get even worse.

But this is not a story about John or about my understanding of medicine. Leadership—good leadership is about connecting with people on a personal level, particularly through the more challenging times of life. My specific successes and failures may not be relatable to many people. But most of us have found ourselves in a deep dark hole at some point in our lives. As parents, we've all faced terrors. As employees, many of us have faced hurdles maddening enough to bring us to tears—perhaps never so true before as in the era of COVID-19.

As I've tried to teach my kids, no matter the challenge ahead of you, learn to find the opportunities hidden within. Perhaps this mindset is a by-product of military service. Those who don't learn to love a challenge don't fair well in uniform. *"Embrace the suck,"* as soldiers and airmen far wiser than me have opined upon this very subject. And in a shout-out to my alma mater, IHTFP didn't become the unofficial, ironically-applauded and esteemed motto because the place was a barrel of laughs (IHT stands for 'I hate this' and I suppose you can Google the rest).

The best leaders understand they are obligated to respond to calls for action and are honored to fulfill such obligations. To serve your country is a privilege afforded to a small percentage of our population. The greater one's ability to contribute, via expertise, experience, and dedicated effort, the greater the personal reward. Not everyone understands this concept, but for those who do, the reasons are self-evident.

Those early days of parenting established a baseline of biological knowledge that I later used when developing a novel emergency respiration system for my first company's record-breaking submersible watercraft. My research resulted in a discovery regarding the way our lungs respond to extreme levels of certain gasses. I well understand many of the biological processes involved in the existing medical crisis, as well as the medicine involved. We have rightly so, been looking to physicians and epidemiologists to help guide us through the COVID-19 crisis. I am neither of those, but there are many dimensions to the existing crisis and even to the medicine.

Infection transmission for COVID-19 turns out to be based on a single factor—the travel of virions, or viral particles, from one person to another, and that is happening primarily in the air. You can't understand the travel of these particles without understanding both aerodynamics and gas dynamics, and I have studied both of those subjects at MIT. My alma mater is widely considered to be the best university in the world in these disciplines. I am at least as qualified to discuss the airborne travel of virions as many epidemiologists and certainly most physicians.

As a military officer, of thousands trained, I was one of only two pilots to enter B-1 training as a tanker copilot candidate and complete that same training as an aircraft commander. I spent another six years developing my skills in leadership as a formation and mission commander, then instructor, and eventually evaluator pilot of what is one of the most lethal military platforms known to man. Yes, a carrier is badass, but try to use its aircraft to bomb a target 1500 miles inland.

As a business school professor, I taught Organizational Behavior and helped to develop new tools for online MBA classes. As an airline captain, I was publicly recognized by my company's CEO for my ability to put passengers at ease in the immediate wake of the 737 MAX accidents at a time when many people were refusing to fly on the airplane.

I use a simple formula that brings many people success: respect, compassion, and good communication. Respect people, recognize when and how they are impacted, and honestly explain the facts to them. The results that can be achieved by doing these few things are remarkable. Even after long delays, my airline passengers thank me enthusiastically, simply for communicating with them and treating them well.

While only a few people may understand the responsibilities of being an airline captain, nearly all of us have overcome high hurdles. Certainly, many of us can appreciate the ups and downs of child-rearing. For most new parents, it begins as a blur, feeling like you better hit the ground running or else. Lisa and I had to hit the ground running at a full sprint. Parenting has been the toughest thing I've done. Tougher than graduating MIT, tougher than Air Force pilot training, tougher than war. If you've successfully helped your kids conquer anything tougher than a skinned knee, you're probably a better leader than you realize.

Today in the White House, we are witness to the exact opposite of superior leadership. No one can understand how bad it is until we understand how good it could have been. I can offer some small notion of that.

In the jobs I've held, failure was never an option. Some things have to be done right the first time. Anyone can lead when times are easy. It's only when your world is coming apart at the seams that the value of superior leadership truly shines through. Good leaders take up the mantle.

In my particular story, things hadn't fallen apart at the seams yet. That comes later.

COVID-19 Stuff

I'm a bit of a news junky, so I happened to first read about a novel coronavirus the first week in January. The only thing that initially registered with me was that the *virus* was described in the article as fairly benign, which was curious because it certainly seemed significant. The Chinese knew by then that the virus caused significant respiratory symptoms and was probably contagious. They knew that it was probably zoonotic, meaning it had recently evolved from a virus endemic to some animal. Zoonotic viruses are scary because they're often "novel," or new, meaning humans have not developed any immunity to them. For this reason, they can be highly unpredictable. This new virus sounded similar to SARS and MERS, both of which had a significant impact on the airline industry. Working for an airline that flew to China, it was natural for me to take notice.

By January 11 when the first death was reported in Wuhan, China, a scary picture was coming into focus. The virus was causing bad and potentially deadly cases of pneumonia. We knew we were dealing with a coronavirus similar to viruses that cause common colds, so the likelihood of contagion between people was strong. Already, the resulting disease had demonstrated it might have all of the elements necessary to lead to a pandemic. Doctors strongly suspected that this virus:

a) Could be spread between people (not just from animal to person);
b) If it were spread by people, was likely airborne;
c) Might be highly contagious.

The danger was something to heed, but China had experience and technical expertise. They also had the benefit of authoritarian rule. There was no reason to think at this point, that China would not contain the problem.

Within the next two weeks, things rapidly progressed. Contagion between people was demonstrated; the virus's pedigree meant it was more than likely airborne, it was clearly deadly, and there was even discussion that it might be spread by infected people before they become symptomatic.

I spoke with my wife, Lisa, and explained that it's rare to have a deadly disease spread airborne by people not exhibiting symptoms. There's been speculation that measles sometimes exhibits these attributes, but that appears to be atypical. Occasionally those with the flu can spread it before being symptomatic, but that is also uncommon and usually lasts less than 48 hours. There was speculation that the novel coronavirus was being shed by infected individuals for five or more days before symptoms appear.

You reach a certain age where your younger self would find amusement for what now passes for pillow talk. I threw my socks in the bathroom laundry basket before walking past Lisa to climb into bed.

"You know the story about Typhoid Mary?" I asked her.

"I guess. She spread Typhoid."

"Yeah, but more than that. Typhoid Mary never exhibited symptoms. She was a pure carrier of Typhoid, a bacterial infection caused by Salmonella. No one knew there was anything unusual about her until one day someone asked, 'How come so many people are getting sick and dying when Mary's around?'"

"And you're telling me this because...?"

"You know this virus from China?"

"Not really." Lisa tries to make up for my obsession with the news by mostly ignoring it.

So I explained what I knew about the virus. And then I said, "Typhoid Mary was a cook who infected 51 people, three of whom died. No one knew she was spreading the disease because she had no symptoms. Once they figured it out, she was considered so dangerous that she spent the last 23 years of her life in quarantine.

"Asymptomatic people rarely spread deadly diseases. Typhoid Mary was one of the exceptions. But with this coronavirus, it's possible for infected people to be asymptomatic yet still contagious—maybe for everyone who catches it. That would mean everyone with this new virus becomes a Typhoid Mary—at least for some period of time."

My wife has raised triplets. It takes a lot to get her stirred up, but I could see her concern. "What's going to happen?"

By this point, the virus had spread to numerous other countries. I said, "If it can be spread by asymptomatic carriers, this could be bad. There won't be any way to stop it. It's gonna go everywhere."

"Here?"

"Everywhere."

American Public Health Leadership

When the world learned of the first case in the United States on January 21, 2020, it was clear that this thing needed to be watched like your wallet on a crowded subway. I'd been surprised that China had let the virus breathe, by which I mean they didn't attempt to immediately strangle it. I thought surely the CDC was putting protocols into place to protect Americans. Surely their people in China would be closely monitoring the situation, and if the Chinese couldn't control it, appropriate US border controls would be instituted. It wouldn't be until a few weeks later that I found out that President Trump had undone those safety mechanisms.

By January 26, the virus had clearly beaten attempts at isolation. The numbers in China were building rapidly, and many people were infected in numerous countries. This is when scientists were more seriously contemplating the nightmarish scenario of asymptomatic carriers. It's unclear at this point exactly what steps the CDC, NIH, and the Department of Health and Human Services (HHS) were taking to brace us for the ensuing impact. We know now that responsibilities in protecting the American public had been grossly mismanaged, and I maintain that these failures stem directly from poor leadership.

With a little investigation, we can detect fundamental inadequacies, even from these organizations' respective websites. The CDC states the following about their mission:

CDC increases the health security of our nation. As the nation's health protection agency, CDC saves lives and protects people from health threats. To accomplish our mission, CDC conducts critical science and provides health information that protects our nation against expensive and dangerous health threats, and responds when these arise.

An organization's mission is the sole reason that those it serves would request or require its service, the sole reason the organization exists. In the military and in business school, I taught students and organizational leaders how to develop a mission statement. I could never impart enough emphasis that a mission statement should be developed with great care and attention, that leadership should make it well understood to all stakeholders, and that it should govern the actions of all employees, leaders, and/or relevant participants.

Already, looking at the CDC's mission statement, I was not impressed. It's an amateurish attempt, filled with awkward language and excessive industry jargon. "CDC conducts critical science"? Who outside of the CDC can define "critical science"?

"Provides health information"? To whom and how?

"Protects our nation against *expensive* and dangerous health threats"? What is expensive doing here? If it's dangerous, is that not enough of a reason for the CDC to react? Maybe they meant expensive OR dangerous, but if you have a typo in your mission statement, you and your organization are not giving it nearly enough attention.

No, this is a mission statement of an organization that is led by people who have not deeply considered what they even do. And if the leaders don't know what they do, how are its employees or anyone else supposed to know?

One might imagine that whatever the CDC was doing (or trying to do) about the novel coronavirus in January 2020, it was a disorganized, half-hearted effort.

The NIH's mission statement is written substantially better:

NIH's mission is to seek fundamental knowledge about the nature and behavior of living systems and the application of that knowledge to enhance health, lengthen life, and reduce illness and disability.

I have a good, unambiguous understanding from reading this statement about the fundamental function of the NIH. On the same webpage, I'm able to view the NIH's goals and their strategies to achieve these goals.

The NIH's mission statement and goals suggest it is not a "health protection agency," or driven by "health security" as is the CDC. Its mission is not explicitly reactionary as is the CDC's, though it is tasked "to lengthen life and reduce illness."

I can reasonably conclude that the NIH will react when directed by governing authorities, but that it is not primarily driven by "health security." As it is tasked to "seek fundamental knowledge about the nature and behavior of living systems," I might imagine that the NIH was initially involved in collecting data such as the virus's genome and perhaps early investigations into the development of a vaccine. Presumably, the CDC was in charge of coordinating pandemic mitigation efforts, but because of its weak mission statement, although it "provides health information" we have no idea how "that protects our nation against expensive and dangerous health threats."

Finally, from the HHS website:

The mission of the U.S. Department of Health and Human Services (HHS) is to enhance the health and well-being of all Americans, by providing for effective health and human services and by fostering sound, sustained advances in the sciences underlying medicine, public health, and social services.

The HHS, which oversees CDC and NIH had a 2019 budget of $1.3 trillion! That was roughly twice the military budget! That's a lot of money. And what does their mission statement reveal they do with that money? "…foster sound, sustained advances in science…." That's the essence of their mission statement. The first clause is good, but the remainder of this single sentence says little else. I guess $1.3 trillion doesn't get you much anymore. If they had put the statement into Grammarly, they might have at least found the misplaced comma, but even that was apparently too much work for this team.

It may sound nitpicky, but that's exactly the point. If you can't precisely define what you do and how you do it, and professionally communicate these facts to relevant stakeholders, ideally with care and concern, how can anyone have faith in you to, for instance, develop a test to detect COVID-19 without preventing contamination from ruining the entire test (which was only the beginning of numerous blunders bungling American COVID-19 testing)? The CDC and HHS failures in test development were no accident. We could have observed last year from their website that these people weren't up to the task.

As the performance of the CDC, NIH, FDA, and other federal public health agencies are examined, several costly missteps have already been revealed. As we discuss these technical failures, let us maintain our focus on leadership and its role in the success and failures of our nation's public health organizations.

Presumably, when the CDC detects a threat, they elevate awareness to their governing authority, the HHS. At the time of this writing, the HHS Secretary is Alex Azar. This is a Cabinet-level position., so if the secretary deems a CDC identified threat to be significant, he/she notifies the president. These actions should have occurred in early January, ideally in a matter of minutes or hours.

It's possible that the president was not notified at all until late January, but that doesn't matter as far as the president's culpability. It's time to quit letting President Trump off the hook because "someone else" dropped the ball. Secretary Azar is Trump's secretary. The president hired and supervises him, and he's responsible for listening to him, as Trump should all the senior officials in his administration. We know the president was notified by late January, at the latest, because of his misleading braggadocio regarding shutting down air traffic to China.

From this point onward, the president made numerous public statements downplaying and ignoring the virus. It was clear to anyone paying attention that a slow-motion train wreck was unfolding before the world's eyes, and no one would be there to intervene.

A First Look at Leadership through the Pandemic

Bleeding inside and outside the body, severe abdominal pain and headache, and rapid death are symptoms that make you stand up and take notice. Many of us may recall the Ebola scare in 2014. The virus had first been brought into the US by a tourist returning from West Africa. Long before Ebola graced our shores, the CDC had workers overseas, working hard to stop the virus's spread.

Once Ebola had arrived in the US, the CDC called for and quickly received nearly a billion dollars' worth of support (not initially funded by Congress, but by other funds diverted by HHS). For what it's worth, it is precisely for reasons such as this that the HHS Secretary is a Cabinet-level position. Sometimes, there are health threats to the American people that are serious enough that they require presidential-level attention.

The WHO also sprang into action, and a dozen countries offered additional support. It's well understood that disease does not respect borders and the quicker a contagion is stopped the better. It's far better to devote resources to stopping the spread of an illness *before* it enters your country. In other words, attack Ebola in Africa and save lives in the US— kind of exactly like the model that Republicans use for terrorism. Inside our borders, we suffered a total of 11 cases and one death due to Ebola. With full respect to the victims, don't those numbers seem utterly adorable?

To be clear, Ebola is not COVID-19. The bodily fluids of those infected with Ebola carry an extremely high viral load, and it is easily spread by those not taking precautions. However, it is not known to be transmitted during its incubation period (before symptoms appear), and it is not easily spread airborne. Also of note: there is far less air traffic coming from West Africa than there is from China. Yet the Obama administration quickly devoted hundreds of millions of dollars to shut down the possibility of the spread of this disease.

Zika had a similar story. Remember Zika, an illness that spread even easier than Ebola? Maybe not, because it was stopped, also at significant expense but before it could spread in large numbers).

To date, with the much greater potential threat of the coronavirus, it is not clear that the Trump administration has devoted any specific resources toward this problem. This is after having previously removed resources devoted to preventing pandemics.

Why *is* that?

One can only speculate. In my view, this is not part of the normal ideological battle of budget priorities between Republicans and Democrats. I believe these cuts were made because Obama acted like a politician, while Trump acts like a certain faction of businessmen, hyper-focused on short-term profitability to the exclusion of the business' overall health.

Politicians are quick to spend taxpayer money for many reasons, often to remain in the good grace of voters. Ironically, that is why many people dislike politicians—so damn quick to spend our money, right? In opposition, there is a mindset adopted by some businesses to avoid expenses that do not show immediate or near-immediate tangible benefits. Unfortunately, this includes most expenses involved in the prevention of bad things that have yet to happen.

This is exactly why we have strong product liability laws—because business people do not have an explicit fiduciary compulsion to be safe (as opposed to an implicit desire for safety that businesses derive by computing the costs to items, such as potential damage to the brand and missed days of work due to injuries and deaths). Without liability laws, some businesses would fall into the temptation of grossly underestimating the costs of 'danger' and thereby minimize expenditures related to preventing the hazardous results of their operations.

Some in business push back on this concept because there are plenty of morally and ethically driven business owners. This is absolutely true, but even when a business' intentions are arguably moral, they are prone to grossly underestimating the cost of danger to the greater industry or community.

For an example, one needn't look any further than the crashes of Lion Air's and Ethiopian Airlines' 737 MAX aircraft. Flawed decisions made by the executives of those Third World airlines, and the American manufacturer, Boeing, led directly to the two crashes. Thousands of flights were canceled, millions of people's plans were disrupted, and millions were financially impacted after the crashes led to worldwide grounding of the entire fleet for years.

All larger companies use specialists in actuarial science to determine the actual dollar cost to different kinds of risks. Statistically, extremely impactful events are outliers, typically so rare, that the actuarial cost does not justify investments to mitigate associated risk. Without governments putting the fear of God into private enterprises with the threat of very expensive legal liability, few companies would mitigate the risk of most dangerous products and services.

To illustrate the concept, we can perform a simplified actuarial analysis: in the case of the MAX, when Boeing needed to decide if they should put a redundant sensor in the base model (which may cost them .0001% of their margin) or make the sensor an option (where there is a .000001% chance of being sued for $30 billion), Boeing made it an option because the small statistical likelihood of danger outweighed even the huge potential legal liability.

In the case of the MAX, we're using fabricated numbers to create a simplification that ignores the liability by Lion Air and Ethiopian Airlines, but mathematically speaking, this describes the situation well. The problem was as much a failure of the legal liability system as it was engineering and management failures. There is no way that Boeing will adequately compensate the millions affected, despite the billions of dollars they will relinquish in damages. Private enterprise rarely has the answer for statistical outliers.

So, what happens when you elect a businessman obsessed with only spending money when totally necessary? What checks and balances are in place to restrain such a politician from taking huge risks with the health and wellbeing of their constituents?

To be clear, businesspersons of high moral character, who have an understanding of public policy, can make excellent politicians. I.e., a good businessman might have done a cost-benefit analysis and concluded that for $1.5 billion (roughly $4 per US citizen) the country could take all reasonable steps to stop the spread of Ebola and Zika. Anything else would be the definition of "penny wise and pound foolish."

By any reasonable analysis, outside of his reality TV show, Trump has never been a good businessman (which should be distinguished from his remarkable skill at self-aggrandizement). His business philosophy was on the extreme end of the spectrum where one doesn't spend money or pay bills unless forced. There is evidence aplenty that Trump would rather deal with the fallout that ensues than pay a bill. This is how he ended up fighting thousands of lawsuits and taking six companies into bankruptcy. Even as President, there've been dozens of complaints that Trump's campaign doesn't satisfy its financial obligations.

Such miserliness does come at a cost. It would be interesting to create an epidemiological simulation applying Trump's 'COVID-19 approach' to Zika or Ebola. What potential disaster might arise, and what associated cost would an actuarial analysis reveal? While we're at it, let's examine how things would have played out, if we'd handled COVID-19 properly. Would we have been able to keep cases down to a tiny percentage of what we will ultimately experience?

The president wasted two months doing nothing. Likely, inaction would have been better. Instead, Trump used his bully pulpit (and when has that term ever been more apt?) to insist that COVID-19 posed no threat at all to America, thereby further minimizing disaster preparation.

Leadership is difficult. All leaders—business, military, and political, make mistakes, and criticism and jokes follow. Often these are not so much mistakes as they are approaches with different priorities sometimes combined with minor missteps. Even well-executed leadership is often criticized and becomes a victim of satire. Lampooning and roasting politicians used to be a time-honored tradition. The slow-motion train wreck that has been the Trump administration's response to the novel coronavirus, beginning in early January and extending into at least mid-April, is not worthy of humor—not in the face of so much preventable death and economic hardship.

Who Else Can We Blame?

To be fair, there is plenty of well-earned blame and criticism to go around. Enough was known, and so much more should have been done. Looking back, I wouldn't have scared my wife in late January unless I had some notion then of the danger in front of us. To be fair, Lisa doesn't take well to change. It's better to ease her into things. But she's not as high maintenance as say, an entire nation. If my wife needed a little extra preparation, I'm guessing it might have been a good idea for the country to also start thinking earlier about a response. The virus had already defied predictions by busting out of China's borders, and the world's governments had defied predictions by letting it get out nonchalantly. Virus metrics show they weren't so lackadaisical in Asia and Oceania (apart from China's initial reaction). Those countries, despite their proximity to Wuhan, responded aggressively and were the least impacted. This includes China! The West's response more closely resembled that of a deer in headlights—with predictable results.

The politicians of Western Europe had the same slow responses as those in the US. Because the virus hit Europe first, they were initially impacted more. In the early stage of treating the virus, physicians were less capable, and the odds of dying were significantly higher. This drove up mortality rates in Europe and New York City. The initial quarantines in Europe and New York were far more decisive than the eventual, overall American response. At best, our nation's reaction was utterly chaotic, incoherent, incompetent, and higgledy-piggledy. There was a heavy premium paid by those who got badly ill early on, and Europe and New York/New Jersey, despite having low infection rates from May 2020 onward, maintain high total per capita mortality figures.

In late January, I didn't know exactly where things were headed, but I had lost faith in the way things had begun. I began to fear that the virus would come to America. You know that book, *Everything I need to know*

I learned in Kindergarten? Everything we needed to know about the danger of this virus we knew by the first week in February.

People say politicians are overpaid. I believe, for what they are asked to do, they are grossly underpaid. When businesses are not receiving job applications from sufficiently qualified employees, do they cut the offered salary in response? Of course not. If we want to put intelligent, hard-working, and ethical leaders in office, we have to quit thinking that paying them less will improve the situation. What we needed was a group of politicians behaving more like sharks or even greedy entrepreneurs– not wanting to be outdone by anyone; on a constant lookout and ready to respond appropriately to any threat or opportunity. What we needed were politicians who would fight for our health like successfully aggressive businesspeople fight for profit. The fact is, back in January, every governor and every mayor of a large city – any jurisdiction that has one or more public health officials as advisors, should have been requesting and receiving regular briefs on the threat. They should have quickly brought up plans based upon existing pandemic guidance, and as it became clear that the virus would not be controlled, they should have started executing those pandemic plans. Many of our politicians were given plenty of warning, but with few exceptions, there is no evidence that they responded appropriately until they found themselves backed into corners—meaning far too late.

We need to dive deeper, though, to shine a light on the CDC, the NIH, Dr. Fauci, Dr. Birx – pretty much anyone working with or for the federal government with specialized medical knowledge relevant to pandemics. Putting aside their actions specific to healthcare for a moment, let's address their performance as related to policy. How many people has Trump fired since taking office? A ridiculous multiple when compared to any other presidency, to be sure. To think that he hires the best is in most cases laughable. He fires anyone who does not readily acquiesce to his foolish notions and conform to his unquenchable narcissism. This absurd ritual has become part of the "new normal."

So, I offer criticism with caution. Anyone standing up to President Trump needs to be prepared for retribution, probably on numerous levels. But people have to sleep at night, too, don't they? Look at themselves in the mirror without shame? Wouldn't you hope some American bureaucrats would have put their country above their positions and careers?

Are my standards too damn high? Shouldn't we be disappointed that none of these scientists, doctors, or other officials were more vocal in opposing the president's absurd denials of reality?

It's reasonable to ask where we would be if, for instance, Dr. Fauci had spoken up aggressively in protest and been subsequently fired in mid-February. He'd probably have been fine, and the rest of us might have started taking chloroquine and injecting ourselves with Lysol. So okay, we'll let poor Dr. Fauci off the hook for now as we can only lay so much upon his shoulders. But numerous other officials could have called news conferences or maneuvered for enough political attention so that Trump (or at least more local politicians) might have been embarrassed into doing the right thing. None did.

***** Because the chronology of this work is important, in later editing, I have left previous analysis intact. Where circumstances later changed and made clarification important, you will observe in subsequent pages that I have added to this work with a dated notation of "Edit" in parenthesis as such: (Edit, August 6, 2020. I'm adding this explanation so that readers understand these non-standard descriptors.)

Failings of a Federation

It would be intellectually dishonest to place blame solely on Trump. There's limited information concerning the advice and information that leaders at the state and local levels received. Everyone in public health should have seen the potential danger and warned their client organizations, and many did, perhaps quite vocally, albeit out of the public eye. How is it then that it took SO long for politicians and/or public health officials to act (and by act, I mean, initiate social distancing measures, close venues, prohibit gatherings, and curtail non-essential economic activity that risked contagion)?

It's possible they were all "Going to Abilene." Many people with a business degree know about the Abilene Paradox which concerns a story about a group of people, one of whom casually suggests traveling to Abilene, TX. The most agreeable of the group responds affirmatively, and one by one everyone else agrees, no one wanting to rock the boat. Once they get there, it turns out no one wanted to go to Abilene. Even the person who first suggested the trip was merely freewheeling, expecting his idea would be summarily rejected.

Let's say you're in charge of Public Health for Virginia as an example. Maybe you don't want to rock the boat with the governor or step out too far in front of neighboring states by playing Paul Revere.

In some cases, maybe in spite of their training and knowledge of epidemiology, they couldn't bring themselves to believe a pandemic was coming. Maybe they let themselves become overly concerned with the economic picture despite their positions as health officials. Or maybe some aren't good enough at their jobs to have understood the threat. Of note, as of mid-May, few health officials seem to have been fired. In one notable exception, Connecticut Gov. Ned Lamont fired his Public Health Commissioner during the crisis.

It is evident that by early February at the latest, any public health official who wasn't warning the politicians in their jurisdiction about the need to prepare for a pandemic was entirely negligent in their duties. Even Trump's economic advisor, Peter Navarro, warned the president on January 29th of the potential of "a full-blown pandemic, imperiling the lives of millions of Americans." To be fair, Navarro is a bona fide hater of China, and it might have served him politically to highlight a virus that originated in Wuhan. But he wasn't wrong, nor did he stretch the truth.

If many of our nation's citizens, including myself, who have nothing to do with public health, could see what was coming, those with applicable knowledge and responsibilities should have done more. Perhaps many health officials elevated their concerns to their mayors and governors and it was primarily the politicians' bad judgment for doing nothing? How could that be, some may wonder?

No need to wonder too hard. The war on science goes back well before Galileo. It's hard to believe that in an age where advanced technology is everywhere, that science could be so dramatically under attack. It comes down to advocacy and the flow and control of information. One must only contemplate the actions of a typical parent to understand that humans make great advocates irrespective of the legitimacy of their convictions. "My kid should be starting at shortstop!" "How could you give my child a C minus on that essay?!"

No doubt, teachers and coaches hear these words from the parents of the least intelligent, least coordinated children. People advocate for corrupt arguments, too: "Smoking doesn't cause cancer!" "Global warming is a Chinese hoax."

Progress can seem unobtainable when we still have at this moment tens of thousands who believe the earth is flat. So, of course, we have a plentiful supply of business owners and politicians adversely affected by stay-at-home orders, who have been happy to deny all things pandemic that might take money out of their pockets or otherwise threaten their power, not to mention, impinge on their freedom.

The war on science has lent fertile ground to pandemic deniers, but there are other factors. It used to be that a high percentage of our (male) population, particularly those destined for leadership, served in the military. Especially in wartime and as a military officer, you have to learn how to make decisions about life and death. I would include a caveat that veterans in support roles (rather than combat/operational) *are not exposed to this 'life and death' experience* and perform commensurately.

Since the end of Viet Nam, fewer and fewer public officials or politicians have military (particularly operational) experience, and it shows. They don't seem to know how to make life and death decisions. We expect businessmen to screw this up – that's why we have those liability laws. But politicians need to be able to make analytical decisions involving life and death. The policies of a police force, the safety of our roads and bridges, the level of medical care and nutrition for the poor— all these issues require balancing life and death considerations against financial responsibilities—and then communicating those priorities to the public to garner their support. It's a skillset few people are born with.

When I first scratched the surface, the data did not support my assertion. There are currently eight governors with military backgrounds, and as a group, they did not perform particularly well against the virus. Digging a little deeper, seven of the eight governors had either been noncombat – lawyers or doctors – or had been enlisted in the military, where they would have had less life and death responsibility. But the worst performance of the lot has been Louisiana Governor John Bel Edwards, who had served as an officer in an army operational (combat) unit—the exact kind of experience that should have prepared him well for the pandemic. So why did Edwards' Louisiana fare so poorly (as of mid-April)?

At the risk of turning this into an epidemiological discussion (a pitfall to which I am about to fail), it's important to look at the data. Figure 2 below compares by state, per capita CoVid-19 cases versus population density (defined by state population divided by the respective state's land area).

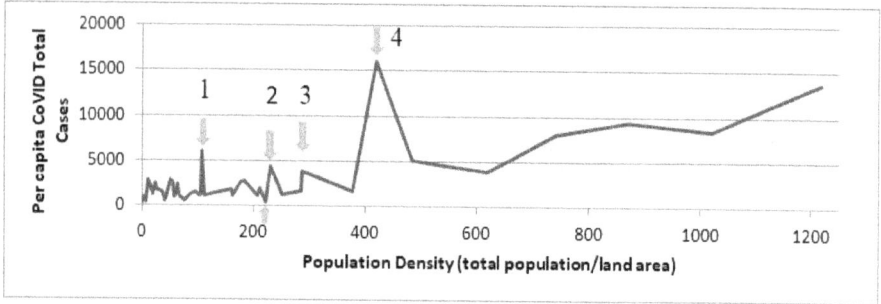

Figure 2

The total number of cases can be a blunt instrument. Among other issues, areas that test less will statistically see fewer total cases. So one can argue that "per-capita total cases" is inherently distorted, but it is a useful tool for the more simple analyses. The correlation of the above graph, a number which states how related population density is to COVID-19 cases, is .77. Anything over .7 is considered a strong correlation, which means that population density has an awful lot to do with how many people become infected. To better understand correlation, a two-axis plot of a perfectly straight line with a positive slope (sloping upwards) would have a correlation of 1, meaning a perfect correlation between the two variables. A straight line with a negative slope would have a correlation of -1, meaning a perfect inverse correlation, which basically means, as one variable goes up, the other goes down proportionately.

The graph indicates what epidemiologists know well and what the rest of us might intuit, that states with greater population density spread more disease, even on a per capita basis. This is simple science and math, which will be true nearly everywhere and for any contagious disease.

Figure 2 also highlights spikes (denoted by arrows)—outliers as statisticians would call them. The bottom (unlabeled) arrow (a few millimeters right of 200 on the horizontal axis) points to a state doing especially well. It is not a huge surprise that this state is Hawaii. Every island destination has fared well as of May 2, when this data was collected. That is also not unexpected. It's easy to shut down travel to an island destination.

The strong performance suggests that many new infections can be traced to "travelers" – people traveling longer distances, i.e., interstate travelers. It is then useful to ask, who is currently doing the most intrastate traveling? While this data is not easily obtained, we can make some educated guesses. Truckers are probably up there. There are also healthcare workers. It makes sense that these groups could be spreading a lot of disease. It may also be possible that island residents, by nature, are more comfortable "staying in place."

The top arrows (1-4) are the least lucky states, from left to right, Louisiana, Illinois, Pennsylvania, and New York. Of those, Louisiana (1) and New York (4) are the worst. If we ignore Louisiana for the moment, IL, PA, and NY (2, 3, & 4) contain three of the nation's most populous cities: Chicago, IL; Philadelphia, PA; and New York, NY—respectively, the 3rd, 6th, and 1st most populous. Those three cities also have remarkably high population densities. Philadelphia (the 6th most populous) drives a bigger spike than Chicago (the 3rd most populous), despite Philadelphia having 60% of the population of Chicago. Meanwhile, the nation's 2nd most populous city, Los Angeles, has failed to make California an outlier. What's going on here?

It's apparent that leadership decisions are playing a significant role. California was put placed under a mandatory stay-at-home order on March 19. It was the first state to do so. To date, California has performed exceptionally well, considering it is the most populous state with several of the most heavily populated cities, and possibly the worst homelessness in the nation.

From March 21 – March 24, governors of the following states also issued stay-at-home orders: New Jersey, New York, Maryland, Connecticut, Massachusetts, Ohio, and West Virginia. Those states are colored green in the map below:

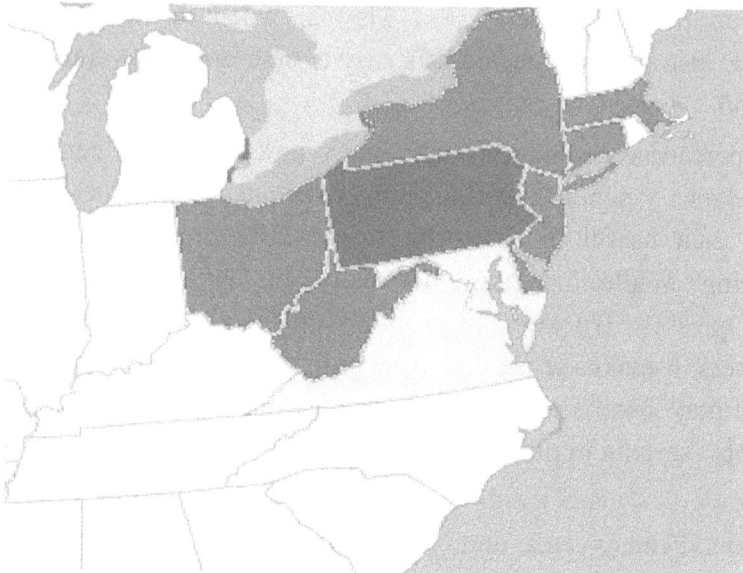

Figure 3

Pennsylvania, in red, waited until April 1 to issue its stay-at-home order. That one-week delay created that costly spike (#2) for Pennsylvania which persisted for months. It's worth investigating Gov. Tom Wolf's thinking, when he kept Pennsylvania open while all the states around him shut down. For what it's worth, Maryland and Virginia in yellow-green waited until March 30, and they didn't fare well either. Of interest, there is almost no correlation between when each state in the Northeast shuts down versus the respective governor's political party.

Back to Figure 2, what about the big spike in New York (4)? People are going to be discussing New York for a while. I think it would be useful to mentally place ourselves back in March 2020:

On March 17, New York City has about 400 new cases, on that day alone. The city is about to get slammed, but the context is important. Americans have been taking a "dip your toe in the water, and then ease in slowly" approach to social distancing and quarantine. It's not what reality demands.

It's desirable to give companies, schools, and other large organizations a few days to shutter their doors in an orderly manner, which is all the more reason why social distancing should have been initiated earlier. White-collar companies with intelligent leadership have had their employees working from home for some time—some as early as January. And there have been all kinds of "guidelines" – suggestions for social distancing, which many (if not most) Americans have begun to adopt. But without mandatory orders, there are far too many interactions between people to keep the virus from getting out of control.

New York Mayor de Blasio is calling for a "shelter-in-place model." He recognizes the need to mandate the greatest feasible level of social distancing possible, but he doesn't think he can legally shut the city down, believing such an order has to come from either the governor or the president. The semantics are interesting. It's not clear what to call the order, who can issue it, or if it's even legal to be executed by any level of American government.

It has to be understood that this COVID-19 worldwide pandemic is somewhat unprecedented. There have been pandemics before, but the current situation is quite different. We have better science and biology as well as an ability to remain at least electronically connected unlike ever before. A vaccine is likely within 18 months (edit: substantially sooner, now), and before that, viable therapeutic treatment to mitigate some of the virus's effects is definitely achievable. So there's a definite logic to a stay-at-home order. There are also logical arguments against such an order. It's all uncharted territory.

What's clear is that few politicians have the balls to shut down any segment of the American economy. If a shutdown is to be the strategy, though, it is absolutely critical to shut down as soon as possible. Why?

Mathematics and psychology inform us by offering the following guidance:

1) Humans are primarily two-dimensional thinkers. We understand things well when we have to account for two variables, generally an independent variable, which can also be thought of as an input variable, and a dependent variable, which is often the observed output. Beyond two variables:
   a. It gets difficult to graph. At best, we can draw a three-dimensional graph on (2D) paper, but unless we can rotate the graph around on all three axes (as we would any other three-dimensional object), we can't see what's happening. And when we get to four dimensions, we can't use visualization tools well, so we resort primarily to mathematical formulas.
   b. Calculating the math becomes exponentially more difficult as the number of variables increase. There are many situations where we can't explicitly solve multi-variable mathematical equations. In those cases, we must resort to creating models.
2) Models are simply that. We construct a best guess at what is happening. There are always assumptions involved in modeling; that is one of the major differentiators between using a model versus computing a more exact answer.
3) Sometimes these assumptions can be wildly inaccurate, and when they are, the model will usually (though not always) be wildly inaccurate.
4) Models begin with *initial conditions* – the state of your system before you begin to manipulate it, generally in time.

Depending upon what you are modeling, small changes in initial conditions can have immense effects upon your model's future state – its predictions.

5) We don't often need to assume initial conditions; we can observe them from reality, but even then, if our observations are inaccurate, the model can be way off.

6) If you want to understand anything about epidemiological models, understand that these models agree that when facing an impending pandemic EVERYTHING gets MUCH better the quicker EVERYTHING possible IS SHUT DOWN. Shutting down even slightly earlier results in:
   a. Far fewer total cases
   b. Far fewer deaths
   c. Far less stress on the healthcare system
   d. A shorter shut down period and therefore
      i. Far less economic pain and damage to the economy
      ii. Less emotional stress on the population
      iii. Less secondary effects that social distancing naysayers warn about – i.e., suicides, drug problems, domestic violence
   e. Easier, cheaper, and more effective contact tracing
   f. All of the above is pure science and math – objectively derived and proven. All fact and zero opinion.

I can't emphasize enough what has been said by many. You can't heal the economy without fighting back the virus. Most people are not going to risk their lives or the lives of their loved ones to get a cheeseburger or sit in a movie theater. In mid-March, the economic realities of the public's health concerns should have been old news to nearly every US governor. On March 19, as Gov. Gavin Newsom is shutting down California, New York has 1770 new cases. De Blasio is still "requesting" a shutdown of New York City. Cuomo complains that a "shelter in place/stay at home" order will be counterproductive if adjoining states don't do the same—a challenge to his neighbors and a subtle rebuke of national leadership. Since every one of the continental United States adjoins, Cuomo is implying either the entire country remains open, or the entire country "stays at home." Besides, Cuomo doesn't want to get left at home if everyone else goes to Abilene—meaning Cuomo isn't ready for the heat that Newsom is receiving.

Trump continues to wildly downplay the threat of the virus. His pandemic strategy, which we'll eventually cover in detail, is perfectly incoherent.

On March 20, there are 2,950 new cases in New York, and Cuomo, probably operating on only a few hours of sleep, has finally had enough. The pressures on him have to be immense. It's clear that New York City is headed for a full-blown pandemic. Nothing can change that, though Cuomo must realize if something isn't done soon, he will oversee the nightmare scenario of oversaturating hospitals, and the fatality rate will skyrocket. Other governors are facing similar pressures, but the notion of shutting down New York City – the center of world finance, home of the UN, perhaps the closest thing the world has to a capital – seems unthinkable. (Full disclosure, I grew up mostly in Upstate New York but attended PS22 in Flushing, Queens. So, I may have an elevated view of the Big Apple.)

Cuomo plugs his nose and jumps into the stay-at-home pool, but his order will not officially take effect for two more days, on March 22. He calls it, "New York State on Pause," fearing other labels sounded too drastic. It all sounds drastic. It's also too late.

The next day, March 21, Illinois and New Jersey follow California's lead, becoming the second and third states to "stay-at-home." There are 3,254 cases in New York that day, and 4,812 on March 22, when Cuomo's order is finally in full effect.

To be entirely fair to Gov. Cuomo, it takes time for some of the case data to catch up, so he had initially been presented with lower numbers.

More importantly, he mans up like no other politician has or will. Cuomo says what Trump should have said: "I accept full responsibility. If someone is unhappy, if somebody wants to blame someone, or complain about someone, blame me. There is no one else who is responsible for this decision."

I cannot emphasize enough that these should have been President Trump's words. The best thing for the country would have been to shut everything down as soon as the inevitability of a pandemic was clear. Unfortunately, it took weeks for some governors to stand up against the political pressure to keep businesses open. Even lacking a federal order (as some doubt there was a legal avenue for such an order), Trump could have given the nation's governors plenty of political cover to get their states closed earlier. Instead, the virus was allowed to run rampant.

For those paying attention, there was another oversight: The TESTING!

We'll cover testing in more detail, but suffice to say, there were virtually no tests accomplished by mid-March. Available data offers an estimate of somewhere between 500-2,000 tests administered by March 15. Subsequent investigation reveals that there were over 3800 total COVID-19 cases in the US on that same date. COVID-19 diagnoses were primarily presumptive – if a patient had the symptoms, they were counted and treated as COVID positive. That totally hampered early efforts of contact tracing, where health officials interview and trace the contacts of every infectious or potentially infectious person. Those people who are exposed close and long enough for disease transmission to be possible are then directed into quarantine until it's proven they did not catch the virus. Done properly, contact tracing can stop even second or third order contacts from spreading. I.e., let's say Bill became infected visiting his aunt, and the next day, he spends an hour at lunch with Linda. Then, the next day, Linda spends an hour at lunch with Helen, all four of them should quarantine, regardless of symptoms, once Bill's aunt's status becomes known. But if Bill's aunt never gets tested, no one is sent into quarantine, and the disease just spreads.

Early in the US, no one with minor symptoms was tested, and these people spread COVID-19 like wildfire. Think about how many people you (used to) interact closely within a typical day. With 3800 cases, we should have been testing ten times that number at a bare minimum. 25 to 50 times would have been desirable in a perfect world. By March 5, we should have tested over 100,000, but we'd only tested about 1,000. Is there any wonder we never had a chance?

Our efforts to understand the disease have been hampered from the start because we did not monitor how it initially spread. No symptoms meant no diagnosis, and in most cases, even symptoms meant no diagnosis, until they became severe. The one statistic that most people agree upon is that there were (and are) more COVID-19 positive individuals than have been documented. Even at the time, it was abundantly clear to Gov. Cuomo where the New York numbers were going. Many became afraid the entire country was headed for the Italian pandemic schedule. Italy was the first, after China, to turn into a red-hot mess. As of May 2, 2020, Italy had 209 thousand total cases. The US had over 1.1 million. From early April onwards, the Italian schedule looked pretty good.

New York would eventually reach over 10,000 cases a day, off and on, for over 3 weeks. If New York had shut down on March 17, when the caseload was less than 10% of what it was on March 22, would that have reduced the infection rate by 90%?

There's more to it than that. Cuomo's order wasn't exactly like flipping a switch. New Yorkers had already modified their behavior substantially. Many citizens were staying in place well before and after March 22. However, people were often doing a poor job of social distancing.

Determining how many fewer cases there might have been or lives lost is too big a math problem for these pages. In one recently publicized estimate, if the country had initiated a stay-at-home order one week earlier, we would have saved 40% of the lives lost in New York. Needless to say, many of those lost would have lived if Cuomo acted sooner.

He's a bright guy, and it probably didn't take him long to realize his error. He never had to think about life and death in numbers like this before this. In March 2020, he was thrown into the fire, and we can see how the experience informed his every move for the next several months.

As I write this on May 3, many states are about to open up. To quote Yogi Berra, "It's déjà vu all over again." This time, though, we have a choice at where to set the "initial conditions" for what will be a new model. It's a new model because things have changed quite a bit since mid-March. People are wearing masks in much greater numbers and generally keeping a greater physical distance from others. Our infrastructure has, at least partly, adapted. But the math hasn't changed. The fewer COVID positive individuals there are in an area that is reopening, the smaller the next wave will be.

I can promise that the states that are patient will benefit greatly. Those that are opening tattoo parlors and bowling alleys (yes, looking at you, Georgia) will pay a price. In general, states with substantial or growing numbers of COVID-19 positive individuals who relax social distancing guidelines will see substantially fewer positive cases and deaths.

Not Gov. Cuomo, though. Fool him once, shame on him; fool him twice.... Cuomo is one of a handful of governors who will not repeat his earlier mistake. In New York, much to the annoyance of many businesses, there is rigid discipline to the quarantine. While most upstate counties are permitted to open up, the epidemiology dictates that in New York City, where population density is so high, anything greater than a minuscule of positive cases could rapidly fuel a catastrophic new wave of infection.

There are also hundreds of mayors of major cities that play a role in the safety of their citizens. How did it happen that in March, every one of the nation's executive-level politicians waited too long? Some acted quicker than others, but nearly all were too late. Was it some kind of groupthink/Abilene paradox? Deer in headlights?

When it became time to reopen the economy, the same impossible choice had returned. Would we extend the quarantine to keep the infections low but wreck the economy, or let the disease run rampant and potentially kill a million or more?

I believe our politicians continued to be in denial. It was inconceivable that we would shut down our economy and voluntarily throw ourselves into a major depression. And it was unthinkable to let more than a million of our citizens be killed. Keep in mind, at this point it was still not well known how deleterious CoVID-19 could be to survivors.

Step to the left and get hit by a truck or to the right and get hit by a car. Some point to a potential third alternative, splitting the difference between a strict lockdown versus no reaction at all. Later, I'll have explicit words concerning such a "compromise" strategy.

Leadership Matters (except when it doesn't)

What of poor Gov. Edwards of Louisiana—remember, the military officer who should have done better?

Gov. Edwards appears to be largely a victim of circumstance.

Let's return to February 25:

There are only 15 officially confirmed cases in the US. The Louisiana/New Orleans governments have devoted time and resources attempting to assess the virus's impact on their state's unique activities. They decide keeping Mardi Gras on the schedule represents a minimal risk—too small to turn away a billion dollar's worth of business to the local economy. No other large gatherings had canceled, so neither would Mardi Gras (which is more of a season than an actual day).

By March 9, there are still Mardi Gras activities—not blowouts, more like aftershocks from the big party. It's on this date that Louisiana has its first confirmed CoVID-19 case. The next day, the state begins shutting down street-level events. By March 16, there are 33 new cases and 3 CoVID-19 related deaths. Edwards orders further closures of bars, gyms, movie theatres, and he limits restaurants to take-out only. Governor Edwards has NO intention of going to Abilene. It's a brave move, effectively shutting down the economy of New Orleans ahead of the entire country. It's a good bet the governor spent the next week appeasing angry business owners.

The math of the virus does not treat him any better. A week later on March 23, there are 335 new cases in Louisiana, and Edwards officially shuts the entire state down, only a day after New York did. The Big Apple was registering over 10 times the New Orleans numbers.

Louisiana still spikes quickly, reaching 2,726 cases on April 2. This offers a unique data point. Unlike many other spikes around the world where families and friends went out and caught the virus together, the NOLA population shows a mini spike the third week in March before the big spike on the 1st week of April. The data suggests a first round of infections of tourist industry workers managing the poorly timed Mardi Gras festivities in the first week of March. Over the next several weeks, those workers then brought home and spread the virus to family members in a second and possibly third round of infections. Interestingly, unlike the rest of the nation, Louisiana cases come down about as fast as they rise—an indication that the quarantine, once finally put into place, was well executed.

It's difficult to look at Edwards' actions in a greater context and be critical, particularly relative to the rest of the country. He actually had one of the first stay-at-home orders in place, only behind California, Illinois, New Jersey, and New York. And they all had far more cases. The math is clear that shutting down even sooner would have saved lives, but in shutting down when he did, Edwards did save lives, particularly relative to other governors.

One might ask, if Edwards had sharply curtailed economic activity only a day after the first COVID-19 case was observed in the state, how could he have shut things down any sooner? And why would he? That's exactly the point. We know now that the virus had started spreading throughout the world well before we noted its presence.

For a novel virus that often presents with flulike symptoms, this should not have come as a surprise. What should be obvious now is that we should have shut down transmission of the virus at the first indications of danger. This is a lesson that may already have been forgotten as of early May.

Two other governors deserve specific mention. First, Gov. Inslee of Washington, where the nation's first hot spot develops. He's the first executive-level politician to face the virus in his territory.

He wanted to have it both ways. He was vocal and aggressive, hoping his citizens would stay home voluntarily, keeping him from having to issue an order. It took until March 23, when it became clear that the virus was quickly spreading despite his tough talk, for Inslee to issue a formal stay-at-home order.

When we look back at the data before May 3, it's clear that Inslee's earlier appeals for social distancing kept the numbers down. Cases peaked on March 26, so a significant number of people would have changed their behavior in the March 12 to March 20 timeframe.

The other notable governor was Jim Justice of West Virginia. Some reports affirm there was only a single documented case in the state on March 24, when he issued his stay-at-home order. Republican Gov. Justice truly wrecked the curve. West Virginia is a mostly rural state with fewer international and domestic travelers than its neighbors, but even accounting for those advantages, West Virginia fares extremely well. I probably can't overstate how well Justice "punched above his weight."

On a per capita basis, West Virginia was only bested by Hawaii (with its unique natural advantages), Alaska, and Montana, both of which have drastically lower population densities. West Virginia is the model that everyone should be trying to emulate. Surely other governors were getting similar advice from their public health advisors, but only Gov. Justice listened. Despite his success, the state and its governor somehow avoid the limelight. Maybe his health advisor pressured him with incriminating pictures? I'd love to know more. I suppose successfully leaving the public in the dark is a measure of success in American politics.

(Edit: July 28, 2020. West Virginia continues to punch above its weight, and Hawaii continues to have the least number of infections in the nation. Louisiana kept it together for some time and then totally lost it. It's not clear why. On July 11, Gov. Edwards issued a mandatory mask order. It should have come earlier, but he's still well ahead of states like Florida and Texas. Louisiana is primarily a red state with a Democrat governor. Edwards received a lot of blowback from local Republican politicians, and Republican constituents may be ignoring the governor's orders for social distancing and masks to spite him. I expect Louisiana will or certainly should receive special scrutiny from epidemiological researchers in the future.)

What about the rest of the governors? We can recycle the data from Figure 2 and eliminate our 5 statistical outliers to create Figure 4. When we do, we see in mathematical terms, a straight plotline with a high correlation of .92 – meaning that population density is incredibly influential in disease spread. There are a handful of small spikes on the left end of the chart. In all of the states represented by those spikes, you'll find a meatpacking plant and/or a prison system. If we were to remove the caseload from those plants and prisons, the line would be even straighter.

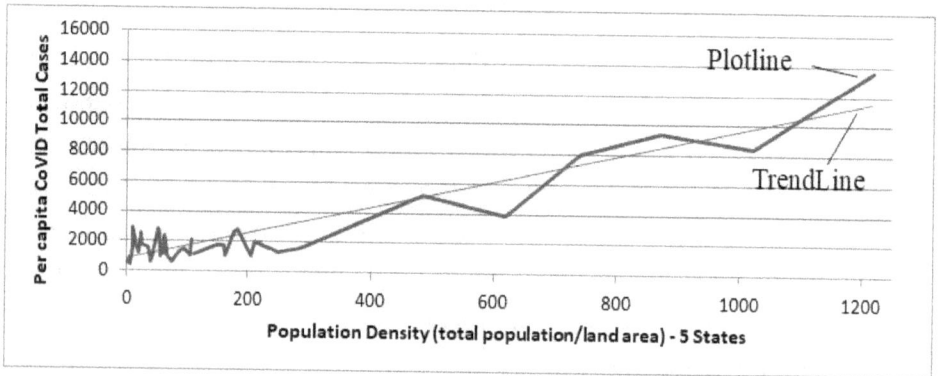

Figure 4 (per capita cases vs. population density, as of May 2)

One might argue this is an odd commentary on state leadership. In observing the straightness of this line, its .92 correlation, one could argue that it hardly mattered from state to state what measures were put in place, nor when they began as population density appears to play the overriding role. That would be mathematically dishonest for several reasons. First, nowhere along the line is it perfectly straight. Every point or bend in the plot represents an individual state. If you compare the actual performance of each state – every point where the plotline bends – relative to the thin straight trend line in Figure 4, you'll note each state performs a little above or below. How much above or below the trend line represents an incremental amount of illness and death that did or didn't happen in each respective state based upon factors other than population density. Leadership strategies account for a substantial percentage of this incremental amount.

Second, the Figure 4 plot, as depicted is misleading. The magnitude of the scale, at densities exceeding 1200, and per capita caseload at up to 14,000, artificially distorts the appearance of variations at the smaller magnitudes charted on the left of the graph.

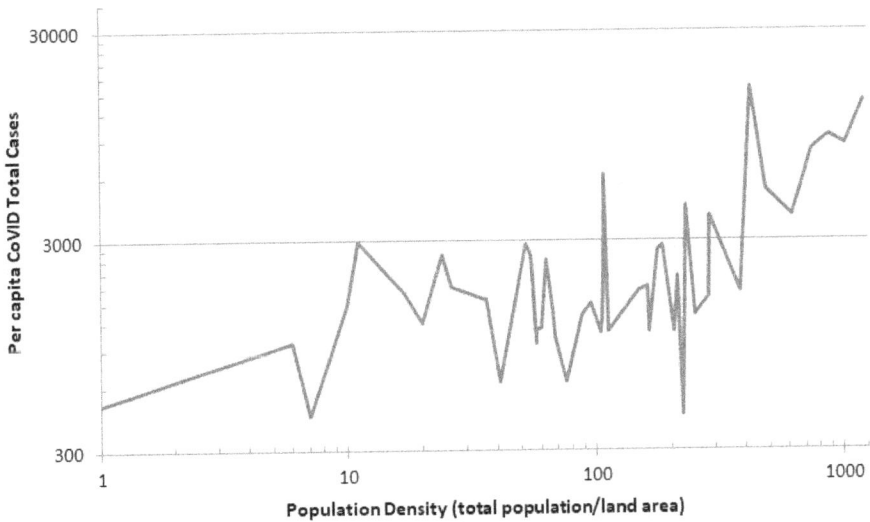

Figure 5 (per capita cases vs. population density – logarithmic scales)

Figure 5 shows definitively that leadership matters. Believe it or not, this chart is drawn with the exact same data as Figure 2, the chart with the spikes. But here we use what is called, logarithmic scales for our axes. Log scales are used to visualize data when analyzing low and high numbers in a single dataset. I could have blown up the left side of the chart (and chopped off the larger numbers on the right), and that would have shown how different the performance was for the less densely populated states. The log scale chart is a more elegant tool that

65

demonstrates how deceptive the original chart was, without having to truncate any of the data. We can still see the general correlation trend from low to high population density, but Figure 5 highlights notable differences in the infection levels of each state, independent of population density.

What does that all mean? Simply this: Leadership matters.

An Elephant

There's one of them 800-pound elephants with us. And a donkey, too. I'm not sure how much the donkey weighs, and to be honest, the elephant's weight is also in question. I'd love to divorce politics and partisanship from this entire book—more than you know. I consider myself an American patriot above all else. The plurality of my adult years I spent in New Hampshire where a person such as myself can proudly remain an independent, in no way beholden to any political party. I live in Florida now, where I have to declare a party to vote in a primary. I place a high value on my right to vote, but an even higher value on my independence from political parties. So I haven't voted in a Florida primary in seven years. Please don't tell my kids.

Independent does not at all mean dispassionate or lacking strong opinions. Both parties (and their supporters) make plenty of mistakes they should be called out for! I'm perhaps too often compelled to believe I should be the one calling them out. So I'm kind of a recovering social media political warrior-evangelist. I have wasted too many hours of my life arguing with online trolls, believing that a cogent argument will change a closed mind. I once believed the time spent was worth it. It's a dangerous fantasy placed inside our heads by the geniuses of Silicon Valley, a mental affliction for which abstinence is the only known cure. In writing this book, I sometimes feel like I've fallen off the wagon, which is one reason I'm fighting hard to steer clear of partisanship. But politics certainly cannot be divorced from leadership, and partisanship certainly cannot be divorced from politics. It needs to be addressed. I'll try not to write too much on the subject, but as you're about to bear witness, I'm going to fail.

Like a longstanding family feud, I've been in an ongoing battle with partisanship that reaches back decades, yet one story remains cemented in my mind. Back in 2004, the aviation industry was still in a recession stemming from the 9/11 attacks. There was a possibility of me losing my airline job, so I became an aspiring novelist and tried to get a book published. I was absorbed by this ridiculous notion that I'd be able to replace an airline pilot's salary with that of an author. I was advised that any professional writing gig would be a good start on the way to publishing my first novel and ultimately fame and glory. As I have always been a student of politics with a distaste of partisanship, I thought I might be able to do a good job writing a political column from a non-partisan viewpoint. It made perfectly good sense to me, as polls often show many people with political views on slightly left or slightly right of center, and everyone seemed to be growing tired of partisan fighting and gridlock. Somehow this niche, which seemed to me more like a chasm, was going unfilled. I wrote up a pitch for a column along with a couple of sample editorials. Then I made an appointment with the editor of the local paper, the *Union Leader*, in Manchester New Hampshire.

The Union Leader was at the time, a center-right leaning newspaper, with a slightly more Conservative editorial section. Since this was a reasonably small operation, I somehow managed to score a meeting with one of the paper's assistant editors. I believe I may have included a resume in my request letter – perhaps they thought I was going to help them blow the lid off the whole chemtrail conspiracy. Anyway, after a few pleasantries, I pitched the guy my non-partisan concept. At first, he stared back at me like I had two heads. After he realized there was no punchline, he simply asked, "Why would we want to do that?"

That's it, that's the story. I responded to the man, but it was irrelevant to this discussion. The whole point was that to this gentleman, who I eventually came to realize well represented the journalism industry, partisanship is The Point. It was irrelevant that I might develop a readership and that a non-partisan column might help sell a few papers. Partisanship *is* the brand. Every organization of the journalist ecosystem has staked out territory along the partisan continuum, and to stray from that would be kind of like asking Ford to make a motorcycle. Could they do it? Sure. They don't want to; it doesn't fit into their *"product mix."* As someone with an MBA, this was obvious in later reflection. At the time, I faulted the newspaper for what I considered to be their absurdity.

Turns out the absurdity wasn't with the newspaper but with human nature. Partisans make up the larger part of news consumers, and partisans prefer news that fits into their respective worldviews, even at the cost of blatant inaccuracy. People in the center and those that favor accuracy versus validation of their worldview don't consume as much news. The market for reasonableness is a loser.

These economic pressures have driven journalism further and further from the center. The dystopian result has been the loss of fundamental truth. There is no longer A Truth. There is Our Truth or Their Truth. Our Facts or Their Facts, and guess what—no one is interested in Their Facts or Their Truth. Truth has been murdered or at best is held prisoner, and with so many people now vested and rewarded by the status quo, I'm not sure how we fix this.

If most of us are governed by confirmation bias, is it even possible to convince anyone of anything they don't already believe? The other half of neural perception, emotions, in many ways bypasses cognitive reasoning. Activate a strong enough emotion, and you just might change a mind. What are the strongest emotions? Those of our ancient "lizard brain" – fear, anxiety, greed, lust, anger. They are the emotions least influenced by rational thought, uninterested in truth or science. They are also the emotions of tribalism, a place our brains go when we feel least secure.

Though I suspect partisans on both sides disagree upon whom, one political party seems to have benefited more by capitalizing on this collective "fight or flight" reaction. Conservatism is an ideology vested in the status quo. Every event, every domestic or international incident, arguably, every moment in time presents the possibility of opportunity and/or threat. All things being equal, it is in the nature of progressives to frame necessary change in terms of opportunity, whereas Conservatives more often perceive danger. The threat of global warming illustrates my point well. Progressives are inclined to build an entirely new "green" industry around minimizing humanity's carbon footprint. Progressive businesspeople are excited about all of the new technology that will be introduced and all of the new jobs that will be created. Conservatives are focused on unproven fears of increased costs and lost oil industry jobs (despite the results of the Obama Administration's green initiatives, which drove down gas prices and didn't cost oil industry jobs). Have I sufficiently demonstrated my disdain for partisanship?

In today's environment, tribalism has become a fundamental need on both a personal and global level. It has come to control much of the world around us. People require their news and even recreational media agree with their lifestyle. If you're typical, your social media feeds are heavily biased toward your ideology because you rarely click on posts that contradict the ideas of those around you.

Besides tribalism and the loss of truth, there's another force driving us toward partisanship. Over the last several decades, increasing amounts of power have been handed to a small number of individuals at the highest levels of government. How has that happened?

Once again, it's a matter of simple math. We stole power away from individual congressmen.

How?

By eliminating earmarks.

Huh?

Let me explain: the not so young may remember hearing something about a "bridge to nowhere." It was around 2005 when Alaskan senators tried to attach to legislation a provision to spend $300 million on a bridge from mainland Alaska to the Ketchikan airport, which at the time could only be reached by ferry. The bridge would have serviced a relatively small number of people. It was therefore dubbed the 'Bridge to Nowhere," by politicians with a particular agenda that had little to do with the bridge. The marketing effort in vilifying this short stretch of expensive roadway was not an effort to save taxpayer money nearly as much as it was a way to eliminate earmarks from the congressional legislative system.

Earmarks permitted congressmen to include "pet" legislation (legislation directed toward their constituents, typically to the exclusion of the rest of America) in any related or unrelated budget bill. On the surface, eliminating earmarks seemed a good idea, but here's why it wasn't: we send our politicians to Washington to get things done. No matter where you live, there are important things that need to be funded in your state that don't mean a hill of beans to the other 49. Earmarks were the best tool for Congress to *wheel and deal*. The system increased bipartisanship and the approval of more legislation.

Congress members had more power. If they couldn't get what they wanted from their own party, they could cross over to the opposition to cut deals. Party leaders had a harder time keeping caucus members in line. If a majority of the group wanted legislation, even if it didn't have the leader's support, they were more inclined to bring it to a vote. After all, the cost of antagonizing individual legislators was higher when there was always a risk of losing votes to the other side. Even the president had to respect this power from time to time. But now, where's that same motivation for our leaders? Gone. Individual congress-people have nowhere else to go, short of defecting entirely from their party, which some, though very few have done. There is little motivation for Congress members to even be civil to those on the other side of the aisle.

Though it was not without abuses, earmarks were the primary lubricant to the legislative process. Today, if a member of Congress needs to have legislation passed, they are beholden to their political parties, which really means beholden *to the leaders* of their respective political parties. Nothing gets done in D.C. today unless it has support from Trump, Pelosi, and McConnell. Is it any wonder so little gets done? With only three people calling the shots in American Government, I'm struggling to differentiate our current system from that of an American

Politburo. America, in the strictest sense of the word, has become an oligarchy.

In 2011, when the ability to include earmarks in legislation was effectively banned by the Tea Party's new congressional rules, the intention appeared innocent enough. Earmarks were generally considered "pork," a pejorative term for unnecessary/wasteful government spending. Fiscal Conservatives had been rallying against earmarks for years, in spite of their understanding that loss of earmarks would mean loss of power by individual members of Congress.

The process was not without corruption, but there were avenues to address excesses. The "bridge to nowhere" amendment was successfully blocked without changing rules, as were many other wasteful earmarks. Some were passed, though, and it doesn't take a lot of money spent in Liberal districts on Liberal causes, and vice-versa, to get voters outraged. The practice of earmarks died in the second half of President Obama's first term, without meaningful opposition by the president. It was in my view one of President Obama's biggest political mistakes.

It needs to be said that the death of the earmark had primarily been a goal of the Republican Party. It was couched within fiscal conservatism, but its primary purpose had been to advance a greater, right-leaning agenda. Many Democratic causes relied on earmarks for funding. The elimination of earmarks shifted spending to more Conservative ventures. Meanwhile, the resultant hamstringing of the political process has resulted in a more impotent, less effective, and less productive federal government. The depiction of the government as more of a problem than solution is a longstanding goal of the Republican Party—a goal in which it has succeeded.

If it makes me sound any less partisan, I believe that Democrats are largely schmucks. For anyone needing the definition, because I want to be clear here, schmuck is a Yiddish word for penis, in other words, a pejorative term somewhat equivalent to dick. I've used it here because I'm struggling to definitively convey what's wrong with the Democrats.

Somehow an insult without true meaning seems to fit. Primarily, I am bothered by how ineffective they are at battling against Republican power grabs. How difficult is it to publicly state, "Hey, the Republicans don't want government to succeed. They want our efforts to fail. If that's what you want, vote Republican. If you want a government that will work for the better interest of the people, vote Democrat." Or words to that effect. How difficult would that be? I watch the news regularly. It's so rare to hear anything approaching this level of sincerity.

I will also add that I'm particularly bothered by the policies of the Far Left and certainly the Far Right. Can't we all agree that Republicans get some things right, and Democrats get other things right? Voters should feel beholden to our country, but the average voter should owe no allegiance to party.

Who am I kidding? I recently voted in a local election for a bunch of judges and lower-level officials. Nowhere on the ballot or even online was there any mention of party affiliation. I could find no voter group summaries for these officials. I had to do all the research on my own. It took hours. I think it's a reasonable question to ask how many of our citizens are willing to devote hours to researching national candidates like a president, senator, or congressperson? Think about how many of us vote at all. The Party system is an endorsed cheat sheet for the lazy American voter. Zero studying required.

The two-party system sometimes looks good on paper. When it works, it works well. The majority party controls the government, and the minority party, by intention, becomes the watchdog, monitoring the majority for slipups. The minority, with concurrence of the voters, holds the majority accountable. But what happens when the majority does everything or most things right? What role is left for the minority? What happens to a system that was designed for conflict when the natural source of that conflict is removed?

This is where we see the true toxicity of two sets of facts, two truths. Because having two truths is no better than having no truth, and without truth, political conflict simply becomes two opposing sides in disagreement, vying for the title of most bellicose advocate.

The other "potential" problem with the political party system occurs when one or more parties inspire devotion to party over country. Ironically, policy becomes irrelevant. The whole point of a political party is to advance a defined agenda, and yet with blind devotion to party, the failure of agenda becomes a *fait accompli*.

For the record, I did not get offered that political column, but I did keep my flying job, which I suppose was just as well as I had three hungry kids to feed.

Partisanship and COVID

I try to remain cognizant of the fact that as we age, our perceptions change. New things become apparent to us as our understanding of the world matures. So maybe I've been delusional up until now, but my recollection is that in crises of America's past, our two political parties found a way to come together, at least in so much as to the country and the world, they would present a united front. I think I can be forgiven for believing in the context of today's shit-show that this must be my imagination conjuring up some naïve, nostalgic interpretation. For the younger of you though, ask around. I'm certain most people my age and older would agree that historically, when the going got tough, Congress got a tad more touchy-feely. From the McCarthy hearings and the Watergate era, through the transition of the Bush to Obama administration which happened in the midst of the 2008 financial crisis, mutual respect and cooperation didn't come easy, but it was generally accepted as an end-goal.

The entire evolution of partisan discord is too ugly and lengthy a tale for this discussion, suffice to say that what sits at the core of this plague of divergent opinion is the proliferation of alternative facts. It seems, no matter the issue in contention, each side is able to manufacture a set of "facts" to support their assertions. In most cases, the "facts" claimed by the opposing sides are mutually exclusive. Common sense and simple logic dictate that at best one or perhaps neither side is correct.

The implications for important issues are dire. Take, for example, the issue of global warming. The Left's assertion is that climate change is happening, is man-made, is accelerating, and if not appropriately addressed, will bring about catastrophic consequences in the not too distant future. If the Right is correct in its opposite assertions, then the substantial expenditures devoted to mitigate climate change represent an immense waste of money and resources.

Getting the answer wrong to climate change will result in significantly negative consequences to the entire world. The global population, with the exception of North Korea and the American Republican Party, accept climate change as a real and imminent threat. Somehow the Republican Party is nearly unified and resolute in its continued denial, even against an overwhelming majority of the scientific community and 7 billion others in opposition.

Americans have a history and tradition of rebelliousness, but this seems to be something new and clearly dangerous. Though the climate change story is playing out in a protracted drama, the *gifts* of partisanship to the COVID-19 crisis have bestowed upon us a relatively more rapid cataclysm.

And now we must needs discuss President Trump. At first, the threat of the virus was effectively a *hoax* that would have no effect on America, then it was going to quickly go away, and then…. Good grief, I just can't. Injecting disinfectant, hydroxychloroquine, there seems to be no comment too absurd, too patently stupid, to derail the cohesive, disciplined allegiance of Trump's supporters. On May 22, 2020, there were nearly 100,000 "officially" dead—there were likely more, but among the Trump faithful, this is not a dangerous virus at all.

With a death rate currently three times that of the next worse country, Trump's America is finally number one at something—and by a substantial margin. The president was certainly right about one thing. We have definitely become tired of winning. *"Please, please, it's too much winning. We can't take it anymore,"* is a direct quote from at least one of his lovely rallies. I guess he nailed it. Doctors and scientists have pointed out that a successful quarantine should look like a non-event, where everyone climbs out of their dens of hibernation, after almost no ill effects, and declares, "What was the big deal? Why did we have to go through this?"

Thanks to incoherent messaging, the sabotage of lifesaving guidance from the medical community, and particular thanks to late starts and weak restrictions, America's quarantines (50 state quarantines and many more municipal quarantines) have had on average, dismal results. And as of the time of writing this, it's only getting worse. Somehow, among Trump's supporters, 100,000 dead and counting is no big deal.

As we enter the Memorial Day Holiday, while America averages 25,000 new cases and 1,500 new dead a day, and with all 50 states easing quarantine restrictions, we do not appear well-positioned to see meaningful reductions in infections. Perhaps if as a nation we could agree to honor the recommendations of those smarter than us in the medical and epidemiological communities, we might have a fighting chance. But partisanship has attacked the science, and so a large segment of the population believes that facial masks either don't work or make us sicker. They see no value in social distancing guidelines and fight quarantine restrictions of any kind. Worse even than the deniers, are those who are indifferent to the fact that the virus is killing older people. As data suggests the infected young appear to have minimal symptoms, this group of people would sacrifice the older and sicker segment of our population in exchange for their own unfettered personal freedoms. In other words, *it's too big an inconvenience to put on a mask to save the lives of strangers.*

At many stages, the president had opportunities to lead the country through this crisis with grace and intelligent governance. Instead, he has led the charge in taking the most ridiculous positions at every step along the path to death and infection. He is like some odd caricature of himself, contradicting the rest of the federal government at every opportunity. With something as simple as wearing a mask in public, which epidemiologists believe would prevent as much as 75% of infections, our president has decided to create a partisan divide.

In the military, there's a saying: *The troops eat first.* It's a message of servant leadership, that you take care of your troops, and they will take care of the mission. Trump would never understand this concept. *He* eats first. Everyone else comes after him. He should have been the first person to put on a damn mask. Science tells us this without question. Trump's stupidity with many things, but even with something as simple as not publicly wearing a mask, has and will continue to cost lives.

With millions flaunting their defiance of science, it is likely that we will sustain or grow the current level of carnage for at least the next several months. Flare-ups and hot spots are likely, and the emergence of a true second wave is more than possible. If this book were a novel, the president would be the villain.

In many ways, truth proves to be stranger than fiction. There's no pretending otherwise. New Yorkers know Donald Trump all too well. Throughout his life, our current president had an obsessive need to be in the limelight, and he has made himself a public figure in New York City's news for decades. Transparent self-promotion became his avocation, and if he excels at anything, it is this. He was able to parlay this specific skill into building a valuable brand—that being his name—which he has made every effort to display in every possible venue, and with no cessation, even after he took office—in clear violation of civil law and the Constitution itself.

While it's generally true that "all press is good press," there comes a point where overexposure leads to annoyance, and it's safe to say that among New Yorkers, Trump reached that point a long time ago. Accordingly, Clinton won Donald Trump's home town of New York City by 90%. Clearly, a little bit of Donald Trump goes a long way, or as we might say in a loose parallel to Benjamin Franklin's quote regarding fish and houseguests, after three years, most of us are noticing the stink.

If you're a Trump supporter, this is merely evidence of the cluelessness and out of control liberalism of New York. It's simply fascinating how a substantial portion of his family, those who have worked for him before and during his Presidency, and the general public of his hometown who know him best have no regard or respect for him, yet his supporters aren't bothered by this in the least.

Of note, what attracts certain Americans to him are the exact qualities that annoy others to no end. Trump supporters have gotten and continue to get exactly what they wanted, which is why that hard 35% of the population continues to support their guy, despite the indications that show him to be the worst president ever.

Some Americans simply don't want a "politician" as president, nor do they don't want to listen to an "elite." By elite, they obviously don't mean a person of wealth, rather they don't want someone who makes intelligence and competence a high priority for leadership. They prefer someone with apparent brawn to anyone with brains. Some Americans simply adore Trump's combativeness, his unwillingness to cooperate with anyone inside or outside of the country. In today's divided America, some people's *flaws* are other people's *features*.

Testing—the One (Really) HUUGE Screw-up

At the beginning of any new challenge, particularly when one finds themselves out of their element, one of the best things you can do is to go benchmarking. Examining the successes (and failures) of those that have acted before you is quintessentially fundamental. So of course, the Trump administration put every effort into doing the exact opposite.

Nowhere has this been made clearer than with the debacle of COVID-19 *testing*, which has already been discussed by the media in great detail. There are two different types of tests. Nasal swab and saliva tests involve the detection of the actual virus, officially labeled SARS-CoV-2. This is the more important test because the presence of an active virus is a prerequisite to spreading the disease. There are also tests to look for virus-induced antibodies. Such antibodies indicate evidence of past infection and possibly some level of immunity. I suspect many books will be written on testing, and those books will generally not be read by the public, because it's all so complicated.

It is clear that the country's leading experts made substantial mistakes in the development of both types of tests. The reliability of public information detailing specifics of the mistakes is currently in doubt. It's going to take some time to figure it all out. Even the Wikipedia page is (as of this writing), misleading on a number of fronts.

What appears evident is that tests were developed by other countries and made available to the US by the WHO sometime in January. We did use some of those tests but rejected offers for more in the expectation that we would generate our own, which we presumed would be more accurate. Instead, mistakes in the creation of our own tests led to a waste of critical time, from early February until mid-March when almost no testing was accomplished in the US. The technical nature of those mistakes is well understood, but irrelevant to this discussion.

Before the first failed test had even been produced, the US should have been working hard to develop a contact tracing strategy. That strategy would have made clear the need for far more tests than what we could quickly produce ourselves. This conclusion would have in turn led to a strategy to obtain all of the *foreign* tests that we could. Regrettably, there appears to be minimal to no evidence of any federal effort at contract tracing, at any point in the course of the infections. State efforts at contact tracing were almost entirely inhibited because federal action and decisions were required to obtain the tests needed.

The bottom line is that once the virus was on American soil, the Trump administration's actions and inactions made it impossible to conduct anywhere near the desired level of testing. The possibility for appropriate contact tracing (by the Federal Government or the states) then became hopeless, and that's why we never had a chance to moderate early spread of the virus.

The exact opposite was happening in other countries like South Korea, Singapore, and Taiwan, all of which demonstrated early successes in combatting the virus. Plainly put, we had a roadmap available, to avoid economic hardship, illness, and death, but we said, "No thanks, we'll find our own way."

Setting aside the mistake in not obtaining more foreign tests for the moment, one or more people at the CDC, under the overall supervision of the FDA and HHS, were responsible for creating a flawed test. There's no doubt these people must feel awful, even devastated. But where does the buck stop? With the scientists? How about their supervisors, who hired them and put systems in place to ensure that when the nation NEEDED SOMETHING ESSENTIAL DONE RIGHT, it would be done right?

Or does the liability fall upon the leaders of those organizations, those with poorly worded mission statements, who may not have thought hard enough about the importance of their positions and the responsibilities that they held?

The buck should reasonably stop with the president who has shown little care and even less respect for science—a president who made it a point to take money away from pandemic response, not because of any particular ideology, because he doesn't seem to have any, but seemingly out of spite because the previous administration had made pandemic response a priority, and this carnival barker of a president has made an ideology out of working to reverse everything accomplished under his predecessor as though he was some spiteful ancient Egyptian Pharaoh striking from history any record of some unloving forefather.

Would a better leader had a staff that would have hired more talented scientists? Possibly. Better rewarded and inspired those scientists? Almost certainly. Funded and put in place better control systems to ensure triumph when we desperately needed success? Absolutely. Had better staff in related agencies who might have more quickly caught serious mistakes? It's difficult to believe otherwise. In learning that the American effort to develop a test was failing, executed a contingency to obtain more foreign tests? How could anyone believe otherwise?

Even lacking all of the above considerations, I suspect that if we simply had a president who did not have such a disdain for science as well as such an elevated opinion of his own ability to take on all the functions of the entire federal government, it would have been more likely that we would have created a successful SARS-CoV-2 test from the very beginning.

A Deeper Dive into Biology

At the time of my kids' birth, our home was in Abilene, Texas (so I know all about *going to Abilene*). This was a two-and-a-half-hour drive away from the Ft. Worth hospital, where I was to become all too knowledgeable in the respiration and blood transfusions of NICU infants. For three months, Lisa and I had been living in a small room in the Ronald McDonald house adjoining the Fort Worth hospital.

Did I mention I'd left the Air Force a few months prior, and that the kids were born nine days into my airline training? As it happened, that training had been in Forth Worth, and when Lisa went into premature labor, the Abilene hospital referred her to the bigger city, as Abilene did not have the resources to care for three babies as premature as ours. My friend Roger called to tell me that Lisa was being airlifted, and I actually beat her to the hospital.

My airline was extraordinarily decent and offered me as much time off as I needed. For better or worse, studying and learning is how I cope with stress. After five days off, I had learned much about prematurity and all about the NICU equipment. Lisa had been released following her C-section and was doing well physically, and I was probably getting on the nurses' and doctors' nerves with all my questions. As we had three new mouths to feed, not to mention an extraordinary number of bills that singleton parents never see, I decided to return to my job, which was at the time, training. It was a good decision, getting me away from the NICU for a few hours, and after class, I would return with my books to study. The NICU staff got a kick out of me reading my aircraft tech manuals to my children.

All in all, we were fortunate. Throughout the rollercoaster ride that defines most NICU experiences (ours having greater dips and dives than most), we were able to hold things together. Relatives visited from out of town, friends stopped by from Abilene, and my best friend, Roger the physician, visited as often as he could and never failed to pick up the phone.

John's abdominal operation had come and gone, leaving an awful abdominal scar, but he otherwise seemed to be slowly getting better. He came off the oscillating ventilator within a day, and with the help of some diuretics, he started excreting the extreme level of fluid that had accumulated in his tiny body.

A few weeks later, Jim and Mary were released from the hospital, which should have been the cause for great joy. Lisa took them back to the Ronald McDonald House because John was still a long way off from leaving the NICU. Medically, John had stabilized, and his organs were functioning better, but following the elimination of excess fluid, he had lost weight overall and was spitting up too much of the formula he was being fed.

Meanwhile, my training had ended and I had started flying passengers around, leaving Lisa to figure out how to care for Jim and Mary in a small room in the Ronald McDonald house, with almost no support. And this wasn't caring for two healthy newborns. Jim and Mary had been sent home with heart/respiration monitors, which would go off all day and night, sometimes because a sensor had fallen off, and occasionally because one of the kids would actually take a mini-vacation from breathing for a while.

They all spit up more than their fair share of meals. Lisa and I are both thin, a genetic trait that wasn't serving our kids well in those months. God bless her. Mostly on her own, Lisa took care of Jim and Mary for nine days, before we realized it made no sense. When I was flying, she could only visit with John briefly each day. Caring for the other two was literally a 24/7 job. Meanwhile, an army of friends back in Abilene was anxious to help. We made the difficult decision to have Lisa take Jim and

Mary back home to Abilene, leaving me to visit John sporadically, usually before and after my working trips out of Fort Worth.

Our NICU practiced what is known as kangaroo care, which begins as soon as the babies are off the vent. Moms and Dads go topless, and the baby lies in a diaper upon the parent's chest, offering skin to skin contact. The benefits are indisputable. Their blood pressure drops, which indicates less discomfort, oxygen saturation rises—all the vitals improve as soon as the baby hits your chest. It improves the parents' morale, and probably our vitals too. In our case, with Mary on my chest, there was another benefit. She would take her itty-bitty little hands, wrap them around some of my chest hair, and pull with all her might. While I didn't much care for it, it certainly seemed to lift Lisa's spirits, and Mary didn't seem to be the worse for wear.

With Lisa back in Abilene, John was now only seeing me for a few hours a week. At first, his growth slowed. Then it stopped. Then he started losing weight—and this was in the context of him having fallen well behind appropriate growth when he got sick. The doctors said there was nothing to be done but wait for things to improve. The nurses continued feeding him in hopes he would quit spitting up so much milk.

I asked John's doctors if they thought he was ready to come home to Abilene—that maybe he would do better if he could be with his family. They advised against it. They said he was still too sick. The nurses thought it was a bad idea, too. Lisa wanted no part of it. She had two tiny babies at home, both with monitors still going off regularly, and she saw no reason to doubt the doctors' opinions. My friend Roger the physician, waffled, though I suspected he thought it rash. I asked Jim and Mary's pediatrician, though. He was willing to be John's doctor if I brought him home. Technically, John wasn't receiving care in the NICU that couldn't be done at home or in the Abilene pediatrician's office. Of course, with a baby born at two pounds who had already spent months at death's door, any number of serious medical emergencies could have happened.

I never fashioned myself a doctor or doctor wannabee. Not then, not now. I knew that the NICU doctors were some of the best. They knew so much more than me, but I seemed to know something they didn't. Tennis.

There's a saying in tennis: "Never change a winning game, always change a losing game." Keeping John in the NICU apart from his family was a losing game. That was clear to me both cognitively and at a gut level.

The tennis comment might sound flippant, but my aviation background informed me as well. Like physicians, pilots must regularly make life and death decisions. Sometimes it's a bad day. The weather is bad, or the jet is bad, or something else in your environment is putting your life or someone else's at risk. Most of the time, pilots have specific, well-defined, and documented procedures to follow when things go wrong. Sometimes though, you're the first pilot to face a problem, and you have to come up with a solution yourself. Every So Often, "the book" tells you to do one thing, but you end up having to do something very different to save the day. Not everyone proves to be up to the task. There's a Darwinian flavor to all of this—more so in aviation than in medicine. A doctor can screw up big time and continue his career. Pilots, not so much. Generally, pilot mistakes are more *catastrophic*.

If you know any professional pilots, particularly out of the military, you will likely detect some arrogance—maybe not on the surface, but somewhere. A pilot is the kind of person that would tell all the doctors, and the nurses, and his spouse that they're wrong and that he knows what's best for his son. So I did.

I gathered that third car seat and all the other baby necessities. Returning home from my next trip, I had the hospital discharge my 3.5-pound, 4-month-old son, AMA – against medical advice.

The nurses were experts at swaddling, and as they wheeled John to my car, only his tiny yellowish face was visible, peaking out of a tightly wrapped blanket, the same one that most of America's children seem to come home in. John sucked patiently on his pacifier, that typical poker face that babies offer not betraying his opinion on the business of his first long car ride home. The nurses were nice enough about us leaving. They helped me get John into the car and wished us well.

It was a difficult 2.5-hour drive home. Nobody was on my side. John's monitor occasionally sounded off, just to remind me of the stakes. He was yellow from Jaundice, but at least his blanket hid how he was swollen from kidneys that were still not entirely healed. He didn't look well, though I knew his issues could be treated at home. He had yet to keep much milk down since his bad transfusion, and those issues had only gotten worse after Lisa and I left him to be fed by the nursing staff. God bless them, their work is admirable, but they were not his parents.

John received a warm welcome when we got home. I did not.

Lisa's anger for me, however, proved to be short-lived. John started feeding well and keeping his food down immediately. *Immediately*—state again for emphasis, I suppose because when you're a bit cocky, you enjoy reveling in your successes. John started gaining weight, and his jaundice and systemic swelling faded.

I went against the experts, but I wasn't wrong.

Leaders who want to lead well rarely have the luxury of being wrong. Leadership can be lonely, but good leaders do what needs to be done. When shit hits the fan, good leaders need to draw upon all of their resources, get the best possible use out of them, and then make the best possible decisions. Sometimes, those decisions will make few people happy, at least initially. But if they're good decisions, nearly everyone will (eventually) come around.

There is an important difference between my actions in the NICU and Trump's actions with the coronavirus: Discipline. For four months (and realistically, ever since our kids' births), I put the time in, did the research, and listened (not necessarily obeyed, but always listened) intently to those around me. All of those actions required discipline, a quality our president seems to lack entirely. Trump is fond of saying that he reacts instinctively, listens to his gut. If you haven't first put the work into understanding what's going on, listening to your gut is only guessing. Actually worse. If you're making decisions based upon limited information, this can be statistically worse than random guessing. A little knowledge is truly a dangerous thing.

Regarding *black lights* and *Lysol*, what can I say? There is a substantial inadequacy of our president that never seems to be discussed. Many of those given an opportunity to lead have done so in supervising individuals within one's own specialty, for example, pilots supervising pilots, nurses supervising nurses, etc.

Once you reach a certain level of leadership, you have to manage and lead people with specialties you may know little to nothing about. Not every leader can do this well. It requires soft skills, mainly an ability to assess and inspire people through interpersonal connection, rather than hard skills of directly assessing technical abilities.

Donald Trump is doubly cursed in this area. He has little to no soft skills. Specifically, he is a terrible judge of character as evidenced by his befriending of numerous felons and dictators while shunning all manner of decent human beings. But his Narcissism (with a capital N, because I'm currently at a loss to better emphasize the word) convinces him that he knows better than everyone. In this context, everyone who works for him. He knows "more than the generals," can "solve healthcare in a day," is "really good at science." My sense is that he truly believes these things, so when some anchor at FOX puts an idea in that fact-challenged cerebrum that contradicts a leading expert, Trump is convinced that he is correct and the expert clueless. Is there any doubt that Trump was told by Dr. Birx that black lights and Clorox offer Zero potential for therapeutic value? There shouldn't be after seeing her not shocked, but so humiliated that she seemed to be trying to mentally phase into a different dimension, during that now-infamous press briefing. Yet Trump decided he knew better and publicly shared his "wisdom."

For these reasons, no one can work for him for long. Trump's subordinates grow frustrated with his inability to adopt the viewpoint of another. Often, he has fired them because he believes that firing people is an actual talent. Ironically, as has been pointed out by the media so many times, he is not even adept at firing people, electing instead to delegate others to inform said staff of their new status.

As an aside, if you know more than an expert that works for you, and you are not a trained, bona fide expert in that particular area yourself, you are not "really smart." You've either hired the wrong person, or you are too narcissistic to know better, or you are so far over your head at your current position of leadership that you have no clue as to what is going on. When good leaders get together with their staff, they are frequently far from the smartest person in the room. That is in many cases the mark of a good leader. It also explains why bosses who are arrogant jerks are often bad at their jobs. Leaders with a need to believe they are smarter than everyone around them generally offer limited opportunities for their members to shine. In other words, they sabotage their own teams.

So where did that leave our country, when the entire world was facing a pandemic? As stated, the buck has to rest with the president. Ultimately, it doesn't matter if no one told him or it wasn't properly explained or he misheard, or the sun was in his eyes. Trump owns this awful pandemic response that has been catastrophically costly in lives and treasure. He broke it, and he will own it until the end of time. And though others have made mistakes and played their roles in making things worse, after so many public pronouncements of the virus being insignificant and saying that it will go away like magic or any of the utterly childish (...no 'childish' is unfair to children, I meant to say asinine), the utterly asinine things he said, we can rest the blame quite firmly onto the lap of Donald F. (yeah, I know that's not his middle initial) Trump.

Somehow, he got it in his head, maybe via the FOX echo chamber, or some other *highly reliable* source of information, that the world's experts were all wrong, and that he and he alone was right. He must have thought that it was going to be so sweet when he showed everyone how smart he was and how stupid the scientific "elite" community had been.

So that is how the most powerful country in the world, the country with the greatest biological and medical resources in the world, the country with the most Nobel prizes awarded in science.... Oh, for fuck's sake, we screwed this pandemic up from here to Neptune. Even with additional warning time ahead of the rest of the First World, we are far and away leading the entire world in our high levels of disease and death. This is an embarrassment that exceeds our defeats in Viet Nam, the Bay of Pigs, and probably every other major failure of our country combined. Combined! Such is the enormity of the needless loss of life and damage to our economy.

And still, the mistakes and damage persist! The president is so amazingly deficient in humility that he continues rebuking science, encouraging people not to wear masks or exercise social distancing. After numerous studies discounting his claims, Trump is still recommending hydroxychloroquine, which has now been associated with damage to the liver, heart, blood, and kidneys. Moreover, the drug's use for COVID-19 as either treatment or prophylactic, limits the supply for those with a bona fide, medically prescribed need for the drug. Our president is literally a menace to the collective health of our nation.

The Statistics Problem

What makes the president so dangerous is that many are still willing to believe him. I think it may be useful to take a step into the president's brain to try to figure out what is going on. The human brain, in general, is strongly coded to recognize patterns. In general, this serves us well. It helps us learn and facilitates good judgment. Studies show a strong correlation between the ability to recognize patterns and a person's success in both school and career.

The way in which we see patterns is dictated by our examination of the world around us, something scientists refer to as empirical observation. Those who work with statistics understand that empirical data is meaningless within the bounds of any statistical analysis. This means that we may observe what appears to be a trend, such as several patients taking hydroxychloroquine and getting better, and be fooled into believing that the drug is an effective treatment for COVID-19. Trump has reportedly taken hydroxychloroquine after being exposed to people with COVID. It's likely some family and staff have as well. It would appear to Trump if a half-dozen people that he knew had taken the drug and not gotten COVID that the drug *clearly* prevents the disease.

Despite our brain's interpretation of these conclusions as valid inferences based upon logical analyses, there are numerous problems with such conclusions. First, there is the issue of sample size. Some people will observe three or even fewer people (particularly when it is people they know) who got better while receiving a certain therapy and conclude with near certainty that this therapy is curative. You might later tell them that a study conducted on the 'treatment' showed that 95% of a large sample of those treated either got worse or no better, but because of the mind initially recognizing and codifying a pattern, as well as the mind's related tendency toward confirmation bias, a surprising number will be disposed to discount the 95%.

Where sample size is adequate, numerous statistical pitfalls still remain. There can be intentional or unintentional selection bias, where people chosen for a particular study will have a certain predisposition toward a certain outcome. There is placebo effect. There are statistical variances that may invalidate results lacking any firm correlation. There is even measurement bias where researchers may make false assessments based upon their own internal biases. In the case of hydroxychloroquine, I can see clear indications of one or more of these biases in the presentations of every one of the physicians reporting positive results.

The remedy for all of these bias problems, the gold standard for assessing the validity of treatment, is the "randomized double-blind placebo-controlled" (RDBPC) study. Every FDA approved medication is subject to RDBPC investigation as bare minimum protection against drug manufacturers falsely elevating a drug's efficacy.

The problem with sick people, especially the gravely ill, is that they can be so damned desperate. Any potential treatment or cure that offers a glimmer of hope may be viewed as a clever purchase. This makes them terrible consumers, and it's the reason why the hurdles to bring drugs and other treatments to market are so high. And even with RDBPC studies, there can be issues. It is not uncommon for follow-up studies to refute the results of their predecessors, even when those studies are accomplished properly.

I'm going to take a rare moment to defend the president—in particular, his inexplicable clinging to hydroxychloroquine as a legitimate treatment. Conventional medicine does not offer much in the way of fighting viral infections. In recent years, some antivirals with limited range and effectiveness have entered the market. These medications have not been nearly as effective in treating viral infections as antibiotics have been in treating bacterial infections, even today with all the problems of antibiotic resistance. While there are excellent vaccines against certain viral infections, viruses have a nasty habit of mutating. Some vaccines, such as for the flu, must be given every year yet still provide limited effectiveness.

As biological entities, viruses are incredibly simple; SARS-CoV-2 only contains 15 genes, making it a Darwinian dream. Unlike more complicated organisms that have protections against mutations, viral mutations are far more likely to result in a successful alteration. And of course, the rapid reproduction of viral particles means many generations in a short time span. Alterations of a single nucleotide could drive anything from a disabling change, which would only kill that specific particle, to a consequential change that could make the virus more contagious. Evolutionary pressures ensure that mutations that make the virus more successful are the only ones that endure. Unfortunately for hosts, meaning us, success for a virus means greater contagion (though the good news is that successful viruses tend to be less lethal – dead hosts are not nearly as effective at spreading a virus as live hosts). Viruses, such as HIV, have so far proven perfectly elusive against any attempts of defense by vaccination because they continue to successfully mutate. What we refer to as "the common cold," (which refers to a disparate group of viruses including some coronaviruses) has been particularly bothersome in circumventing most attempts at medical intervention.

Not all but some legitimate studies have shown that zinc medications when taken early on in common cold infections, shorten the length of those infections. I'm going to focus on the part about "when taken early on." In none of the hydroxychloroquine studies have I seen data in which the drug was administered early in the infection (Edit: 7/29, There are now some ongoing studies on early administration of chloroquine derivatives in combination with other meds to treat COVID-19, but those results are not yet available.) Why is this important?

An Engineer's Analysis of Hydroxychloroquine

Several studies have demonstrated that zinc has antiviral properties, to include disabling coronaviruses. Scientists don't understand zinc's mode of efficacy, but coronaviruses all have similar structures. It's a reasonable hope that zinc may work similarly against SARS-CoV-2. One of the problems with zinc, however, is that it isn't easily absorbed inside cells. This makes it a poor treatment once a virus begins entering, attacking, and replicating inside of cells.

Other in vitro studies have shown that hydroxychloroquine is a zinc ionophore, meaning it helps zinc pass through cellular membranes. Can you see where I'm going with this? Potentially, the two substances (zinc and hydroxychloroquine) working together can disable coronaviruses. On May 8, results of what appears to be a legitimate study conducted in New York City hospitals have shown indications of this combination being effective in treating COVID-19. (Note that I have referenced few external articles because information is changing rapidly. In this case, though, since it is so controversial, I am posting a web reference: https://www.medrxiv.org/content/10.1101/2020.05.02.20080036v1).

Viral infections begin when we are exposed to virions—the individual viral particles. For SARS-CoV-2, we know that when virions land in the respiration tract and the eyes, the virus employs ACE2 receptors to enter human cells. Once inside a human cell, the virus steals cellular material to reproduce itself many times over. Generally, the virus destroys the cell thereby spilling into extracellular space, including the bloodstream. From there, the circulatory system transports the virus to attack an entirely new bunch of cells and so on, and so on (thereby causing the COVID-19 infection). Zinc appears to inhibit viral reproduction.

There is at least one legitimate study demonstrating zinc without hydroxychloroquine as being an effective treatment for COVID-19. How could that be without the hydroxychloroquine helping it to penetrate cellular membranes? Logic suggests that zinc attacks viruses better in extracellular space in the bloodstream. Certainly, in the absence of an ionophore, it's tough to make a case that zinc is killing viruses inside cells if the cells won't let the zinc pass through their membranes.

Zinc as a successful treatment for common colds offers confirmatory evidence. Taken early, once in our bloodstream, zinc becomes available to fight those first generations of viruses that enter our bloodstream after being replicated inside the first infected cells. If we wait too long, those viral particles penetrate new cells and replicate quickly in subsequent generations, and it soon becomes too late to stop the viral advance. But if we have the zinc in our blood early enough, in some cases, people with common colds get immediately better. Hundreds of fellow airline crew members that I have asked take zinc either prophylactically or as soon as they have cold-like symptoms. Despite being exposed to more viruses than an average adult, my observations over the last two decades since zinc medications became available is that crew members get sick less often. Yes, empirical data has its limitations, but it is not inherently without merit, particularly when datasets are large enough to be statistically significant.

It will be an interesting moment in time, though, if and when a legitimate RDBPC study shows the combination of hydroxychloroquine and zinc to be an effective treatment. Trump would certainly declare "victory," despite the fact that he has been claiming that hydroxychloroquine by itself is an efficacious treatment for COVID-19, and that has been disproved resoundingly by medical studies. It is only in combining hydroxychloroquine with zinc and perhaps other antivirals that it may offer any potential therapeutic value.

The reason this relates to leadership and why I have invested several pages to discuss it is to once again demonstrate the important notion that decisions made by "gut" or hunch can be legitimate, but only when backed up by some sort of disciplined and deliberative process. With certainty, the president could not present anything resembling a cogent two-page analysis for why he is touting hydroxychloroquine.

In examining his early support of the drug, he may have been referencing either directly or indirectly the results of Dr. Vladimir Zelenko, who was prescribing hydroxychloroquine with zinc and Azithromycin. Getting the details correct is one of the president's many deficits. In this case, the details of adding zinc and perhaps the Azithromycin are important. According to the New York Times, Hannity saw Zelenko's YouTube video, and the rest was history. Viewing a single TV spot is what passes for disciplined and deliberative research in the current White House.

Here is the far more disturbing problem with Trump's chloroquine marketing campaign. Like the masks, it has become political. In response to some doctors who want to prescribe it to COVID patients because it is advised in their best individual judgment, some patients are refusing the medication because of the controversy. Some doctors may be avoiding the drug for reasons that extend beyond their best medical judgment. Like the virus, Trump's insinuation into medical decision-making is costing lives. I wonder how many people in previous discussions regarding healthcare have been adamant about not letting the government come between doctors and patients, yet today, support *Dr. Trump's* nationwide hydroxychloroquine remedy? Is he currently doing anything of consequence that is not costing American lives?

For anyone who would consider taking hydroxychloroquine without a valid prescription or medical advice, be prepared. Most people who fought in the first Gulf War were given chloroquine as a prophylactic against malaria. Everyone I know, including myself, quickly quit taking the drug as it makes you feel absolutely awful. We assumed malaria couldn't be any worse. As I understand it, hydroxychloroquine is a slightly less toxic version of chloroquine, but as announced in the press, it can still have *deadly* side effects. Taking it without a valid medical reason is ridiculous.

Epidemiology 101

Earlier, I introduced data indicating a correlation between schoolkids' math performance versus each country's COVID-19 infection rate (as of April 22, 2020). I promised to further explain the chart, and I wouldn't break a promise.

I removed Eastern European countries from the dataset because they have far fewer international travelers and lower population densities—they were not providing an apples-apples comparison with the remainder of the chart's first-world countries. Viral infection spread is clearly a complicated process to define, with many relevant variables influencing outcomes. The fact that there is any significant correlation at all is a huge statement. Of course, we need to ask, "Why?"

I wrote in the introduction that the successful countries know how to do the math, and to some degree, that is most of the explanation. Epidemiology is at its root, a statistical analysis of human behavior. Darwin made it clear long ago, that organisms better adapted to their environment will survive beyond the temporal footprint of others.

SARS-CoV-2 is a novel coronavirus with unprecedented behavior, but it showed itself early on to be an airborne spreader. Social distancing and masks have been endorsed by the world's epidemiological community to be the best tools to minimize airborne infections. Some populations, as a whole, understand this better than others—better than us. We also have to consider the possibility that countries that invest emotionally and culturally in mathematics education are more likely to be governed by politicians that are more science-minded and science-driven. Consider that Taiwan, despite its close proximity to China and its population of 23 million, has experienced a mere seven total deaths due to COVID-19.

Does anyone believe it is unrelated that the Taiwanese vice president was a practicing epidemiologist?

The intransigent ignorance of Americans is costing lives. This is one of several cautionary tales in this book. Our failures in education are coming at an immense cost. Ironically, these failures are not driven by a lack of education investment. Where money is important, it turns out to be as much about how and where that money is spent versus how much.

More important is how we view math and science culturally. We respect the gadgets that science and technology provide us, but we have little to no respect for the underlying sciences and technologies that help create them. We permit sacred cows, such as religion, to take precedence over scientific understanding. Case in point, religious special interests reject the scientific concept of evolution. They offer as a false equivalent, creationism, an artificial construct that attempts though ultimately fails to lend scientific justification and credence to the Judeo-Christian biblical creation allegory.

I am not a particularly religious person, but I would never suggest to anyone that they *abandon God*. I understand the implications of such a directive. In America, though, we are abandoning science, and that has implications as well. One need only look at the COVID-19 statistics to understand.

* * * * *

While it is true that exact epidemiological determinations are highly complex, we only need to understand some basic principles to improve the chances of health and survival for ourselves and those around us:

1) For any level of virus, the greater the density of people, the greater the spread of the disease. That's simply math and science.
2) Wearing any kind of mask limits you from spreading the virus. The better the mask contains and filters your exhalations, the less

likely you are to spread the virus. I've seen many relatable explanations for why and how this is so. I prefer this simple demonstration: Put your hand about 8 inches in front of your mouth and blow into it. Feel that? That's air from your lungs (which may or may not contain viral particles, depending upon if you are infected) hitting your hand. Now wear any kind of mask and try the same thing again. You will not feel air from your lungs hitting your hand.

a. Unlike the smell of perfume or tobacco or farts, all of which follow the Gibbs-Dalton ideal gas mixture law, whereby those "smelly" molecules push apart from each other so as to spread extremely rapidly, virions are simply carried inside liquid particulate which spread via air currents.

b. You can smell *smelly* things while wearing a mask, even an N95 mask because those molecules are far smaller than a coronavirus.

c. The bottom line is masks mitigate the spread of viral particles.

d. Wearing a mask does not meaningfully increase the amount of carbon dioxide that you are breathing. With some mask and full-face shield configurations, there may be an inconsequential increase in the amount of carbon dioxide uptake—not even as much as the level of carbon dioxide that has been contributed to the atmosphere by humans.

e. Wearing a mask does not "recycle" the virus. If you have it, you have it. The level of virions shed is an extremely small amount, relative to what would already be in an infected body. The mask won't hurt you.

f. Masks are primarily helpful in keeping *you* from spreading disease to *others*.

g. Nearly any mask will likely give the wearer some protection, but N-95 masks and any system that offers equivalent or better filtration offer better protection. Those wearing of N-95 type masks can protect themselves from becoming infected by others.

h. These masks can only reach their potential for effectiveness when sealed properly against the face. During inhalation, the predominant amount of air entering the body from the nose and mouth enters through mask material.

3) The odds of becoming infected with COVID-19 and the severity of infection appears to be strongly correlated with the viral load one is exposed to. The current belief is that it takes about 1,000 virions to acquire COVID-19. With exposure to higher viral loads, there is a likelihood of having a worse case of the disease. The viral load in hospitals due to infected patients is many times higher than anywhere else. This is why many young and healthy doctors, particularly early on, were experiencing more severe cases of COVID-19.

4) Different activities affect the likelihood of spreading and catching COVID-19. Sneezing is the worst. Try sneezing inside with sunlight shining on the area where you sneeze. It's a real show (unless you're wearing a mask)! Coughing is obviously bad. Singing is also surprisingly bad. Various "super-spreader" events inside the US happened at some kind of religious service where there was plenty of singing. This is why various state governments have put strict limits on religious services. It's not an attack on God. It's an attack on the virus.

5) The current best guess is that it is rare to catch the virus without the equivalent of about 15 minutes of close indoor exposure to an infected individual. Indoor airflow patterns can have a significant impact on virus transmission. Airflow can facilitate spread, but some flow patterns can help prevent transmission. Generally, higher airflow is better.

6) Transmission while outside appears to be rare. A single sneeze or cough in the face could easily do it, though—even outside. Sitting

close together in still air outside for long periods would also be ill-advised.

7) While six feet of separation is not a magic number, it's a good guide for avoiding exposure and infection where the air is still. Virions will travel with air currents, so if you're walking directly behind an infected person for any amount of time, six feet may not be nearly enough, particularly if they are actively infected and breathing heavily, or coughing, sneezing, singing, etc.

8) Washing your hands frequently and keeping things sanitary are probably important and certainly won't hurt anything. The latest guidance is that only a small number of infections are occurring from touching infected items, but by keeping things clean, you won't be one of those few to get sick from touching a contaminated surface.

9) While you're at it, try not to touch your face. I dare you. Try.

10) A previous COVID-19 infection *should* make you immune from future infections, for some unknown length of time. If and when a vaccine becomes available, that should do the same thing.

   a. Because there are no guarantees on the length of time of immunity, it is critically important that once a vaccine becomes available, we vaccinate the entire world within some reasonably short period of time. The virus can only survive if provided a consistent supply of new infections. With herd immunity, where roughly 70% of a local population becomes protected, the spread of a virus becomes rare. Permitting rampant spread means more generations of viral reproduction, particularly if there is a lengthy wait for a vaccine, which increases the possibility of a dangerous mutation.

   b. Immunologists have proven statistically that vaccines are extremely safe. Minor adverse vaccine reactions such as temporary pain and or minor swelling at the ejection site do occur, but severe reactions such as anaphylactic shock are rare, and reactions that cause death or permanent disability have been nearly non-existent in the last several decades. The risk of the vaccine has to be measured against the dangers of the virus itself. Scientists are confident that none of the COVID-19 vaccines in development in the US represent a greater threat than the virus, at least for those with a normally functioning immune system. Consider in this context getting the vaccine for you and your family at the first available opportunity.

c. It is possible that a vaccine will be available by the end of 2020 (edit: July 29, 2020—it's nearly certain that at a minimum, some essential workers will have an opportunity to get vaccinated before the end of 2020, with vaccines available to the rest of us shortly thereafter). But it's not impossible it could take much longer. It is also not impossible that an effective vaccine will never be created, though this virus has given scientists no reason to expect this. My money is on having a vaccine available (at least to some) by December 2020 (edit: July 29, 2020—by late September to mid-October. And that's in the US. China has already vaccinated their military. Political pressure to deliver some sort of vaccine by the election will bear attention. There are excellent medical and societal reasons to accelerate vaccine development, but politically, any non-medical interference in the process will likely backfire. Polls show that a majority of Americans believe the president is untrustworthy. There is growing sentiment, even among Republicans, that the president may force a vaccine to be released before it is proven safe. Infants, the elderly, those immunocompromised, vaccine deniers, and the uninsured are all unlikely to be vaccinated. Children are not likely to be vaccinated in large numbers until the vaccines have passed additional confidence trials. If less than 65% of our population is protected, there is minimized herd immunity, and the aforementioned groups won't be safe. The most likely way to steal away the success of a vaccination program is to have excessive numbers of people avoiding the vaccine out of government distrust. Medically, though, there's too much money being thrown at the problem, and too many different groups working the problem to not expect technical success.

d. So far, vaccine development has been moving swiftly.

e. Finally, vaccinations do not offer immediate immunity. For most vaccines given today, doctors tell you to get inoculated at least two weeks before any potential exposure. As long as the course of COVID-19 takes for many individuals, this period may be longer. We will have to wait for the science to know for sure.

It's important to clarify something about the wearing of masks. As some continue to cite: epidemiologists, physicians, and other relevant experts first suggested in the January to March timeframe that unless you are a health professional, you should not expect any benefit from wearing a mask.

They did this for several reasons. By that point, they were not certain as to the major avenues of disease transmittal. They understood that the virus could be spread airborne, but it might have been predominantly transmitted by touching infected surfaces. There had yet to be studies on the effectiveness of masks at preventing COVID-19 transmission, so they could not say *with certainty* that masks would be useful. Experts also realized that people inexperienced with masks would not wear them properly sealed. Breath bypassing masks limit their effectiveness. Primarily, though, public officials were troubled at the time with the limited supply of PPE available to health professionals. What might have happened if we ran out of healthcare workers?

The Trump administration made it consistently clear that they would at best offer limited federal assistance in helping local regions access PPE. The administration had given up an opportunity to obtain an abundance of masks early in the year, so the possibility of running out of supplies was quite real.

Some have legitimately asked, why didn't the experts tell us to make cloth masks or wear bandannas at the outset? The unsatisfying answer is that they didn't *trust* us. Federal officials believed that if they made any mask recommendations at all, people would buy up all the masks they could find. They were probably right because in some places, this was happening anyway. Any run on masks would have cost the lives of first responders. Unfortunately, the deception came at the cost of credibility.

It's reasonable to ask if it could have been handled any better. Having been forced to lie early on, maybe public health officials could have later pivoted to positions of greater candor. They could have explained their reasons for initial deception while endorsing a rigorous educational campaign on the importance and function of masks. We have to wonder, though, was the public ready for that level of candor? There's a reason why few honest people are successful in politics. Like Nicholson's character explained in *A Few Good Men*, maybe the public just can't handle the truth.

Ultimately, all you need to know about Epidemiology 101 is to wear a mask and steer clear of sizable groups, particularly inside. Until you have immunity. *And when a vaccine does become available, GET IT!*

COVID-19 101b

(Edit: September 12, 2020:

Trump lies. Verb or noun? You decide.

Some view political lies as a necessary evil component of the political process, but when do lies cross the line? After your president tells 100 lies? 1,000? 10,000? Trump blew through those milestones like a kid blowing out birthday candles, with the same repugnance of saliva and germs typically donated to a ten-year-old's birthday cake. Should the line be drawn when a president's lies are responsible for one or more deaths? Have we reached the point where a president lied, thousands died, and our nation can't agree with anything resembling unanimity that we've got a huge problem?

When Bob Woodward released his tapes of Trump saying the opposite in private of what he was saying in public, there was shock and outrage. But in the same way people failed to see how the Access Hollywood tape had forecast Trump's abuse of power, people in this moment fail to see that Trump, in publicly contradicting his understanding of the virus, is telling the world two remarkable things. These lies indicate that he doesn't respect his voters. But even more significantly, he made it clear that he thinks his supporters are stupid! He knows that they're too stupid to understand the science, too stupid to independently seek out the truth, too stupid to comprehend that being wrong about this virus could cost them or their loved ones their lives, and too stupid to make the conservative, reasonable decision that the risks of denying science outweigh the rewards of walking around mask-free at an indoor rally. I'm laughing now because I don't want to cry.)

The more Americans understand the following undisputable facts, the healthier and safer our country will be:

1) This virus is NOTHING like the flu. *Symptoms* of COVID-19 for some, especially early in the course of the disease, can be flu-like despite the following differences:

   a. About 20% of (known) COVID-19 cases require hospitalization—substantially higher than the flu.

   b. About 80% of (known) COVID-19 cases are mild or asymptomatic—substantially higher than the flu—particularly the percent of asymptomatic carriers which is NOTHING like the flu.

   c. The mortality rate is still in question, though we know it increases substantially with age (more than the flu). The flu though, represents a greater danger to young children. My research suggests the overall mortality rate for the US lies somewhere in the range of 0.4 to 1.8%, as compared to the flu, which has a mortality rate of 0.1%. COVID-19 by any reasonable estimate is substantially more deadly than the flu. Of note, death rates will vary by the age of the population, as well as numerous other factors related to the availability and quality of healthcare. Also, mortality has been varying over time as detailed in the chapter, "Mortality Takes a (Mini) Holiday."

   d. COVID-19 is more contagious than the flu. The flu has an R naught (a variable epidemiologists use to express the contagiousness of a disease) of approximately 1.3. The COVID-19 estimates are all over the map, but they're in the range of 2 - 5 and will vary with time and location-based upon quarantine measures in effect.

   e. The flu is primarily a respiratory infection, which sometimes leads to pneumonia in severe cases. COVID-19 appears to be an infection of the circulatory system and can affect the lungs, blood, brain, toes, and most any organ in the body. In rare cases, some children have developed severe inflammatory responses, and the disease has proven lethal for some of them.

f. A common distinguishing symptom of COVID-19 relative to the flu is a loss of or change in taste and smell. If you have flu-like symptoms in combination with symptoms associated with stroke, such as confusion or facial paralysis, there is a strong possibility of COVID-19. Of course, any stroke symptoms require immediate medical attention. (edit: July 30, 2020. The determination of a COVID-19 diagnosis has varied over time. No single diagnostic has been free of error. Clinicians have been using some combination of chest X-ray and CT scans, blood serum levels for certain inflammatory markers, patient symptoms, and a SARS-CoV-2 nasal or throat swab (PCR) test. As the swab tests have been taking too long to return, clinicians have relied primarily on those other indications).

2) There is still no firm determination as to whether or not COVID-19 infection leaves you immune to future infections. The WHO has made this clear. The CDC has been more reassuring, suggesting that immunity is likely with prior infection. This is a critically important question, because if prior infection does not lead to immunity, the likelihood of finding an effective vaccine quickly, if at all, is in doubt. (edit: July 30, 2020, these fears appear to be overblown. Evidence suggests that suspected reinfections were a result of inaccurate testing. Edit: August 25, 2020—a 33-year-old male in Hong Kong was assessed by scientists to have caught COVID-19 twice. Determining reinfection has been complicated by the

ailment's atypical tendency to wax and wane over a long period. Because of the low incidence of suspected reinfections, the suspicion is that for some small number of individuals exposed to different strains of the virus, their particular immune systems did not recognize the different mutation.)

3) One treatment that offers particular promise is convalescent plasma wherein antibodies are donated from the blood of survivors of the disease. As time goes on, the number of potential donors goes up (and we hope the number of COVID-19 positive cases goes down). (edit: August 25, 2020—Trump managed to politicize convalescent plasma by compelling the FDA to authorize Emergency Use. The fact is that tens of thousands of physicians have already been using it, and it is likely saving lives, but there have not been sufficient (RDBPC) studies on this treatment, so some doctors are saying the Emergency Use declaration was inappropriate. Initial studies indicate that convalescent plasma is most helpful when administered as soon as possible. This was expected, as infected individuals will produce antibodies after some period, by which point the donated antibodies are made redundant.)

   a. The drug Remdesivir has been clinically shown to shorten hospital stays for COVID-19 patients and may also reduce mortality.

   b. As all these treatments act with different modalities, their therapeutic effectiveness might be additive. For example, Remdesivir and convalescent plasma offered together might prove more effective than either individual treatment alone.

   c. New information concerning treatment options is being published every day.

d. Partly due to improved treatment as well as increased mask usage and social distancing, transmissibility and mortality have been decreasing over time.

4) There is a gold standard for how to successfully emerge from a pandemic quarantine. Though stated with minor differences, the following measures were announced by none other than President Trump, as the necessary process for states to emerge from quarantine:

   a. Get your infections down substantially using masks and social distancing/quarantine to the maximum extent possible.

   b. With low numbers of infections, begin aggressive contact tracing. Those who are exposed to infected individuals must strictly quarantine themselves and be tested at a minimum of 14 days after exposure. Only if these individuals remain infection free for 14 days should they be released from quarantine.

   c. Ease quarantine restrictions slowly. Where infections show signs of resurgence, reinstitute previous measures up to full quarantine, if necessary.

So much has been said about testing. Public health experts, and by extension the media, have been misleading and presenting the need for testing as a unidimensional problem. It's rare for them to explain that *who* you test is as or more important than how *many* you test. It's somewhat important to test patients that are assumed to be COVID-19 positive. A firm diagnosis is important for doctors to be able to have confidence in their treatment; the epidemiologists need to have accurate information to assess how the disease is spreading; and patients must know when they are COVID-19 positive, so they can quarantine appropriately. But for patients with classic COVID-19 symptoms, an assumed diagnosis is nearly as beneficial to the patient as one confirmed by testing—particularly when testing resources are scarce.

The MOST important people to test are those who might test positive but show little to no symptoms. Of course, we're all supposed to be quarantining anyway, but until people exhibit meaningful symptoms, many do not consider the possibility of contagion seriously, particularly with respect to keeping socially distant from household members or those with whom they have close contact. Those definitively symptomatic are more likely to quarantine themselves, and certainly others will avoid them. The "no-symptoms-maybe-sick" are the most important people to test. These are people who have either been directly exposed to COVID-positive individuals or have engaged in high-risk activities, such as attending large indoor gatherings without a mask. While unknowingly positive, these people will spread disease until they're made aware of their status.

Let's call them "needits," because they need the test, and I need a word to label them. How is it that we determine who should be a needit because we have nowhere near enough tests?

That's where contact tracing comes into play. Anyone who has been sufficiently exposed to a COVID positive individual becomes a needit. Once you contact and identify those needits, THEY get tested. For any of those needits who test positive, they are your new infectious people, and then all their meaningful contacts become new needits. With a low number of infections, this is doable, but you either need to have a fast test or a lot of tests.

Imagine you're a contact tracer. You call an individual who had COVID exposure, and you tell them to take their at-home instant COVID test. It's not *instant*, though – it takes 5 minutes, so you wait on the line for the test to complete. The test comes back negative, and you say great! Without that test, though, you have to presume that they have the virus, so you have to ask them about everyone they've been in contact with since their exposure to the virus.

The infection threads that are created by multiple generations of disease transmission are like a river tributary system. The contact tracers must pursue every individual tributary and functionally cap each one by quarantining. Without rapid testing, the river continues to flow, and you have many more tributaries to trace. Eventually, if you cap the flow of disease transmission of every 2nd, 3rd, 4th, etc. generation tributary, you stop the flow and put an end to the disease. Anyway, that's how it's supposed to happen.

There are three problems with the American contact tracing program:

1) Epidemiologists tell us we need to be doing five - ten times more testing than we currently are doing (or have the capacity to do). The unusual variation in how this disease presents in various people adds to the challenge. Current guidance is that individuals will begin to test positive anywhere from one - fourteen days from virus exposure. So ideally, it makes sense in contact tracing to test the needits at least twice—once after about three days and once near the fourteen-day point.

2) There appears to be little contact tracing being conducted by governmental agencies. It's not entirely clear why. Most of the contact tracing that I can detect appears to be driven by larger private corporations that are doing some limited contact tracing for their employees and in some cases for customers.

3) The biggest problem though is that contact tracing is a laborious, burdensome process. Think about the many people each individual is exposed to in a single day. When one of my airline's flight attendants goes to work, she might have incidental contact in a three-flight day to over 450 passengers, and close contact with over 100! After work, there might be a subway trip somewhere and then dinner with friends and family. We failed at contact tracing when we thought there might be less than 50 infections nationwide. If we can't get our infections down to much lower levels and our tests back more quickly, contact tracing is going to be extremely limited in its ability to meaningfully reduce disease transmission, let alone eliminate it.

* * * * *

The president has been channeling both Dr. Jekyll and Mr. Hyde in his pubic comments. On April 17, Mr. Trump briefed America on the wisest science-driven guidance then available, concerning how to best emerge from quarantine. From May 7th on, his recommendations had *evolved* to the following:

1) Forget what (the president) said before about how to safely *open up/end the quarantine*. We don't need to do any of that.
2) Masks – maybe they work, maybe they don't. Wear them, don't wear them, doesn't seem to matter.
3) Social distancing is costly to the economy, costly to jobs, and costly to the stock market.

    Not sure social distancing ever did anything anyway. Get as close to strangers as you like. Get close, even if you have no reason to, just to annoy the "libs."
4) Football and athletic events in general are REALLY important. We need to get back to them, and we need to fill the stands with fans.
5) Hydroxychloroquine is wonderful! Take it if you have the virus. Take it if you don't. What have you got to lose?
6) A vaccine will be available REALLY soon!
7) The virus will melt away, no matter what.

It is not simply the inaccuracy of information that is problematic. It is the president's colossal failure of leadership. He should have been the first damn person to put on a mask, and he should have been wearing one frequently in public to model appropriate behavior. It's only fair to also include Governor Cuomo (who gets special mention as he is appearing on TV more than any other politician, except perhaps Trump), but other politicians have also appeared in public without masks. I understand the argument that they may be sufficiently distant from others at the time of their appearance, and/or that it is difficult for them to -be properly heard with a mask. Regardless, politicians have to find a way to model appropriate behavior. It's what leaders do. (Edit: July 30, 2020. Cuomo did eventually start modeling a mask on camera.)

That we have so many people not wearing masks in public is more a failure of the American politician than it is a failure of the American public. Many parents have heard the principle "catch your kids doing something right." Politicians need to adopt a similar mindset. They need to be caught wearing the damn masks, even if it means putting them on when they know it's unnecessary. Sure there is a danger in appearing "staged," but there is a greater danger in citizens pointing to Trump or any politician not wearing a mask and feeling justified in going without. It's worth emphasizing praise for Joe Biden, who despite his limited public footprint, has been regularly seen either wearing or at a minimum having a mask on his person.

* * * * *

Public gatherings and social distancing represent another complex set of issues. President Trump's statements and recommendations on this topic are problematic because his motivations are purely political. He knows his reelection bid hinges upon the success of the economy. As he sees quarantines and social-distancing efforts as antithetical to a successful economy, Trump has been frequently scornful of disease controlling measures. He also understands how badly all of the deaths reflect upon him, and he wants to appear in command of the pandemic response. He's not anchored in reality. It has been somewhat pathetic to watch him flip-flop between his encouragement to practice social distancing versus his calls to "Free Michigan" et al, possibly based upon continual reassessment of how much disease and death the American public will tolerate and still support his reelection.

As for the nation's "reopening plan," the utter dysfunction, at most levels of government, in adhering to even a small percentage of CDC guidelines is staggering. These malfunctions are only enhanced by the media's failure as their role of watchdog. Few states are sticking to the criteria that the Trump administration established and announced would be necessary before nonessential public activity should resume. And no one is talking about it, least of all anyone from the White House. It's as though Moses came down the mountain with the Ten Commandments, and everyone just shrugged.

The media has been highlighting the large numbers of people not appropriately social-distancing or wearing masks, but not in reference to the reopening guidelines. There may be a combination of reasons for their silence:

1) Trump's outrageous behavior simply does not permit in-depth scrutiny of the ridiculous things he does because he is consistently assaulting us with more and more shocking statements and actions.

2) Ever since his failure to get Mexico to pay for *The Wall*, few people, other than some supporters, take Trump's pronouncements seriously. He doesn't have a staff to execute and enforce his tweets. On those occasions when his Cabinet attempts to fulfill one of his pronouncements, he typically undercuts them with some brand-new whimsical order. And on those rare moments when some highly divisive policy is enacted, they have consistently been thrown out in court. Trump replies with angry tweets for 2 - 36 hours before forgetting his intentions within a few days. The Trump administration may be the most feckless government in the history of the Western world.

This does not mean he's incapable of generating enormous damage. Trump has always been at best a president to his voters and *his* voters only. Most of his voters have probably been quite happy with the arrangement. Since COVID, though, Trump's association with his voters may be causing substantial hardship. It is a frightening scenario that he has encouraged citizens to congregate in larger groups and avoid mask usage, not based upon science and medicine, but instead an immoral and misguided political strategy.

The Big Problems with Data

There is a big problem with the way that people understand numbers. If your job involves any kind of autonomy, you've probably been encouraged to make data-driven decisions. If your organization is serious about such directives, they've likely instructed you in some of the tools for understanding statistics. Why? Because it's the only way to make sense of a large amount of data. Consider your daily commute. If arriving late means you'll be fired or severely penalized, you'll want to know your *maximum* travel time. If you're considering a job change, you might be more interested in the *average*. Average and maximum values can help you make data-driven decisions. They are far more useful than a list of commute times over the last thirty months.

There are more sophisticated statistical tools, like *correlation*, introduced with Figure 1. I've taught enough over the years to realize once we're talking numbers, the eyes start glazing over. I'm going to play the mean teacher for a moment, and smack you on the knuckles. Take another look at Figure 1, back in the second chapter, and ask yourself, what is the most important lesson from this chart?

Simply this: America's weakness for mathematics is literally killing us. Our fellow citizens are dying because we don't know how to interpret data properly. If we continue on this course, we'll eventually realize our future is constrained by deficits in America's collective mathematics comprehension.

There's another BIG problem. It's the *bigness* of pandemic related numbers. Currently, Google states that there are 328.2 million people in America. It's the third-largest population in the world. We are well eclipsed by India and China, but 328 million is still an immense number. The high standards set by Americans require extreme precision to keep even the simplest parts of the American economy moving. If an Indian citizen dies eating some bad lettuce, it is an isolated tragedy that the government may or may not address. If an American citizen dies of the same (a 1 in 328 million problem), millions of heads of lettuce representing millions of dollars will be destroyed. It's a news story. People stop eating lettuce. People may lose their jobs. Companies are affected. Stockholders lose money. Particularly, due to the loss of money, a great deal of attention goes into establishing the highest possible standards for the safety of every single food item in the country. Americans have high standards. We expect a lot from our institutions. Or at least we used to.

Where individual responsibility is expected (where the danger of a product is commonly understood), the tradition is quite different. We don't force tobacco companies to create safe products. Smoking is our Right! *Caveat emptor*, let the buyer beware! The result has been millions dead due to lung cancer.

Then along comes COVID-19, where the high standards of collective responsibility have been colliding with the exceptionally low standards of personal responsibility. As we currently live under Republican governance, we have mostly been favoring the personal responsibility approach to fighting COVID-19.

Polls indicate the majority of Americans understand the common sense of wearing a mask. Many of us, though, find masks to be uncomfortable and the risk of infection low. They would argue that we don't live in a risk-free universe. In nearly everything one does, there is a risk. Some have decided that the freedom of acting irresponsibly is worth the risk, but they fail to comprehend the effects when their behavior is mirrored by millions of their peers.

A simplified analysis can explain the challenge. Let's say 10% of our population on some given day decides to go out and not wear masks in public. Of those 33 million, 2% of them are actively infected. Of those 660,000, 2% do something like sneeze without covering well or have lunch with some friends while they are 3 feet apart, and they infect on average two other people. The result is 26,000 new infections. Of those 26,000 we can expect that approximately 500 will die. We must also realize that those 26,000 new infections add to our total number of infected, so that the next day, the new infections will grow.

It's all very innocent. Of the 10% of our fellow citizens in public without masks, only 2% do something wrong. It doesn't *feel* dangerous. As of June 8, there are roughly 20,000 new infections diagnosed in the US each day. That is only six-thousandths of one% of us! Our odds of getting sick are really small. Of those who do get sick, the odds of getting seriously ill or dying are far smaller. Why worry about it?!

Because in this country there are 328 million of us. When we multiply our admittedly minor stupidity over and over 328 million times, we end up with 20 thousand diagnosed infections and a corresponding 500 deaths a day. Additionally, those we infect go on to infect others, and so on and so forth. Caseloads build exponentially, which means the numbers grow slowly in the beginning. At some point, if left unchecked, that growth accelerates rapidly. Remember, it was only a handful of infected individuals who entered the country, and the result has been millions infected and over 100 thousand dead. Our actions affect everyone! My stupidity today might kill you two months from now.

Our brains are not equipped to understand that math. Sure, we can understand it in an academic sense. But when you take your mask off because you're in a place where few people are wearing them, you don't feel stupid with your mask off. You feel stupid with your mask on, because social pressures mean more to us than math. It's tragically ironic that far-right "freedom" activists who don't believe in wearing masks are referring to those who do as sheep. They are trying to make the argument that people are thoughtlessly following the "party line" of wearing a mask. It is instead the social pressure to not wear masks that is now killing Americans in primarily red states.

It just doesn't *feel* like your stupidity is causing 500 deaths a day (edit: July 30, 2020. 500 dead a day was close to the minimum. We are now close to 1500 a day). But it is. That's the problem with statistics. We just don't see our role in the big picture.

There is yet another challenge in getting our citizens to do the right thing. Our traditions and rights to individual freedoms are colliding with our societal traditions and obligations for safety in our everyday lives. This is the fundamental political conundrum laid in our laps by COVID-19. Because we are currently led in this country by a man who is cognitively and emotionally a child, we have yet to have this intelligent conversation, at least in the national spotlight. I mention it now in the context of the numbers. Those who espouse freedom are concerned with the rights of 328 million to live and work as they desire. In opposition is a tiny six-thousandths of a percent that will pass on an infection. It's obvious to those who emphasize freedom that the rights of the many should not be infringed upon by the few.

Those that espouse safety are working a vastly different math problem. They add up a pandemic average of around 1,000 deaths a day, which would amount to a third of a million a year. They add to that those who will be partially or permanently disabled and add the hospital costs in dollars and the loss of healthcare workers. They know that infection spread is an exponential problem, meaning two infections today will mean four next week, then eight thereafter, and so on. Suddenly, this small risk of the *few* has turned into many millions who are directly affected. This group concludes that this extremely large sum of life and treasure easily overrides the minor inconvenience and annoyance of responsible behavior, at least until a vaccine is available.

COVID-19 – The International Edition

One of the best ways to assess America's success with respect to COVID-19 is to examine the successes and failures of other countries. In a monolithic sense, I think we can safely say as it relates to American leadership, the benchmarks set by the rest of the world puts our nation's response to shame. With less than 5% of the world's population, America accounts for over 25% of the COVID-19 fatalities. There is no sufficient explanation for this extreme level of death, short of severely incompetent leadership.

To be fair, this statistic paints an unfair and incomplete picture, at least in the early days of the pandemic. America has more world travelers and therefore had greater initial exposure to the virus. Additionally, we are a large country with very substantial cities. If you remove just New York City alone, our statistics change substantially. (edit: July 30, 2020. The distinction of removing New York City matters less and less now that the virus is out of control in southern states.) Perhaps most significantly, our federal system of government makes national edicts difficult relative to other countries.

But there can be no letting our government off the hook once we examine the entirety of its response.

*　*　*　*　*

For two days, I've been stuck trying to figure out what to write next. Maybe that's because I understand these paragraphs that follow should define the significance of this book—the reason for time spent not otherwise binge-watching Netflix, playing tennis, or helicoptering over my three 21-year-olds. But frankly, I don't know what words possibly capture the apocalyptic level of incompetence, irresponsibility, ignorance, and to borrow a word from Hollywood, *Idiocracy* exhibited by the president and members of his administration. The only thing that comes to mind is to recount a brief story.

I served in the Air Force with my dear friend, Roger, who is the physician I previously introduced. I don't recall for certain, but I believe his workload increased substantially when he returned to being a civilian. For me, becoming an airline pilot meant a more leisurely schedule. Roger had scoffed at the restrictions that the FAA placed upon airline pilots not working long hours. He once said to me, "In the ER, we work 24-hour shifts all the time. Sometimes as a surgeon too. It doesn't make sense that you pilots have such a leisurely schedule. How are the airlines supposed to make any money?"

Thinking for a moment, I answered, "As a doctor, if you have a bad day at work, somebody might get a bit sicker, maybe even die. Maybe even two people die if a doctor has a really bad day. If I have a bad day at work, 200 people could die. I think that's worth a little extra sleep."

To take this a step further, if the *American president* has a bad day at work or makes even a single bad decision, thousands or more could die. What happens to a country when its president can't make an appropriate decision on a life or death matter for six weeks or more? *What does it mean when we have a president who can't lead his way out of a paper bag?*

That's what we've been dealing with. That's why my words matter. It's no less important than life and death, not for a few, but for many. Hundreds of thousands, as it turns out. To anyone who believes we've discussed the American leadership failures of the pandemic in sufficient detail, I would say, "Get ready. We haven't gotten started yet."

* * * * *

We have, by far, the most number of cases and deaths in the world, but we have a large population that makes per capita mortality rate a fairer metric. With that number, America is currently the 9th worse out of 215 countries (put another way, 207 out of 215)—certainly nothing to brag about.

Let's not gloss over this too briefly. We're America. Even the least patriotic among us when I was growing up understood that American exceptionalism was more than a fictional construct. But in this one basic and telling metric, 207 out of 214 other countries have had healthier and safer responses to the pandemic. America, with the greatest number of Nobel Science Prize winners, arguably the best university system in the world, with medical facilities that are among the best, and drug companies that lead the world in therapeutic medicine is 207 out of 215? The failure of a country to manage per capita mortality isn't some random statistic. This is the equivalent of a patient with a blood pressure of 60/20 right before they code.

Worse yet, when we drill down and look at the eight countries that are supposedly inferior to us, our response looks even worse! Two of these are San Marino and Andorra. I had to look them up because I've never heard of them, and I fly all over the world. They are so small as to be the definition of statistical outliers. Between them, they have less than 100 dead as of June 15, and the two together have had one total death in the last month. On the whole, they are doing better than us.

Sweden is one of the eight. They have made a conscious (and many would argue, highly misguided) decision to let the virus overtake their country in the hopes of achieving herd immunity. Because Sweden has put zero effort into stopping the spread of the virus, they should be removed from this particular analysis, but we will return to discuss the interesting aspects of Sweden's response in greater detail.

Belgium is also on the list. Many have also considered this country an outlier, as they are counting COVID-19 deaths more liberally. On an apples-to-apples comparison, they likely have fewer dead.

The remaining four are France, Italy, Spain, and the UK. The UK is an interesting case. They began with an approach similar to Sweden's. They anticipated minimal intervention and had expected to simply ride out the storm. Then their Prime Minister, Boris Johnson, who some refer to as the UK Trump, came down with COVID-19 and became so sick he ended up in an ICU. After that, the UK decided that the Swedish strategy was not at all for them. But in delaying their response, the damage had already been done. Discounting Belgium, San Marino, and Andorra, the UK has the highest per capita death rate in the world.

As for Italy, France, and Spain, their performances are nothing to be proud of, but…. They do appear to be the Louisianas of Europe, which is to say that they've been somewhat victims of circumstance. As major tourist and international travel destinations, they were the first countries outside of China to get substantially hit. The initial seed numbers of infected people appear to be high in those countries. Although the three countries were slow to initially respond, they have had highly effective quarantines. The daily new case curve in Spain is representative:

Daily New Cases in Spain

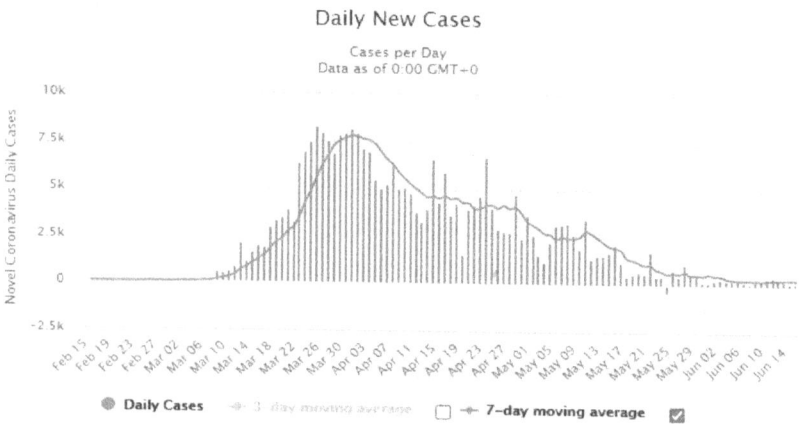

Figure 6:

From www.worldometers.info/coronavirus/country/spain/ As of June 17, 2020

Once a country lets the virus in, they can't do much better than Spain, although most of Europe is similar. Discounting anomalies, short of Sweden that made no effort to stop the virus (and America), every First World country has a similar curve. Also of note, every one of the eight countries with higher per capita mortality than the US has substantially higher population densities—the UK population density is over seven times ours. As you may recall, population density plays a critical role in disease propagation. In any reasonable analysis, we are distinct from every other country in the world, in terms of our failure to manage public health.

Looking at the American curve:

Daily New Cases in the United States

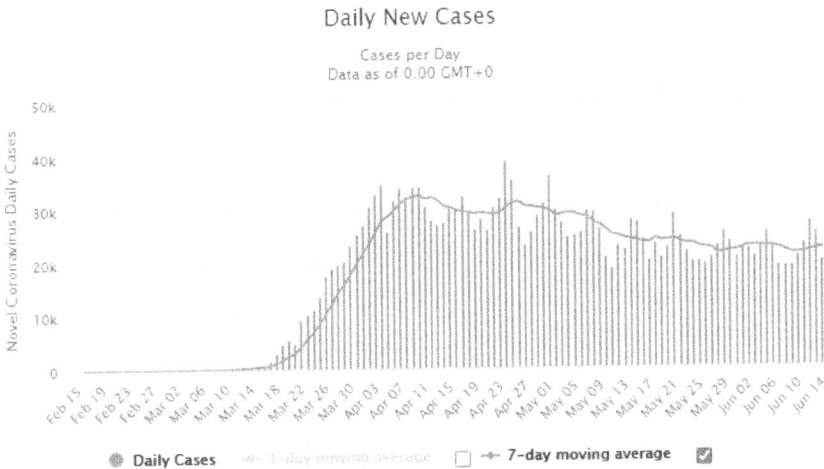

Figure 7:

From https://www.worldometers.info/coronavirus/country/us/ As of June 14, 2020.

This curve only resembles Sweden's curve in its failure to draw down meaningfully from its peak. The new case count grows until over 30 thousand daily cases, before very slowly inching down and plateauing in the low 20 thousands. (edit: July 30, 2020. This chart was drawn when the American infection rate was at its lowest. Cases have exploded to over 70,000 and may not reach the lows of May for the remainder of the year.)

The US continues to be an amalgam of 50 states. Initially, the case count was quickly sent higher due to the infections in New York City. Once The Big Apple got the virus under control, the remainder of the country has been taking turns permitting virus spread and as a result, we have a mostly level curve. As of June 14, the future looks dismal. Some cities are beginning to see significant outbreaks, just as restrictions are easing.

How is it that the United States of America, with all of our resources—natural, financial, medical, and all of our brainpower would be dead last (or next to dead last) out of the world's hundreds of countries? We should be looking back and saying we did it best, or maybe next to best or at the very least, in the top ten. Not the *bottom* ten!

As of June 15, we are beyond 115,000 dead and counting. Projections are pointing to 200,000 by the end of the summer. The number one responsibility of government, above all else, is to protect the safety and well-being of its citizens. This is arguably the greatest failure by any American government in the history of our nation, a national disgrace, and history in the making. The implications of this failure go way beyond our ability to respond to the coronavirus.

The tragedy of the American problem is the plenitude of low hanging fruit left to rot. With each passing day, America could have looked to the successes of other countries. Policies such as universal mask usage in public, increased per capita testing, and increased restrictions against public indoor gatherings were keeping case counts low throughout the world. If American leadership had been making data-driven decisions, we would have saved many lives.

The WHO?

The World Health Organization has exhibited odd, unexpected incompetence regarding this pandemic. Any speculation on my part regarding *why* would merely be conjecture. Answering this question would be a job better suited for an investigative journalist. However, it's worth considering how it is that the organization appears to not be living up to its usual high standards. Before SARS-CoV-2 came along, the WHO had for decades played an instrumental role, along with the CDC, in keeping the world safe from the spread of disease.

There is a legitimate basis for Trump's criticism that the WHO was late in their January 30 declaration of a public global health emergency, though in my estimation by only by a few days. I believe they were more delayed in their declaration of a world pandemic, which amazingly did not occur until March 11, weeks after millions throughout the globe had begun proactive measures in anticipation of a pandemic.

Part of the issue is semantics. They might have been looking at some minimum number of infections before using the term, "world pandemic," but regardless, a clear and present danger existed, and the WHO was not sounding alarms as aggressively as it should have been. Still, there is no evidence of Trump's accusations that the WHO altered its findings and recommendations based upon China's sensitivities. It makes even less sense considering that country contributes less than 12% to the WHO's annual budget, in comparison to the US which contributes 22%.

The WHO has had other suspect behavior, most notably by their lead technologist's June 8 statement contradicting a defining characteristic of the pandemic, that asymptomatic COVID-19 infection transmission was *"very rare."* This statement was then quickly walked back the next day by other WHO officials. There was otherwise broad agreement among the scientific community that asymptomatic carriers were responsible for a large percentage of disease spread. It's possible a lack of consensus over even rough estimates of that percentage may have contributed to the confusion.

In general, the WHO assumed a role in responding to this pandemic that was more limited than with previous infection outbreaks. It could be that the organization found itself ill-equipped to manage the bizarre political climate of the moment. Consider the following:

1) The WHO waited until January 30, 2020, to declare a world health emergency, and then President Trump (and the American science community) did little in response.

2) The WHO could have and should have been more critical of the American administration's head-in-the-sand reaction to the virus. America's response remains a severe threat to the health and particularly the economy of the world. WHO officials should have said more, but didn't, possibly out of established policy and rules about avoiding political conflict. Nevertheless, the seriousness of American neglect should have overridden these considerations.

3) The WHO is staffed by mostly American scientists from the CDC. The notion that they would exhibit any strong allegiance to China is unrealistic.

4) The WHO's budget is too small for the job that they need to do. Part of their problem is that dwindling budgets have hollowed out their staff and capabilities. To punish them by denying more funds is absurd. The WHO does an incredibly important job that makes the world a safer place for all of humanity, America included. Call to replace the management, call for an investigation, do other stuff if you must, but don't defund them. Unless you're hoping for more disease and death.

In consideration of the above, one possible conclusion is that it was *American* pressure from CDC bureaucrats that kept the WHO from getting more aggressive in their declarations of danger. America has more influence with WHO scientists than China. After January, when the international community shut down travel to Chinese destinations, President Xi had lost his incentive to downplay the virus, whereas President Trump's incentives were just beginning. One can only imagine the frustration among WHO scientists over the US withholding funding if it turns out it was primarily American pressure that delayed their pronouncements.

The Third World

Some of the Third World's answers to COVID-19 will be inferior to the US, but it is truly an apples-to-oranges comparison. The Third World encompasses some of the densest population centers in the world; they have minimal discretionary money to pay for items like PPE or ventilators, let alone the inability of some countries to treat any significant number of hospital patients. They cannot borrow money at close to zero interest rates, as we can still do. They do not have the luxury of being able to quarantine most of their population. If they shut down their economies, they will lose more people to starvation than to the virus. Determining the metrics of caseload and mortality is a greater challenge. Likely death and disease will be underreported, diminishing the value of these metrics, particularly relative to wealthier countries.

It sucks to be poor. It always has and always will, as long as society fails to embrace its poor to its bosom. Money isn't everything though, by a longshot. As I've explained to my kids from an early age, there are people in the deepest of economic despair that live far happier lives than some of the world's wealthiest. Happiness is a skill to which some are simply more gifted than others.

There's another advantage some poor have beyond their wealthy counterparts. Immune systems, like the remainder of the human body, tend to become stronger under greater demand. The many and various germs to which the impoverished are exposed can create robust immunity. Additionally, COVID-19, to some degree, is a disease of obesity. Impoverishment and obesity don't often go hand in hand. Those who are severely malnourished or simply overweight due to unhealthy diets likely comprise the bulk of disease in the Third World.

Brazil is worthy of mention. It's the country that put the B in BRIC. Run by right-wing populist president, Jair Bolsonaro, easily a far Trumpier character than the UK's Boris Johnson, Bolsonaro famously refers to COVID-19 as the "little flu" and has given it that much consideration. Brazil is a large country with sizeable, developed cities and a substantial population. Unlike numerous third-world leaders who have little choice but to appear fearless against the virus as a substitute for actual medical policy, Brazil has more of a choice. It is not without financial resources, even though its economy has been stagnant since 2015. Where First World nations have a middle class, Brazil has a large underclass of impoverished citizenry, but the country does have sufficient wealth to wage a far more aggressive war against COVID-19. They simply chose not to. Specifically, and more accurately, Bolsonaro has chosen not to.

Because Brazil lives in both the First and Third Worlds, it had enough international travel to seed coronavirus inside its borders in large numbers. Additionally, many of its citizens live in crowded neighborhoods and cannot afford sufficient healthcare, so Brazilians have been impacted by the worst influences of the First and Third World. Since mid-May, they have been number two (only to the US) in the number of positive COVID-19 cases. As they are testing per capita, 10% as much as the US, they surely have far more cases than they are reporting. At the current trajectory, it is unlikely that Brazil will overtake the US in either caseload or mortality. However, their actual numbers will likely remain underreported. (edit: July 28, 2020—The US has finally started seeing the results of self-correction. Red-state populations have appropriately moderated their behavior and caseloads are coming down. Brazil has not been so fortunate, possibly because information does not move as freely as it does for us. The result is that Brazil is poised to take over the lead from the US, at least in per capita numbers, of worst in the world COVID-19 response.)

And Sweden???

Speaking of odd choices, Sweden's epidemiologists made an interesting early choice in electing to aspire to herd immunity. Although it represents a huge risk in being the only first-world country taking this strategy (after the UK abandoned it), it would be unfair to call it an entirely irrational decision. In not quarantining, they avoided a certain level of social angst and certainly inconvenience. It is difficult to see to what end, though. Because their economy is tied so strongly to the rest of the world, they have not avoided economic pain, whereas their total per capita mortality is among the very worst. They are also the only First World country currently experiencing a significant upsurge in caseload, as seen in the following chart:

Daily New Cases in Sweden

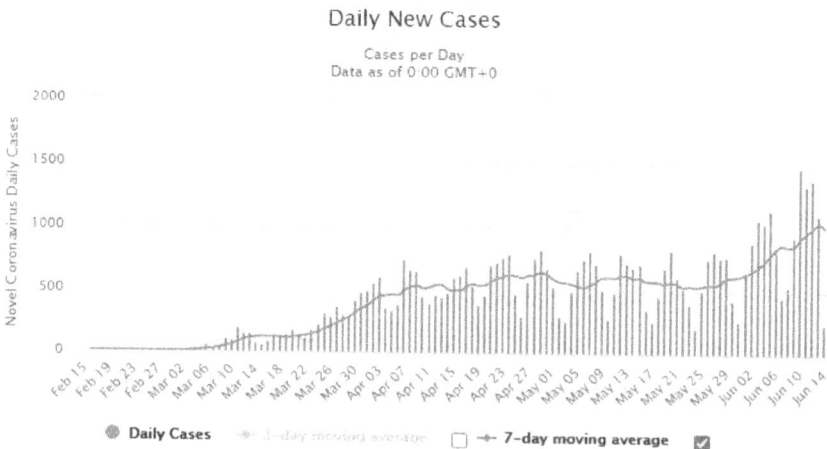

Figure 8:

From https://www.worldometers.info/coronavirus/country/sweden/ As of **June 15, 2020**.

Meanwhile, they are nowhere close to the bare minimum 65% infected rate needed for any meaningful herd immunity. Sweden had likely been hoping for several factors that never ended up working in their favor. Despite the "cold" Swedish culture, with its built-in social distancing, transmission rates have held high. They had hoped to keep their elderly population somewhat isolated while permitting younger people and nuclear families with school-age children to live without restrictions. Unfortunately, infection rates among the elderly have been dreadful therein keeping Swedish death rates stubbornly high. Still, the book has not been closed on the matter. In the unlikely event that an effective vaccine does not materialize within the next 18 months, Sweden may have a head start on herd immunity.

Despite the frightening trend in Figure 8, the mortality rate for Sweden is decreasing:

Daily New Deaths in Sweden

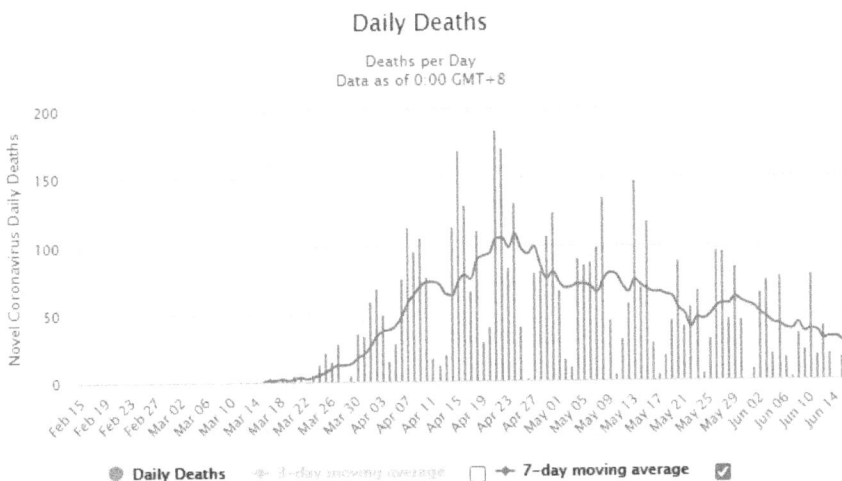

Figure 9:

From https://www.worldometers.info/coronavirus/country/sweden/ as of June 16, 2020

The declining death rate (in Sweden's case, even in the face of increasing infections) has yet to be widely discussed, even in right-wing media. I doubt it will go unmentioned for long.

Swedish Addendum (July 5, 2020): After peaking sometime around June 27, the Swedish infection rate took a rapid reversal and has been dropping precipitously for about a week.

Hmmm. There is nothing about the Swedes' stated approach to account for such a reversal. On the other hand, the Swedish Prime Minister, just three days ago opened an inquiry into the failure of their coronavirus policy. My conclusion is that there has been an insurrection of sorts to their initial approach and that Swedes have, on their own account, taken to wearing masks and otherwise instituted social distancing measures. This would be consistent with their cultural philosophy of "Total Defense," in which every Swede is obligated to defend their nation. This rapid turnabout is particularly telling in the face of the EU's recent decision to prohibit Swedish citizens from entry into other EU nations. Sweden is already an outlier as they are EU members but excluded from the Eurozone due to economic factors. In that way, they have been lumped together with the backward nations of Russia, Brazil, and amazingly the USA. Nonetheless, the Swedes have had the good sense to let their shame be their guides; it seems they realized the folly of their ways and have quickly adopted proper social distancing.

We in the US, at least on the Right and particularly our president, don't seem to be capable of such shame. Of note, Republican politicians to include Trump have recently begun embracing masks to various degrees, but the lack of full-throated endorsements of science will prevent the level of widespread adoption of mask-wearing and social distancing that has made the rest of the world safer. Unfortunately, red-state Americans have taken the EU and other exclusions as badges of honor. They don't seem to recognize how financially costly this will prove to be.

(Edit: September 4, 2020: Sweden had me stumped. Their infection spread rate took a sharp reversal in the week of June 23, so I knew they had changed their behavior. It's critically important to know with certainty what is happening in Sweden because the discovery of an unknown epidemiological influence could have implications to the entire world.

I hypothesized that they must have quickly adopted mask usage and other social distancing measures that they hadn't been using before. I looked for news to corroborate, but I found precious little information online. I went to Swedish webcams to see if I could ID increased mask usage. All the webcams I found are low quality and placed too far from people to see clearly, but I thought I was seeing a high rate of mask usage.

I believe I may have been guilty of confirmation bias. Recent news articles maintain that Sweden has not had any official change in policy regarding COVID-19, and there is no evidence pointing to a widespread adoption of mask usage. There are no logical explanations for the rapid turn of events. A radio news article discussed the possibility that Sweden may have reached some level of herd immunity, even though estimates are that about 10% of their population has had the virus. An interviewed epidemiologist has theorized that the herd immunity threshold might be much lower than the expected 60-70% because of innate t-cell protection from other similar coronaviruses. If this were true, we would expect to see in the infection curve a slow decline from the peak followed by an asymptotic decline towards zero. We see instead a rapid decline to a plateau:

Daily New Cases in Sweden

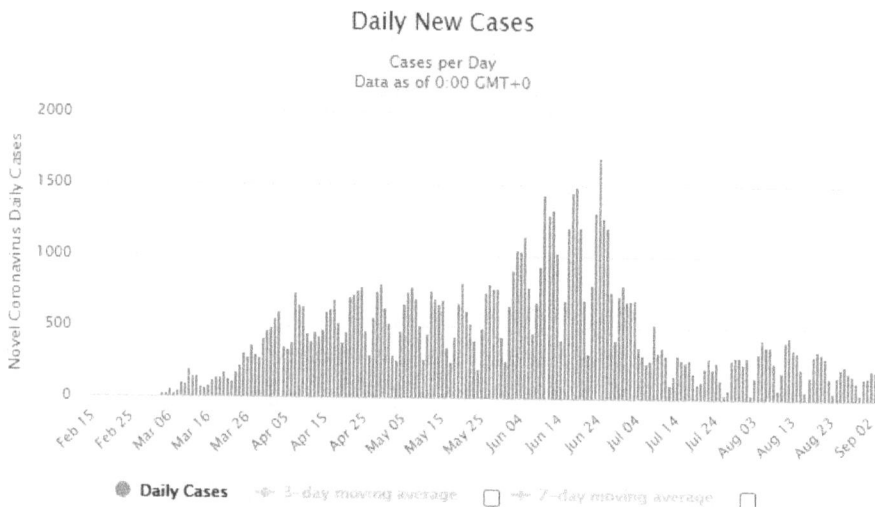

Daily New Cases

Cases per Day
Data as of 0:00 GMT+0

Figure 10:

From https://www.worldometers.info/coronavirus/country/sweden/ as of Sep. 4, 2020

Current evidence points to a combination of three factors. The first is quite simple. It may not seem it to foreign travelers, as European cities are habitually packed in the summertime, but much of Europe takes an extended summer vacation. Those left in the cities have been tourists or tourist industry workers. Of course, this year, there've been far fewer tourists, particularly with Europeans avoiding crowds. The result has been lower caseloads throughout Europe through much of the summer. It's reasonable to expect similar influences in Sweden.

Second, Sweden's post COVID downturn in economic activity was little better than anywhere else in the Western world. Their government's explanation was that this was caused by reduced foreign economic activity. However, recently published data indicates that domestic consumption was substantially reduced. US media has reported that Swedes have been spending far less time inside restaurants, pubs and shops. We can only conclude that they decided to embrace the concept of Total Defense after all. Put another way, Swedes are no more interested in risking lives for meatballs than anyone else.

I believe I found evidence of the third factor while researching the effects of climate on COVID cases in California. Sweden has a relatively cold climate. The rapid reversal in disease spread appeared at the beginning of Summer. In the US, Summer brings many adults inside to escape the heat, but in Sweden, adults head outdoors to enjoy the temperate air. I believe these three factors taken together explain the Swedish curve.

Mortality Takes a (Mini) Holiday

All available data as of mid-June points to a reduction in the mortality rate throughout the world. If correct, this is fantastic news, but why or how is it happening? The answer lies in rapid advancements in medical treatment efficacy. Despite the lack of a vaccine or universally viable treatments, doctors are now armed with several important findings:

1) COVID-19 patients who can't maintain sufficient oxygen in their blood and have therefore been put on ventilators have extremely poor outcomes. Resultantly, physicians are only using vents as a last resort. They are using improved tools, such as high-rate nasal cannula oxygen and ECMO, in which blood is removed, oxygenated externally, and then circulated back into the body. The lower usage of ventilators has saved many COVID-19 patients.

2) Remdesivir has proven to be an effective treatment.

3) Steroids have proven effective in keeping patients off ventilators. Patients treated with steroids have survival rates that are better by a third.

4) COVID-19 is as much a circulatory disease as it is a respiratory disease. For many patients, blood thinners are proving effective. Physicians are learning how to better tailor therapies to individual patients.

5) Physicians treating COVID-19 patients have seen so many of these patients that they are getting years of experience crammed into days and weeks. There is a multitude of important details the medical community is quickly learning in how to prevent COVID-19mortality.

Other factors might also be in play:

1) The use of masks among the public and better social distancing may be reducing the initial viral load for individuals who become infected. This will result in less severe disease and lower mortality.

2) It might also be that higher-risk individuals are being more careful in limiting exposure such that those now becoming infected have naturally higher survivability.

3) People getting infected recently are much younger, on average. This, perhaps more than anything, might account for the divergence between new cases and new deaths.

4) Much about this virus is still not understood. It certainly did not "disappear" with the onset of summer. Infections during warmer months may be less severe. Indoor infections are now occurring inside air-conditioned spaces with faster airflow, which should result in reduced viral loads.

Whatever the reasons, lower disease mortality is welcome news. (Edit: July 30, 2020. I expected a rebound in caseload as America reopened the entire economy. I did not expect the rampant irresponsibility of some state governors to fail to tighten restrictions in the face of rapidly growing infections, nor the rigid obstinacy of so many Trump supporters to maintain their denials of the very simple science of masks and social distancing. The self-corrections to reduce infections are slower in coming than I'd expected, which has caused caseloads to rise dramatically. Sadly, advances in medicine have been partly negated by the large number of infections. The only factor that seems to have any meaningful influence on this troublesome segment of the population to alter their behavior is high numbers of deaths close to home. It takes four to seven weeks of unsafe activity before an increase in mortality is observed. That's at least four weeks of growing infection spread before the first corrective change. The failure of many to comprehend this delay will drive millions of infections.)

The National Discussion You Always Wanted and Thought You Had But Never Did

Though I never agreed with Sweden, I have to hand it to them. Their decision took guts, and more importantly, they made a choice – they didn't just let the virus make the decisions. Not so much in the American White House. Society will eventually reach the point where we discuss all the things the president should have or could have done but didn't. For now, we'll limit it to the most important thing: the development of an overall strategy.

For decades, I have studied and taught cultural change in large organizations. As our country and the world initially faced an impending pandemic, and decisions were being made as to what to do about this new reality, one of the few things that we knew with certainty was that change *was* coming. The fundamental approach that any leader must take toward instituting any kind of change, particularly within a large group, encompasses a few basic principles which can be broken down into the following seven steps:

1) Conduct a balanced discussion and reasoned debate regarding how to address the impending change. There are times when it is appropriate to have this discussion in private although in this particular case, it should have been very public.

2) As a logical course of action begins to take form, work to win support and buy-in among relevant leading stakeholders, which in this case would probably have included leaders of the Democratic Party. This would have, by the definition of the democratic process, involved compromise on both sides. This might seem a bizarre statement in the context of national

politics over the last decade, but I assure you, this is how things have been done historically. One need only look back to the financial collapse of 2008 to see compromise in action. The party in power always gets the final and most important vote, but anytime we have previously faced large challenges to our nation, this was how it's been done. Even at the inception of Obamacare, the Obama administration reached out to Republicans and adopted the majority of Mitt Romney's (former Republican governor of Massachusetts) healthcare plan. Unfortunately, Mitch McConnell was unwilling to take *yes* for an answer. They abandoned any notion of compromise, electing instead to pursue an aggressive strategy of obstructionism.

3) Once there is buy-in amongst as many leaders as possible, institute a campaign to explain to the greater group of stakeholders (in this case the American public) the extent of the challenge and/or change, the reasons why decisions were made, and the importance of gaining as much relevant support as possible.

4) Continue an outreach program, building upon step 3 above, to further consolidate buy-in for the leadership's decision and plan. Explain the weakness in alternative courses of action and reinforce the advantages of the chosen plan. Address those that may be adversely affected by the chosen plan, as there are always winners and losers, and attempt to mitigate any adverse effects.

5) Execute the plan.

6) Continue outreach efforts. Address critics' concerns when possible and continue to reinforce the importance of the plan.

7) Self-correct and adjust the plan to current conditions to optimize results.

No one in the federal government, or local governments for that matter, did anything remotely like the steps above. The result has been limited buy-in by the American public with the result of the *least successful quarantine in the entire world.*

Instead of a logical, organized, fundamental approach, we have had no definitive national quarantine plan, with a result of chaos, uncertainty, protest, unrest, and limited cooperation. Instead of buy-in and support from both ends of the political spectrum, we have had limited support by members of either political party and a perception that no one has gotten what they wanted.

Which conversations might we have had?

Conversation #1: This year we will lose many more lives to COVID-19 than the flu. But what about the next five years? Or ten? Combining five to ten years, the flu's mortality may resemble COVID. What will we do about *that* loss of life?

As of now, nothing. Is it proportional to shut down a large percentage of the entire world economy for COVID while doing little to nothing for a similar loss of life from the flu, just because it occurs over a longer time duration? I don't see how anyone could successfully argue that point. This contention should not be taken as an argument *against* quarantine for COVID-19, but rather an argument *for greater future vaccination rates* and more resources devoted toward the flu.

Conversation #2: What has the cessation of so much travel and commerce done to the American and world economies? A lot of damage, to be sure. Have quarantines saved more lives than they've cost? There has been discussion concerning suicides and starvations. At least in this country, quarantine related casualties will not reach anywhere near what the US has so far suffered from COVID, but it would have been worth it to hear specific estimates of metrics and an ensuing discussion back in February.

Conversation #3: It would have been important to discuss the practical limits of government restrictions. It's no secret that Americans are a rebellious lot. You can only limit people so much from their livelihoods and amusements before they start to push back. The scientists offered a false binary choice. Shut down and social distance or else. It's not the scientists' fault. They were doing their jobs. It's up to leaders, the politicians, to ask if any other solutions are possible. It was up to our leaders to better consider issues such as quarantine fatigue. Instead, politicians responded in a mostly binary manner. Some shut down; some did not or opened early. The scientists were managing the disease, and the politicians were trying to manage the economic needs of their constituents. Unfortunately, our political leaders failed to attempt to negotiate any kind of middle ground.

The problem is that we ended up with a "middle ground" by abdication, and this was probably the worst of all possibilities. Restrictions that could have been safely eased were not. Restrictions that should have been left in place were not. We knew relatively early that we could have safely held outdoor gatherings (wearing masks) with larger numbers. Such gatherings could have been permitted before "opening up." Other wholesale dropping of restrictions in some southern states led to rapid resurgence of infections.

Conversation #4: We learned during lockdown that restaurants would be especially dangerous with respect to disease spread. We could have better incentivized restaurant owners to create outdoor venues, which would have in turn created valuable economic stimulus. Bars could still be made safe by restricting loud music or even any music so people would not have to get too close to hear each other. Plus there would be less reason to sing. Yes, these restrictions would be unwelcome to the nation's pub crowds, but we all have our crosses to bear. Because there was little national leadership, localities did as they pleased, often making decisions egged on by the president. We used to take the sanctity of life seriously in this country. There used to be implications for lives lost due to neglect. What happened?

Conversation #5: Leadership knew in March that when we eventually opened up, there would still be many infected individuals who would seed a new wave of spread. While most of the country was in lockdown, we could have created experiments in certain cities with lower infection rates similar to what would exist when we opened up more broadly. In one city, we might have established mask ordinances. In other cities we could have attempted different strategies. Successful ideas would have been deployed throughout the country.

Such an *experiment* would have been incredibly valuable in three respects:

I) It would have generated valuable epidemiological data to better understand disease spread.

II) Our population would have (in some small sense) become the scientists, creating buy-in and greater overall respect for scientific guidance.

III) It would have (to some degree) taken our minds off of the economic and health/mortality costs of the disease (regularly appearing on the news every night) which would have improved our morale.

One theme I will continue to revisit is the notion that you can't effectively fight the threat of a 'new normal' with the same weapons of the past. I'm just one guy who might have a few good ideas, but there are people out there with larger, faster, and more supple intellects, who if given the chance could likely develop outstanding solutions to some of our pressing problems. America's "cream of the crop" always rises to the challenge of developing market-based solutions to even our worst problems. Unfortunately, our country's rigid reliance on free market solutions proves to be an ineffective defense against national emergencies. The strength of the free market is efficiency; the priority of an emergency must be speed. In America, large-scale rapid response is by design under the domain of the executive branch of the federal government. Too bad no one told them.

Conversation #6: The total bill to the federal and state governments combined might approach something close to 10 trillion dollars! That's roughly half the current national debt, amounting to over $30,000 per individual, or about $122,000 per household of four. A tiny fraction of this number could buy a lot of things—like healthcare, or perhaps cures for cancer or heart disease, which in the long run would save far more lives than COVID-19 will take. Once the pandemic became inevitable, catastrophic economic loss became equally inescapable, but many of the wrong choices were made well before 2020. In a forward looking conversation, we need identify potential dangers akin to COVID-19, and invest in strategies to mitigate these future threats. We also need to have a national conversation concerning federal expenditures for basic medical research. Statistically, a deadly disease is far more likely to cause our demise than a foreign threat. As a veteran I fully support a strong military, but we have to rational decisions that acknowledge that military dollars spent are dollars not spent in saving lives lost to disease.

Conversation #7: What of the rest of the world? Aside from Sweden, our allies and trading partners in the First World have all quarantined. Had we not quarantined, we would have been involuntarily isolated from the rest of the world, at least until we achieved herd immunity or a vaccine. That isolation would have come with an immense economic, political, and cultural cost. (edit: July 30, 2020. Nearly all other first-world countries have reduced their caseloads to less than a tenth of ours, and they have opened their borders to each other. But not to us. *We are isolated now!* Our GDP last quarter dropped by **A THIRD!** We have screwed it all up. By not managing the crisis, we have by default taken the middle road, which in this case has resulted in the worst possible outcome. We are destroying our economy with an ineffective quarantine, and we're killing our people with that same ineffective quarantine. One might hope that watching the American economy implode before our very eyes may motivate some to alter their behavior, but even now, Congress appears set to let enhanced unemployment benefits expire. Without approved legislation to extend benefits beyond September 30, millions who never expected to be in such a position will experience problems of poverty and severe economic hardship.)

Conversation #8: The lack of intelligent national discourse has left us with other deficits and cheated us out of harnessing the full strength of the American ethos. This is the danger of a leader who believes that every good idea must originate from the top.

Several important early decisions could have been made but were never publicly discussed. For lack of a better word, there is a *tradition* in our country of sending our young people out into the world, at the risk of their lives, to protect our greater population, our way of life, and our national treasure. If we can send our young to war, why would we not at least consider that we facilitate the volunteering of young adults to accelerate the advance of medical therapies and vaccines?

What would this look like? Volunteers might be intentionally infected with the virus under various conditions. Adults in their 20's with no underlying conditions who were infected with lower viral loads would have a low mortality rate (though potential lasting effects are still not well understood). This may sound absurd to some, but human trials of various treatment therapies could have saved many lives early on by offering firm data. Certainly, we place far more of our young at risk by sending them off to war. New *realities* necessitate new paradigms and sometimes new ways of looking at old ideas. It might have been shown that the ethical pitfalls of such a program (or something similar) would be too awful to endure, but we never had the national discussions to find out.

Human Psychology 101

I am not a psychologist, nor have I played one on TV. I have taught Organizational Behavior at the graduate level and other courses addressing human psychology and its impact upon cultural change. Societal needs related to altering behavior as a protective response to the threats of COVID-19 are well within my wheelhouse.

Two competing themes need to be addressed. The first is that people never truly change in any substantial manner. There's a lot of support for this position. Recall, if you can, your New Year's resolutions over the last decade. Have any of them stuck? If you are like most of us, you made some initial effort to change but eventually returned to old habits. My apologies for reminding you about it. We're only human, and for the vast majority of us, that's how we roll—wishing, even planning to change, but eventually falling victim to old behaviors and our brains' fundamental patterns governing our natural state of being.

Despite the difficulties in substantively changing our behaviors and the likelihood that such efforts will fail, almost all of us, at some point, make the attempt. And while change is difficult, it *is* possible.

When considering rapid wide-scale societal changes in behavior, two interesting benchmarks come to mind. The first is waste recycling. As a nation, this transition has been a years-long process, but for individuals, the need to separate recyclable waste from other trash was generally thrust upon us quickly. Initially, a large number of people responded positively, while more obstinate neighbors eventually got with the program. Today we still have the outliers—some small number of people who refuse to sort their trash.

The other benchmark is post 9/11 in-flight behavior. This benchmark addresses the outliers specifically. Prior to 9/11, there were a surprising number of in-flight arguments that led to physical altercations, though it was still a relatively small number of people—these were outlier events. Immediately following 9/11, the country adopted a zero-tolerance policy to any in-flight disturbance. In the decade that followed, airborne physical clashes were extremely rare. Even 20 years later, we have not returned to the same level of pre 9/11 violence, though the debate about masks has certainly amped things up.

These benchmarks tell us that changes that inconvenience us with minimal costs of non-compliance, like recycling, take a long time for broad adoption and fail to change outlier behavior, even after an extended period. But when there is a shock to the psyche, such as occurred on 9/11, change can be rapid and all-encompassing.

For family members of those dead or even sickened by COVID-19, I suspect the rapid and lasting adoption of social distancing measures and mask-wear. For many, the mere fear of catching COVID-19 provided that necessary shock to the psyche that has driven a change of habit.

For some, the change to wear masks in public has not been so much a shift in personal habit as it has been an act of conformity. There is truth to the claim from the Right that many people are wearing masks primarily because others around them are in masks. Humans are programmed to conform to the norms around us. Tendencies to follow others have helped humans survive evolutionarily because it is safer to do so. It should be noted that the inverse has been equally true. Darwinism can sometimes be capricious and cruel to would-be trendsetters.

What about washing hands? Or washing packages? Or take-out meals? Certainly, we know less of what happens behind closed doors. People behave differently when they believe they are free from observation. This can make all the difference when conformance is the driving motivation, but the question is still deserving of study. Fortunately, few infections are being attributed to touching infected surfaces.

So, if change is so inherently difficult for the individual, what can leadership do to facilitate individual change? We've discussed the steps leaders should take to enact a cultural shift and compel individuals to change. Internal motivation is particularly important when modifying behavior, whereas heavy-handed control tends to backfire. Give a group of people a reason to rebel and a target for rebellion, and guess what you get? You don't have to guess. The news of summer 2020 says it all.

For any (small "d") democratic leaders seeking to rapidly change behaviors and not desiring mass protests, the emphasis should remain on what amounts to good marketing. These days, micro-targeting is viewed as the gold standard. From a national viewpoint, it would make the most sense to recruit and motivate local politicians, who would be better positioned to make better-tailored *pitches* to their respective constituencies. Local politicians could certainly be motivated by employing COVID metrics to drive carrot/stick reward and/or punishment. Locations need only seed a base level of compliant behavior, and then our tendencies toward conformity will lead to greater adoption.

Micro-targeted appeals toward changing public behavior need to be interesting and informative, and relevant concerns should be addressed. All the typical media channels, from social media, to TV advertising, and news should be employed. Government needs to bear the costs of such marketing, but the effect in lives saved, avoidance of hospital stays, and fewer missed days of work ought to easily result in net-positive benefits to the taxpayer.

Concerning non-conformity, America does face a challenge beyond what most other countries must manage. America is and always has been a country of rebels. Our politics, our laws, our culture, and many of our social practices are broadly influenced by desires to cast off the noose of authority. Governing Americans, particularly at the national level, can be a little like herding cats. Meanwhile, rather than making any attempt to mitigate our rebel ways, Trump has actively worked to sabotage the efforts of local politicians with tweets like "Free Michigan!"

How *should* a government deal with rebels?

When the rebels' ideas have merit, call it a revolution and support them. When there's a large swath of Americans who refuse to wear masks and protest against all efforts at social distancing, there is nothing of merit to support. In that case, it's an insurrection. To tackle an insurrection head-on is not an easy thing. Governments find themselves in a downward spiral in which enforcement fuels rebellion. It can be a problem with only bad and worse solutions. Like the parents of a teenager who refuses to (you can fill in the blank here, but let's just say) "clean their room," you must stop enabling bad behavior by no longer cleaning it for them. You might then believe or hope that once they are living in true filth, they will *get with the program* and clean the room themselves, only to find out that they are more than happy to sleep in between numerous layers of dirty laundry. Alternatively, parents who *set down the law* may find that they win a few battles, only to learn later that they lost the war.

Most parents who successfully survive the teenage years with minimal graying/loss of hair and everyone's sanities intact come to realize that with kids, "Do as I say, not as I do," becomes a guiding principle for how *not* to be a parent.

Insurrections are often acts of righteousness at their cores. The best way to win an uprising is to expose it as a moral failure. This brings us back to Donald Trump, who won't wear a mask or encourage anything close to social distancing. He certainly plays the role of a bad dad extremely well, getting in fights all the time, making all the wrong friends, and having unprotected sex with whoever comes around (I was going to make up a satirical list of misbehaviors, only to remind myself that Trump has a long list of actual misdeeds to draw upon). It then becomes the role of Mom (speaker Pelosi) to figure out how to get the kids to behave.

I would posit that most people who deny the science of epidemiology today rebelled the most as teens. That these folks remain alive, out of jail, and for some, successful, only validates the legitimacy of rebellious ways. Then along comes a father figure, like Dr. Fauci, telling everyone what we should be doing. For some, it might feel quite satisfying to disregard what Anthony Fauci, and any other science "authorities" have to say.

For most of American history, being rebellious has served us well. There is defiance and then there is maliciousness, which comes in various shapes and sizes. We got a strong taste of this early on when Utah Jazz's Rudy Gobert "jokingly" placed his hands all over reporters' microphones and cell phones, shortly before becoming the first NBA player to test positive for COVID-19. Even though he did not realize at the time that he was COVID positive, the intent of his *joke* was to make people uncomfortable. Other examples have been far more egregious. Some people have intentionally attempted to infect others, so much so that police departments started supplying their officers with special "spit socks." These covers are placed over the heads of uncooperative detainees to prevent them from spitting on anyone.

There's something called the Pareto principle, which states that 20% of people cause 80% of problems. In large bureaucracies, it's typically a more accurate assumption that 3% of people will cause 90% of problems. Of those 3% that are your troublemakers, 3% of them cause the biggest problems. So that's 3% of 3% or roughly one thousandth of your population who will cause your biggest problems.

If you have an organization of less than 1,000, you may have no troublemakers at all. If you have 100,000, you probably have around 100 troublemakers. If you have a population of 328 million, you might have about 300,000 people who would be more than happy to pull the wheels off the train. Generally, there's no appealing to that crowd with reason or logic or even self-interest.

Of course, only a small percentage of these severe agitators will care one way or another about SARS-CoV-2, but of those few who do, there is the super-spreader problem. Some epidemiologists fear that a large number of cases are caused by super-spreaders—individuals who might infect 50 or more other people. In most cases, these super-spreaders have been innocent of malice, but in the intersection of statistics and psychology we see the probability that some disease has been spread with ill intent. These would amount to criminal acts, and so to control them, governments have the same problem as with any other criminal activity—catching the individuals and finding enough evidence to convict them. Fortunately, the numbers for malicious spread of the virus appear to be low.

*   *   *   *   *

Of course, for far too many of us, the major psychological impact of COVID-19 will be grief. The number dead, though immense, is relatively small in comparison to our total population. Those lost, who are likely to number well over 200,000 by the end of 2020, may each leave 10 or more trails of sorrow. We can be sure that millions of Americans will be in grief over those lost.

Numerically, more people are being affected by loss of employment and/or income. Small businesses, the lifeblood of the American economy, have been hit particularly hard. Federal grants and loans, though expensive, helped limit the damage, despite the mismanagement of monetary distribution. But with tens of millions of lost jobs, and for many, large deficits between government coronavirus payments and actual salary lost, there is palpable national anxiety over our collective financial future.

People have been transiting the stages of grief, from denial to acceptance and everywhere in between. What does it mean, though, when an entire country grieves simultaneously? If the grief is short-lived, it can be inspirational. History indicates that when the grief is drawn out over a long period, it can be toxic to a nation's outlook and identity. It remains to be seen which category COVID-19 will fall into.

Some challenges, such as the threat of terror following 9/11, brought the country together. COVID-19 seems more apt to tear us apart. For the majority, we are fortunate to have not lost anyone close, nor have most families lost substantial income. For many, the government payments have resulted in a raise, which has brought about other problems. In general, a disparity in different groups bearing the brunt of pain is caustic. Differences in realities breed resentment. For many who have yet to see any meaningful impact, there is disbelief and distrust.

The role (and failures) of national leadership cannot be overstated. It would be useful to educate away misconception. Those who don't see the virus as a meaningful threat should be able to understand how devastating it has been, that it does impact some younger people, and that it can be extremely contagious when no mitigation is in place. They should understand the level of contagion is far lower with simple measures of masks and social distancing. Unfortunately, most red-state politicians are doing everything they can to downplay any adverse aspects of the pandemic. The result has been a lack of validation for those in pain. Many people feel that much of the Republican Party has no empathy for anyone suffering. This is a serious failure of political leadership. Democrats learned this lesson the hard way in the 2016 presidential election.

We should consider if the loss of freedom brought about by quarantine has been a grief event. Anecdotally, it appears it has. Though trite, even the loss of live sports has been reason for some to grieve. There are many kinds of pain that our country and the world are currently experiencing. Though the term *snowflake* may quickly come to mind regarding anyone grieving trivial loss, politicians minimize this pain at their peril. Is it any wonder that as of this date of June 17, 2020, there is so much protest and division?

Politicians are obligated to acknowledge everyone's pain, but that does not mean that they should legitimize the outrage of those whose losses are minor (looking at you, sports fans). Surprise, the president disagrees. Trump legitimizes the outrage of minimal lost freedoms while failing to meaningfully acknowledge the immense loss of life and economic pain. It seems whatever the president ought to be doing, he has an amazing knack for doing the opposite. Such is the fate of an addict's family. We feel lost because we are lost.

As we are incapable of even contact tracing and disease testing, anyone would be foolish to expect that the nation's emotional needs would be addressed, let alone met. But just as you would expect to see an adverse impact in an individual when their pain and grief are not properly addressed, the impact on our country is tangible given the existing level of neglect. For example, it would be naïve to discount the possibility of some emotional projection concerning the current unprecedented level of protests against racism. This should not in the slightest take away from the legitimacy of these protests and those who are participating in them. It's just that given the human propensity for emotional projection, some of the vigor of protestors and counter-protestors alike might be influenced by the COVID pandemic.

$$* \quad * \quad * \quad * \quad *$$

The nature of denial over global warming, the denied value of wearing masks to prevent the spread of disease, and denial of even the existence of COVID-19 can all be considered acts of tribalism. They derive from a cognitive unification of thoughts and actions in lockstep among similarly minded people. Denial experienced following catastrophic loss derives from an emotional reaction to that loss. It is the first step in a grieving process. There is a reasonable distinction between these two types of denial. In the context of tribalism denial requires some level of cognitive dysfunction. Denial due to emotional loss is an otherwise healthy step of a natural process.

I suspect there's an inclination to view the denial of science as somehow specifically governed by party affiliation or ideology. It's not that simple. Denial is not the result of a conscious decision. For those raised outside of a tradition of questioning authority, they are expected to adopt the social norm of believing in the same thing as the significant others in their life. What people ultimately believe is strongly tied to the *tribe* to which they belong. *As the tribal leader goes, so goes all others.* A leader speaks and people follow. That leader may be acting on a consistent ideology or a personal agenda or some random insanity. It doesn't seem to matter.

People might be tempted to ask if there is a cure for such *insanity*. Even in parts of the world where there are literal *tribes*, people are known to occasionally switch allegiances. In the US, where we have families, communities, religious sects, occupations, political parties, and teams, it's easier to switch.

A change in any of those *tribes* requires certain changes of mind. Someone converting to Islam at some point will believe that Women should cover their hair in public. If you become a KC Chiefs fan, you will come to believe that Mahomes is a good quarterback. Humans are programmed to conform to norms, and leaders typically determine the norms. As the leader goes, so goes the others.

The majority of deniers will deny to their last breath. Even in something so clear and obvious as the statistics which show that masks save lives, I have seen no evidence of anyone swayed by argument to alter their opinions or adopt the wearing of masks (edit: August 20, 2020—following Trump's minor endorsement of masks, there has been a noticeable drop in new COVID cases. Correlation in this case could be indicative of causation, meaning Trump's followers submitted to his change of stance on masks. It's also possible the explosion of new cases in the early summer changed behavior. It would take a dedicated study to accurately parse out the reasons for the changes.)

Where masks are mandatory, people do comply—but having politicians that mandate mask usage is a necessary component in this equation. It should not be shocking that there are red-state governors who have prohibited their mayors and other local politicians from mandating masks for their constituencies. One can only label this insanity, placing political advantage above even life itself. Stupidity is loathed to be outdone by logic.

The silly thing is that all it would take to save thousands of lives would be for Trump to start publicly wearing a mask, just as it appears that he has ordered most of his off-camera staff to do. *As the leader goes, so goes the others.* We know that Trump understands the value of masks and testing, but he can't afford to alienate his base. He's disinclined to use the tiniest bit of political capital, even knowing it would save lives. It reminds me of some of those vampire movies—get rid of the lead vampire and you fix the problem. Sure, this desire stinks of naiveté. There are plenty of Republicans eager to take the president's place. Still…no one is as Trumpy as Trump.

The amount of disease that will be spread by those not wearing masks should not be seen as an amusing quirk. A mid-June study estimated that mask mandates had prevented the spread of 450,000 infections in the US. (edit: August 29, 2020—With the country now having been open for several months, and mask usage being more universally adopted, the number of infections prevented by mask usage is possibly in the area of tens of millions, though no recent studies are available to verify this figure.)

As of late June, the majority of people in red states are currently not wearing masks. Think about how much disease is being needlessly spread. As with the case of cigarette smoking and speeding, your right to certain freedoms affects the health and safety of others. The US Constitution lists *life* before *liberty*. American society has always (eventually) agreed that safety takes precedence over freedom, but it does take time for these things to work themselves out. The problem, of course, is that a lot of people will die before the mandating of masks works itself out. In this case, freedom comes at an immense cost. Those who study and honor the Constitution should remind ourselves that's how we know how valuable freedom is.

Lightning Strikes Twice

Only those who have raised an "other-abled" kid know what that's like. In honesty, though I have no regrets, I would not wish it on anyone. In raising John, I learned a lot about myself and a lot about humanity, and I'm not sure I'd be better off giving that back, even if I could. My son is probably, for the important things, better off as he is. His successes do not resemble those of his siblings, but they are nonetheless meaningful to him. He is the happiest of my three kids. His siblings, like the majority of their peers, have anxieties and insecurities over futures that seem increasingly uncertain. Though John has had his fair share of struggles, his personality is dominated by happiness. The only thing he desires of others is friendship.

This is what we wish for anyone close to us: happiness, health, and success. John wins, two out of three. That's not too bad. As far as health goes. Finally, after years of too many physician visits and surgeries, John's health had become mostly a non-issue.

Somehow, though, at the end of 2018, lightning struck a second time. There's a book called, *Brain on Fire*, by Susannah Cahalan, detailing her struggles with a disease called autoimmune encephalitis. The book and the associated movie tell the true story of Ms. Cahalan's months of cognitive and emotional dysfunction—specifically, her insanity caused by this disease. As her book mentions, the movie *The Exorcist* was based upon a book that chronicled the disease progression of a boy that is believed to have had this disease. Some medical experts believe that for a large percentage of those who suffer from psychosis, their insanity was caused by autoimmune encephalitis (known as AE).

The mental degradation of AE is horrific. In the case of *Brain on Fire*, Ms. Cahalan makes it known that for about a month, at the worst of her disease and symptoms, she has no memories whatsoever, a feature of her disease for which she is grateful. Lisa and I could tell you a lot about what she might have missed. In John's case, his behavior succumbed to actions that seemed to match, scene by scene, what the young girl Regan does in the movie. This included trying to shake his bed off the floor and screaming a palette of curse words that shocked his military veteran father. This was all coming from a kid who had never uttered a curse word in my presence before. He even developed a tic where he tried to spin his head completely around, though limitations of the human skeleton kept the rotation down to about 110 degrees. We are not Catholic, but I told several friends, if we were, we would have definitely requested an exorcism. I know it always sounded like a joke to them, particularly with me being very much a man of both science and satire. But I always meant it.

AE is an immunological dysfunction whereby the patient's immune system attacks their brain tissue, causing inflammation which leads to these bizarre symptoms. It was diagnosed for the first time in 2007, and as such, there are very few physicians who understand it well. Getting my son's condition properly diagnosed and treated became a fucking nightmare. John had a difficult to diagnose variant of the disease. To make it that much worse, since his neurologic function is usually abnormal, Lisa and I had to clarify to every nurse and doctor caring for him, what parts of his behavior and capabilities were typical and which parts were new. Lisa and I often had the uncomfortable notion that the nurses and doctors considered our information unreliable.

John was admitted to the local children's hospital three times for increasingly disturbing behavior before we were finally told by the hospital's staff that they had no idea what was wrong with him and that we should take him home and not come back. It took about another month in hell following the final hospital dismissal, before we were able to get him in to see the only bona fide AE specialist in all of Southern

Florida. She immediately understood his condition; we had a diagnosis that first visit. She prescribed a treatment called IVIG—basically intravenous fluid to repair his troublesome immune system. He was expected to receive 4-5 of these treatments over so many months. The first one was quite successful, and John's symptoms eased, not completely, but significantly. After two months of insanity, we finally had reason to hope.

However, the feeling was short-lived. One month after the first treatment, John received the second. Over the following few days, he became progressively worse, falling almost all the way backward. The specialist said that it was extremely unlikely that he could have had an adverse reaction to the treatment.

I understand the scientific and statistical concept that correlation is not necessarily causation, meaning if input A occurs and response B follows, we cannot definitively conclude that A caused B without additional information. I did believe strongly that in John's case, he had an adverse reaction to the treatment, but that didn't matter. The IVIG wasn't making him better anymore, so it was pointless to continue treatment. We had to discuss something more invasive with the doctor.

Around that time, some good luck came our way. I was discussing my son's condition with a nurse employed by my airline. She told me about another of our company's pilots whose daughter had been diagnosed with the same condition and put me in touch with him. In our first conversation, he happened to ask if John's doctors had found a cyst (a benign growth) inside John's nose. They had. I previously asked every doctor John saw if the cyst might have anything to do with his condition, and they all replied, "Absolutely not." The fellow pilot said that his daughter had the same cyst. Her doctors removed it, and she immediately got better.

I was able to find five other similar stories online, though only one described in a reputable medical journal. Still, it was enough information to be compelling. I asked John's AE specialist about it again, and she was reasonably certain it was not related to his condition. I asked her if she thought it would be okay if we had it removed anyway. She said she didn't think it would be a good idea for John to have surgery, minor though it would be, until he was more stable.

I liked and respected this doctor. I placed great value in her opinion. Care to guess what I did?

If you guessed finding an ENT who would operate on John to remove the cyst, "Winner, winner, chicken dinner." And if you got that right, what do you suppose happened to John?

He immediately got better. But I did not mention this, just to highlight another good call. Unfortunately, there is more to this story which will eventually intersect with the pandemic crisis.

* * * * *

George Floyd was slain by a Minnesota policeman less than four weeks ago. It's now June 19, 2020, and Trump is a day away from holding his Tulsa rally, his first such event since the country first quarantined. It's a Juneteenth unlike any other. If you're older than 40, white, and not living in a city, you've probably only recently learned about Juneteenth. Though the president should be judged for white-splaining the significance of the day, in this one instance, I believe the media is unfairly criticizing him. In stating that many, *in his demographic*, were not familiar with the day's significance, I'm confident the President was correct. There are so many appropriate reasons to criticize Trump. *So many*. They could have passed on this one.

Accurate information is lacking from so many different corners. The anchor on CNN was incorrectly admonishing various politicians for their failure to *flatten the curve* in America by holding Italy out as an example. Ironically, we are one of the few countries with an actual flattened curve. I could see the wheels turning in the mind of CNN correspondent, Dr.

Sanjay Gupta, as he tried to figure out how to offer correct information without directly correcting his colleague on air.

Allow me to explain. When the world first began postulating what should be done about SARS-CoV-2, people quickly realized that if the disease was as bad as first envisioned, were we to take no proactive steps against the pandemic, we would see the virus spread geometrically (which is to say it would essentially explode), and our healthcare system would quickly run out of capacity. Millions of people who might otherwise survive with appropriate treatment would die in their homes, on the street, and in hospital waiting rooms, untreated, ultimately casualties of an overwhelmed healthcare system. Meanwhile, ordering a quarantine and sufficient testing and contact tracing to entirely snuff out the pandemic just seemed a bridge too far when we first began this *journey*. So many epidemiologists and doctors settled on the concept of *flattening the curve* as an acceptable middle ground that would avoid catastrophe. For the record:

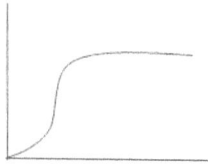

This is a *flattened curve*

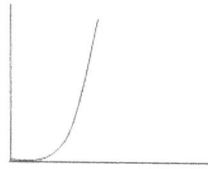

This is the curve if we did nothing

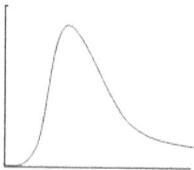

This is the Italian curve

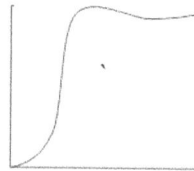

And this is the American curve

Figure 11: The flattened curve

Compared to the curve doing nothing and the Italian curve, the American curve is the only one that has been "flattened," although to be entirely accurate, as of June 19, it is starting to trend slightly up—and I expect it to enter a growth phase soon. But if it were to remain flattened, it would theoretically be in a Goldilocks state of sorts, where we would not be overwhelming the hospitals, but we would not be too restricted by 'excessive' social distancing. Some even argue that a flattened curve is a desirable strategy toward achieving herd immunity.

1) Notice that the American and Italian curves begin similarly on the left. But when the Italians maintained their quarantine a few weeks longer, in America we decided to open up. I don't know any Americans who were thinking, *Well we've flattened our curve now – let's maintain this Goldilocks state.* I saw far more a sense of, *Enough*

164

already. I'm sick of my kids. I'm sick of my spouse. I'm running out of money, and I want to drink at a bar for a change, instead of
    alone   in   my   basement.

Few Americans understood what the plan was because, as I've said, there never was one. Is it any wonder America continues to represent 30% of the dead with only 5% of the world's population?

2) Flattening the curve never made sense as an end strategy. Once the spread of the virus is halted, with a bit more work, a country can get its numbers down low enough to be limited primarily to minor outbreaks. These can be tracked down and snuffed out by extensive, disciplined testing and contact tracing. That's what has been happening in the rest of the First World. Where the American impulse is to get back to work ASAP, the Europeans were inclined to relax and extend the holiday a while longer.

* * * * *

Let's discuss tomorrow's Tulsa MAGA extravaganza. Tens of thousands gathering together indoors, many or most without masks, no doubt shouting and screaming and high-fiving each other. Could there possibly be a better way to put an exclamation point on the failure of Trump's leadership?

I saw a reasonable estimate today of about 1,000 new resultant COVID-19 infections. Those newly infected will bring their disease home and transmit it to others. A reasonable estimate, based on the demographics of the Trump rally, would be about 7-10 deaths from the first 1,000 infections. Does that make sense? They're going to hold a rally to shout about how the Democrats are bad for America, and kill 7-10 people in the process?

Of course, masks will not be mandatory at this rally. One would hope the attendees would be prudent and wear masks, but in a Darwinian twist, the rally will self-select for people who refuse to wear masks under any circumstance, so I expect many will not.

So, why should anyone in Oregon, Ohio, or Florida get too upset about this stupidity? Remember "Six degrees of Kevin Bacon?" Any one of these idiots can be the start of a string of infections that can eventually infect and potentially kill you or a loved one.

With litigation always in mind, Trump is asking everyone in attendance to waive their right to pursue damages due to any COVID-19 infections incident to the rally. The optics of this is terrible to anyone other than his faithful adherents; moreover, it is a foolish legal tactic. I have my doubts about the ability of the waiver to hold up in court, but more to the point, what of those secondary (and tertiary) infections to loved ones or others who signed no waiver? Those people will probably have to get in line though behind the many thousands of people already suing the president.

Of relevance, Trump supporters are pointing to the ongoing series of Black Lives Matter protests around the world with a "Good for the goose, good for the gander" criticism. If one were to set aside all the relevant science for the moment, and let's face it—this is one of the defining characteristics of Trump supporters, it does seem a bit hypocritical for anyone who would have criticism for the Trump rally and no similar criticism for any of the racial bias protests.

Those who do not set aside the relevance of science would respond that:

1) The BLM protests are happening almost exclusively outside, where disease transmission is rare.

2) A large majority of protesters are wearing masks even outside.

3) So far, data suggests an exceptionally low disease transmission incident to protests.

In the interest of being fair, the infections related to BLM protests have not been zero. There is a certain irony in putting lives at risk (even to a minor degree) to protest lives lost. However, the BLM protests represent 400 years of frustration over the amoral institutions of slavery and the ensuing racism that followed emancipation. Everything that most Americans take for granted as inalienable rights – life, liberty, and the pursuit of happiness—has at one time been taken away from our fellow black citizens – even to this day. Our forefathers put their own lives on the line to secure inalienable rights that many of us now take for granted. It would be hypocrisy to deny that same privilege to today's BLM protesters. And again—science—the BLM protests are much safer being outdoors and electing a higher rate of mask usage.

(Edit: August 2, 2020. That Tulsa rally may have marked a turning point. The Trump campaign was spoofed, and an event that at some point the campaign had bragged would have close to a million participants, was attended by only 6,000 people in an auditorium built for 20,000. Ensuing infections were much lower than expected with the notable exception of six Trump staffers and prior presidential candidate, Herman Cain, who would succumb to COVID-19 five weeks later. A string of follow-up rallies were canceled and even the Republican convention was dramatically scaled back.)

* * * * *

I've been asking for years, "When's the bloom going to fall off this (f'ing) rose!?"

People called Bill Clinton Teflon, but Trump has taken this game to an entirely different level. It's been said that Barack Obama brought us Trump, but I think it was Bill Clinton, if you want to blame a Democrat. Obama's greatest crimes were being president while black and wearing a tan suit. Despite his positive qualities, Clinton brought his sex scandals upon himself, his party, and his country. Had he not survived those sex scandals, it's questionable whether Trump would have survived his own. Bill gave Don license.

In surviving some of the most outrageous scandals of all of political history (not merely in the US, but the entire world), Trump has made sport of being awful and then rubbing his misdeeds in the face of the righteous. When the Access Hollywood tape was released, that should have been the end of it. Everyone ever given power and responsibility, even Republicans, realized it wasn't the sex or misogyny that should give anyone pause. I heard a lot of people eventually discount Trump's language as locker-room talk. I've served in the military and been in a lot of locker rooms, and I personally never witnessed any adult I had any respect for speak like that. Still, I could forgive Trump the crudeness and even the misogyny, as it was theoretically a semi-private moment and he's from a different generation. The real problem was that with those recorded words, Donald Trump had shown that if given power, he would use and abuse it to his own ends. At the time, few of us could imagine the degree to which his abuse of power would become the defining aspect of his presidency.

Following the tape's release, Republican politicians all took a breath and waited for the implosion that never happened. The ugliness of the moment was overtaken by a binary choice. Elect the woman they had been vilifying for decades, a person who by definition of Republican rhetoric represented everything wrong with the American political system, someone who would advocate for a political agenda opposite the majority of their collective political objectives... or a man lacking a moral and ethical compass, who was ignorant of most of what his future responsibilities would be. Republicans settled upon the Faustian bargain—a man who would meet the majority of their political wish list despite his "vulgarity." No doubt many hoped at the time he could be *tamed*. Democrats, though, including Secretary Clinton, were left so slack-jawed by Republican acceptance that they did not effectively capitalize on the moment. In my view, too many people pushed misogyny when they should have focused on the abuse of power.

Once it was clear that Trump's campaign was not going to implode from even sinister vulgarity, something novel began to emerge in American politics. The Founding Fathers of America were by today's standards, Liberals. Notions such as freedom of speech, freedom of religion, habeas corpus, citizens as voters and elected leaders—these are all left-leaning concepts (even more so among eighteenth-century elites), despite the professed love of our country's origin from the Right. There is a reason America is labeled a liberal democracy. Conservatism by its nature seems to maintain the norms of the past, but when one looks all the way back to the American Revolution, the Second Amendment and John Adams are the only friendly faces it can see. This explains in part the Right's love affair with the Confederacy.

The Access Hollywood tape, far from being a net negative, gave birth to a Republican epiphany. In Trump, Republican politicians that had felt hamstrung for years by the liberal norms of American democracy, saw an opportunity to shatter the shackles of democratic protections. They realized that if Trump could brag about grabbing women by their genitals without repercussions, anyone hitching their car to the abuse-of-power-train might have something akin to a free ride, safe from even the Constitution. Destruction of the First Amendment, putting kids in cages, cozying up to countries with far-right ideologies, and all of the other norm-shattering behavior of the Trump presidency have never been ideological flaws to his Republican supporters. They're features.

Republican ideology under Trump is what you get when you take Conservative aspirations and boil away the protections of a liberal Constitution. Every time Trump shocked the Western world, even when he was at his most loathsome, he was validating the worldview of his supporters—in this case seeing the world as a dangerous place where the powerful take what they want, and only the strong survive.

Richard Nixon's approval rating, despite his many transgressions, never dipped below 25%. Party loyalty is ultimately just another form of tribalism, stronger than personal ideology or morality for some percentage of us. Trump recognizes that more than most. He has survived countless dimwitted, un-American, both before and after his election win. We have been trained to expect that this man will just scoot past every supposed misstep with his devoted 41% of followers intact, with no expectation that would ever change, unless as I said in the introduction, that Trump somehow sullies his followers' worldview. The Tulsa Rally may indeed have been the unexpected change. Publicly stating he had a million requests for tickets in Tulsa and planning for over 100,000 to show up and fill a huge overflow lot, only to have, by the Tulsa fire department's estimate, about 6,200 attendees, is not a good look for anyone. Trump's supporters' saw him as a political rock star. The primary currency for which Trump could demonstrate his stardom was his ability to fill a stadium. I have little doubt that Tulsa altered the worldview for some supporters. This brand tarnish could last if Trump is unable to replace the Tulsa failures with demonstrative wins; however, right-wing broadcasting and social media has proven effective at corralling those who wander back into the fold.

* * * * *

To a large degree, TV news has been trailing my own writing by two to ten days. I expect within a few days, media on the Left will start talking more about the decreasing mortality rate, which I wrote about last week (edit: August 2, 2020—they did). They may have been holding off, wondering if the large wave of newly diagnosed cases will start showing in the mortality data. Because of the blooming infection rates in primarily red states, death rates are likely to reverse course and tic upwards, but at this point, I expect that will remain clear of multiple thousands of April. (Edit: August 2, 2020, as anticipated, the seven day moving average of mortality seems to be peaking at just over 1,000, though the days at 75,000 new infections suggests we might again see some days with mortality at over 2,000 (edit: August 26, 2020—we reached no higher than 1850, which occurred on July 30). It's a staggering level of death.

Meanwhile, we're at a crossroads with schools. If they open up to in-person teaching in substantial numbers, that *will* result in a boom in infections that could drive mortality back over 2,000 in the latter half of September. A vacuum of leadership should bring alternative leaders to the foreground, but Trump will not play the role of *vacuum* which is essentially to do nothing. He insists on continuous attention which compels him to act out incessantly, almost like a child. Having the country's attention locked firmly on this circus act has prevented better, alternative leadership from emerging.

I only hope communities will quickly self-correct to avoid additional huge losses of life. (edit: August 29, 2020. Though the exact number is unclear, it appears a majority of American schools are not opening up to in-class learning. Of those that open, particularly in more infected regions, rapid early spread of the disease has resulted in many school and university closures.)

Florida, Arizona, Texas, and California are all about where New York was when Cuomo began his quarantine, but these other states have big advantages in population density, public knowledge and preparation, as well as having been given time to bolster medical and other systemic capabilities. (Edit: August 2, 2020—the four states' advantages over New York were negated by populations that for various reasons failed to do their part in minimizing infection spread. Although these troubled states all equaled and even exceeded New York's infection counts, for reasons previously stated, these later mortality rates have so far mercifully remained a fraction of the New York totals.).

Economics 101 (Yes Please, I'd like Some More Quarantine)

Many of us work from home since the pandemic. We order everything from food to furniture on websites, and most of us have been managing our finances on-line for years. Even activities such as home purchases have become 100% electronic. We live in a *brave new* financial world. We shouldn't take it for granted. Twice in the last 15 years, this economic system which satisfies all of our needs to survive has itself been in mortal danger. It might not be a bad idea to better understand economics.

A considerable part of the field of economics deals with statistics. Psychology (which itself is largely guided by statistics) is the other important component of economics. In particular, economists attempt to derive statistics for why and how much humans are involved with certain activities that bear directly upon an economy. In understanding human psychology and using statistical models for human behavior, economists assess the activity and health of all aspects of economic activity. With the help of forecasting techniques, they project these assessments into the future in an attempt to provide usable forecasts to governments, businesses, and NGOs (Non-Governmental Organizations). In other words, they tell us what is happening and is likely to happen with economic matters, which may include details concerning employment, salaries, benefits, sales, production, inventories, construction, population, and related demographics, and behavior trends, such as how we spend free time, work, sleep, and eat.

The economic effects of the pandemic have been catastrophic and unique. Similar to the stock market crash of 1929 that ushered in the

Great Depression, the problems have been worldwide and severe. The economy had been coming off an extended period of growth, and some were saying that the stock market had been a bubble waiting to burst. If you haven't been directly affected financially, you've likely experienced major anxiety related to the crisis.

Unlike 1929, we have independent central banking systems in all of the world's major countries that coordinate with each other and act aggressively to protect financial markets and bolster economic confidence. Economists also have the benefit of hindsight and are thus wiser than the decision makers of 1929. Thanks to eye-watering amounts of cash that came gushing out of federal coffers, we have thus far avoided a substantial economic collapse. Banks and other financial institutions, the scaffolds of our economy, have remained healthy. By avoiding the systemic failures of 1929, businesses have retained the tools necessary to survive, though this was achieved at an immense cost. The $2.4 trillion in government stimulus represents $7500 from each of us. How did we arrive at this $30,000 expenditure for every single American family of four?

* * * * *

At least one American company began directing employees to work from home as early as January 2020. Whenever money is involved, you can always find smart people doing smart things. By this time many employees in China and Europe had been working from home.

Sometime in late February, when it became likely that COVID-19 would soon be spreading throughout the US, I noticed airline bookings were falling off a cliff. This data was extremely telling on two important predictions:

1) Many members of the American public realized that a COVID-19 pandemic was likely and that it was dangerous.

2) These same people recognized the danger of being exposed to strangers in public spaces and were willing to substantially alter their behavior to protect themselves.

It was clear by late February, even before the first government official had put the first limitations on anyone's freedom, that a large percentage of the American population would soon be limiting their own behavior. I must repeat for emphasis, this behavioral change with its associated catastrophic effect on the economy arrived *irrespective of any governmental restrictions*. Anyplace where people gathered publicly would soon be experiencing a huge loss of business. That would include restaurants, movie theatres, public concerts, sporting events, tourist destinations, cruise ships, hotels, and of course, airlines.

Not to be ignored, associated with these changes was the stocking up and in some cases, hoarding of supplies. It wasn't widely discussed or publicized, but we dodged a frightening bullet. There was a legitimate fear that if the Chinese didn't contain the virus, they might shut down much of their production for an extended period. Even if a product isn't directly made in China, there's still a good chance that some component or ingredient is. I told Lisa and close relatives to buy enough of the important non-staple items they couldn't live without—enough to last three to six months. America makes more food than we eat, so although some items might have been (and were) scarce, I knew there would be something to eat on the shelves. The same goes for most staples including toilet paper—what's wrong with you people!? The TP and cleaner shortages were entirely of our own making.

As much as our lives have been altered by the pandemic, this would have been nothing had Chinese factories shut down. Fortunately, this never happened. So as much as China is worthy of criticism for its role in not initially containing the virus, they are worthy of appreciation for their ability to rapidly get the virus under control.

We also have to be grateful for the current state of technology and commerce. The ability to order online from companies like Amazon as well as all of the online food options meant people could avoid many trips outside their homes. I'm near certain someone will do a study of all the lives that were saved because of electronic commerce. And of course, technology from companies like FaceTime and Zoom have played an incalculable role in not only keeping many commercial activities going, with television media being just one example, but in improving the world's morale by letting everyone remain better connected.

And yet, the net loss to the domestic and world economies is unprecedented. Nearly all large businesses win or lose on the margin. I can best explain what this means with an example. 85% of total capacity is a typical metric for how much production needs to be fulfilled for a typical large company to break even (though of course this number will vary based upon industry, location, and other differentiators). If they can sell 90% of their capacity, that's fairly good; if they sell only 80%, that's fairly bad. So small deviations above and below the breakeven point make large differences in financial performance. Operating at 1% below breakeven means losing money. No loss is sustainable; bigger losses cause rapid damage, but no matter how fast, businesses can only lose so much money before they are "out of business."

I couldn't predict exact numbers, but I was confident at the time that somewhere around half the American population would take the virus seriously. If your business needs 85% to break even, and you have even a few days at 50%, that can be incredibly costly. That is what was staring us right in the face. How long it would take to get fixed was the most frightening aspect of the dilemma.

How were we to address the substantial economic pain triggered by that 50% who were going to lock themselves away from normal economic activities, like going to work, shopping, or travel? The eventual fix is to compel these people to feel safe to return to normal activities. Obvious solutions to provide that sense of safety would be to develop a safe and effective vaccine, herd immunity, effective therapeutics, and/or reduce the spread of contagion.

Our president has been regularly seen ham-fistedly pushing on all these levers. His problem is that this is an issue of confidence, and lying tends to be somewhat caustic to maintaining confidence. As Trump's presidential brand has been heavily vested in destroying confidence, his actions are toxic to everyone's efforts. He starts talking about vaccines, and confidence in vaccines plunge.

In the short term, we had needed to do something back in March to stop the rampant spread of the virus, and the only tool we had at that time was to quarantine. Quarantine became synonymous with shutting down the economy and was therefore seen by some as destructive. This is completely incorrect. As a properly executed quarantine leads to a reduction in the spread of disease, it was also the only tool available to offer a sense of public safety. The lower we drove infections down, the more people would feel safe, and the more they would later participate economically. We needed to have the most austere quarantine feasible to drive infections down as close to zero as possible. That has been the successful strategy taken throughout the First World, Sweden excepted. People are unwilling to risk their lives for discretionary purchases.

When you cut your business in half or more as restaurants had to do, the cost of opening the doors was so high that it couldn't be justified. Bars, bowling alleys, and all other manner of businesses where the public meets all faced the same roadblock. Many businesses lost 50% or more of their customers almost overnight, again before any governmental "stay at home" orders were issued. Few businesses can sustain 50% of their revenue for long—certainly not without making undesirable changes such as firing staff, raising prices, and/or reducing services.

Without government intervention, we were facing an environment where many businesses would operate at huge losses while creating environments for spreading enough disease to catastrophically overwhelm our medical facilities. We risked the nightmare scenario in which a large percent of the population became infected simultaneously, driving a mortality rate much larger than what we would experience with a "flattened curve." This would have been the largest lose-lose business decision in the history of man.

Those interested in data-driven decisions would consider the 1918 flu pandemic to be the best benchmark available. In two years, over 25% of Americans and about 35% of the world's population became infected. At the time, a large number of our nation's rural inhabitants benefitted from geographic dispersal. Few people owned cars, and they certainly weren't making two trips to Walmart or going out to eat every other night. Today, if we had made no changes to our behavior, COVID-19 could easily have spread to 50% of the American population within three months. With 165 million infected, a frighteningly high percentage of people would have gone without hospital care. In those conditions, we would have faced a mortality rate of at least 5%, amounting to the deaths of over 8 million Americans! That's what we were facing without a quarantine.

At some level of pain, drastic measures would have been required to control spread. We could have seen the cessation of every last bit of non essential commerce, ultimately costing far more than any planned quarantine. So, although it's not entirely intuitive, the cost of quarantine for a pandemic-level disease is inversely proportional to the severity of the quarantine. The stricter the quarantine, the better it is for the economy! How is it that this fact so rarely made the news (*even after Governor Cuomo said it*)?

Once a government orders a quarantine and the population obeys the order, the infection rate reverses and eventually dies down to lower more easily contact-traced numbers. Under the right conditions, a population can reach zero infections, or at least a level low enough to contract trace and limit further spread. The science was clear on this. We had seen it done successfully in China in February (though skepticism should be the rule with Chinese reports). While it was clear that no democracy would be able to institute as severe a quarantine as they did, the science clearly shows that the earlier and the more severe the quarantine, the quicker the virus can be brought under control.

* * * * *

It is difficult to point to a bona fide leadership decision throughout the entire pandemic made by the president. To be clear, Trump and his administration made very few decisions related to COVID, either good or bad. Actions that might have appeared to have been decisions simply weren't. Trump only shut down air traffic after the airlines quit flying. He closed the Canadian border only after the Canadians asked us to. No stay at home order originated from Trump or any federal official.

All of the federal/CDC guidance on the number of people permitted to gather was simply that – guidance, not a directive and certainly not mandatory. It was the States that set their own quarantine rules, and the States that lifted them. Some took a restrained responsible approach and were rewarded for it. Increasingly though, as public impatience grew, some governors gave in to populist sentiment and eased restrictions too early and too loosely. The cost in lives and money of this failure of discipline, particularly in my state of Florida, will prove to be substantial.

For months we received a daily schizophrenic cacophony of presidential nonsense that left people at best, confused, and at worst, angry and resentful over quarantines they felt justified in violating. In part because the Federal Government took intentional steps to diminish the national supply of PPE, Dr. Fauci et al had to institute the ridiculous initial position that masks would not help prevent the spread of the virus. It's hard to believe, but *the federal government was selling its supplies of N95 protective masks to international buyers in February* (as reported by the Wall Street Journal on March 30). The federal health agencies failed to be proactive in their reversal of mask recommendations. By the time of their flip-flop, a large number of Americans were consistently wearing some kind of home-made/improvised covering or had purchased masks commercially. The prevalence of citizens wearing masks was may have even been the signal to the CDC there was a sufficient mask supply to reverse their recommendations.

Kids are not wild about taking medicine, but my kids at least figured out that if they wanted to get better quickly, that's the route to go. How are there adults ignorant of this concept? Social distancing and masks are the medicine of the moment. Those not taking their medicine are costing themselves and the rest of us dearly.

The needless loss of lives and treasure is mind-blowing. As of June 23, because of our high level of disease, the European Union is seriously considering not letting Americans into any member country when they open up their borders on July 1. The EU have now lumped us in with the BRIC countries of Russian and Brazil. Your assessment is correct if you recognize our new status as a statement of condemnation worthy of humiliation. Though these types of measures can often be negotiated away under less stressful times and when relations are better, I'm doubtful of any easing of the restriction anytime soon. One can only guess at the effect lasting restrictions will have on international business, places of tourism, airlines, hotels, and cruise lines.

I'm no historian, but it seems to me that this is what it looks like when a great power begins to fall. We are about to be expelled from the First World. It is not simply a failure in scientific understanding; it has become a failure of morality.

Dictionary.com defines manslaughter as: "The unlawful killing of a human being without malice aforethought." If you open up a business or hold a rally, knowing it's extremely likely that people will get infected and some of them will die—that suggests forethought. That makes Trump's Tulsa rally worse than manslaughter. Even if it was done out of willful ignorance, it still amounts to manslaughter. As so many are fond of saying, particularly on the Right, ignorance is no excuse for breaking the law.

It's not likely that anyone will ever be tried for murder or even manslaughter because they knowingly created conditions that lead to one or more COVID-19 deaths, but from a moral standpoint, such loss of life is inexcusable. Nearly 120,000 Americans are now dead due to this virus, and many of them did not have to be. People are walking around knowing or suspecting they're COVID-19 positive, spreading disease that will lead to loss of life. If that is not a criminal act, what is? A lot of people are going to exit 2020 with blood on their hands. There may be no possibility of legal repercussions, but they should not take comfort in the government's failure to penalize. Anyone with any sense or religion or spirituality has to understand the tremendous karmic debt some are incurring.

Show me the Money

President Trump reliably touts the success of the American economy, such that it is, as his greatest achievement. You and I and a few hundred million of our neighbors are the president's boss. We can't adequately supervise him, if he's snowing us about his accomplishments. Many of us understand that the president has a limited ability to affect the economy, particularly to the upside. It might be a good idea, as we head to the polls, to better understand the role that the government leadership plays in managing the economy.

Economists now understand that if you throw a bucket-load of money into a failing economy, you can avoid an economic catastrophe. The government's reaction to the 2008 crisis was, in my view, a masterful work of art, but it was not without controversy. Philosophically speaking the more rigid free-market economists of the world have despised any government attempts to mitigate economic downturns on purely ideological grounds. It seems that no measure of success would have them rethink their analysis. They took it as a *prima facie* conclusion that any interference in *the markets* by government leads to inefficiencies and must by definition be less than optimal.

Had this philosophy ruled the day in 2008, it's likely that President Obama would have presided over a depression in his first term in office, which likely would have led to a Republican president in 2012. Strange as it seems, the minor murmur from right-wing economists over the $2.4 trillion invested to save the economy under Trump was dwarfed the banshee outcry over the $800 billion invested to save the economy under Obama. One can see how economics cannot be disentangled from politics.

In both 2008 and 2020, the government ignored the neoclassical, or free-market approach, opting instead for a Keynesian approach. Keynesian economics informs the philosophy that inhibiting free market forces with strategic governmental input can positively alter economic outcomes. The free market does some things incredibly well – far better than any government agency could ever do. Driving down the price of computers and other electronics, while improving their performance (Moore's Law) is a great example. There are also some things for which the free market is and has been entirely unsuitable. Fighting a war, the first moon landing, and healthcare are prime examples.

Can you imagine on December 7, 1941, FDR taking bids from private companies on who would run the war effort against the Nazis? The free market depends upon the availability of information and a requirement for participants to be able to accurately value goods and services. Buyers must respond to increased prices with reduced demand (and vice versa). Sellers must respond to reduced demand with a reduction in prices and will generally increase prices in response to increased demand. It is these balancing forces that drive highly prized market efficiencies. These forces don't balance overnight, though, which makes the free market system poorly adapted to emergency conditions. Where balancing forces are weakened or absent, efficiency is reduced or destroyed.

If you need insulin to survive, you will pay $100, if you have it. If you don't have the $100 or health insurance, well… you don't survive. If the price goes up to $200, you'll pay that. And $300, and so on. If you need something to survive, you will pay what you have—no amount is too much. In healthcare, the "free market" is not a market at all, but more of a blackmailing shakedown. Sure, eventually, another insulin producer will enter the market to offer insulin for less. The problem with this is three-fold:

1) The new producer does you little good several months after you needed the insulin to survive.

2) Newer drugs have patents, so other companies are not even allowed to enter the market for the first 17 years.

3) There's minimal incentive to offer the drug for less. Everyone is paying if they have it, and with insurance, the cost to the consumer is the same no matter what—insurance will pay, no matter the cost. If a second company offers insulin for less, the cost to the patient with a copay system is likely the same. Why should a patient make a change? The $300 insulin is working. Maybe the $200 medicine won't. It's hard enough to get people to change their cell phone service. You think they want to change their insulin manufacturer?

For those who don't have insurance, they probably can't afford to pay much if anything out of pocket, so there's no incentive for companies to capture these consumers unless the drug is fairly inexpensive. The few that do pay out of pocket and can afford expensive medications aren't a substantial enough group to incentivize the drug companies to drop prices.

Substitute knee surgery or dialysis or the majority of other health services for insulin, and the problems remain, the greatest of which is that the information needed for consumers to make "rational market-based decisions" is absent. Metrics on the performance of various doctors, hospitals, and other healthcare providers are difficult if not impossible to come by. Neither is Yelp, with all due respect, sufficient to drive *rational market-based decisions* in the healthcare marketplace.

In those few cases where people self-pay for healthcare, they frequently travel to another country where they can afford airline tickets, hotel rooms, a mini-vacation, and of course the actual medical procedure, all at a fraction of the cost of having the same procedure done in the US. And this is often completed with a healthcare provider with statistically better outcomes than what is available at many US facilities. This is how bad healthcare is broken in the US—all because too many Americans believe that we should have a free market for healthcare.

In the midst of COVID-19, NOBODY IS MAKING RATIONAL MARKET-BASED DECISIONS! Many if not most people are terrified of losing their jobs, their retirement funds, and their homes. Just like people need to have faith that the virus is gone before they start traveling for anything unnecessary, people need to believe that if they buy beef instead of chicken or tuna instead of Ramen, they will not soon lose their jobs and regret the more expensive purchase. Rational consumers certainly don't want to buy a car or a house if they think they may be losing their job. When the government floods the economy with stimulus money, people spend where they may not have otherwise done so. The economy avoids economic catastrophe.

It must also be said that businesses do not respond to public emergencies with the public's well-being as their highest priority. Many do not consider the public at all when analysis reveals the public good to be irrelevant to their bottom line. It's likely some in the Federal Government believed that because there was a public need for test kits and swabs and masks and other PPE and ventilators and hospital beds and all these other things – somehow market forces would make this all possible with zero facilitation from the government.

Yes, over the course of years, the market would respond. We don't have years. We don't have months. People who need Remdesivir today don't have days. *Market forces don't make these things happen.* There is a greater profit to be made from having 100 ventilators too few than 100 too many. During most emergencies, the needs of a civilized society are opposite that of market forces. In the long term, the cost of responding to emergencies may be far exceeded by any potential short term market-based return on investment (ROI). But ROI can also include intangibles like peace of mind or a very long term ROI like saving a young girl who grows up to invent a faster microchip. Unless a business finds a way to monetize such greater societal good ROIs, a market-based approach will never lead to the best possible solution for greater societal good. We must therefore conclude that the only way to successfully manage the logistics of serving the healthcare needs of a nation during a pandemic is to have the government actively involved.

In 2008, the government poured billions of dollars into the US automotive industry. No business entity would have made such a risky investment—the risk-reward profile for a profit-driven company wouldn't justify the risk. But society benefits greatly from keeping companies out of bankruptcy. Following the government's 2008 financial infusion, none of the major car companies went out of business, nor did their suppliers, and very few jobs were lost. Union contracts were renegotiated, and decisions were made to make US cars more competitive with the rest of the world. Meanwhile, Americans maintained the option of purchasing American cars because those companies all survived. AND ALL THOSE BILLIONS OF DOLLARS WERE REPAID TO THE US GOVERNMENT/TAXPAYER—WITH INTEREST! Having the government invest in its people turned out to be a great investment. It was truly win-win-win. What more can you ask for?

And yet, free market economists *still* view the automotive bailouts as gross overreach. Their stated preference was to see American manufacturers fail, to be theoretically replaced by more efficient companies. On behalf of the hundreds of thousands of workers in Michigan who kept their livelihoods and maintained reasonable compensation, as well as the rest of America that benefited from an economy that was protected from an unnecessary depression, all I can say is fuck those stupid fucking morons. Sometimes, government is the answer.

People on the Left complained that some jobs were lost overseas. True. They were. The only cure that can save every single job is the flawed ideology of socialism. Certain elements of socialism make sense, such as an economic safety net that minimizes poverty along with all of the health, crime, and other problems that accompany the poor. But there is logic in the Conservative argument to incentivize behavior that contributes to the betterment of society. The human species is prone to codependence. Give a *fisherman* a fish, and he will eat for a day. And for *some*, wait until you bring him another fish or until he is really, really hungry before he throws a fishhook back in the water. The most successful economies today find a way to balance capitalistic and socialistic elements. Increasingly, balance is one thing sorely lacking in the creation of American policy.

Much has been decried over the amount of money made available to US banks during the '08 economic crisis. Some argue more money should have been given to homeowners to reduce defaults. From a moral standpoint, I can't disagree. From a practical and economic perspective, money that flowed to the banks gave them the safety to be able to keep making loans, which then, in turn led to business development, jobs, home purchases, and the successful payment of mortgages which ultimately led to economic health. Let's not forget that most of the money invested was eventually returned to the government. But this did not keep some homeowners from getting unfairly evicted.

* * * * *

Once the dismal economic projections from the pandemic were understood, there was no debate over the need for stimulus. Exactly how much and where the money should go inspired no such consensus. One common complaint about the '08 stimulus, made by people who at the time were unwilling to budget more funds, is that the ensuing recovery was too slow. Another complaint, more popular in hindsight, is that more needed to be done to help individuals and smaller business entities. These complaints resonated with Congress, who in 2020 responded accordingly. The $2.4 trillion will likely amount to a down payment. At least one more immense tranche of funds is expected, though currently, there is limited political will from either side for another big expenditure.

One of the most contentious debates among economists today is exactly *where* to invest financial stimulus. So much money has been spent that Conservatives have no stomach for additional Liberal investments, and vice versa. (Edit: August 4, 2020—congressional leaders remain deadlocked on a stimulus package. There is talk that congressional Republicans don't want to "waste" money in enhanced unemployment as they believe that a second Trump term appears doubtful. They seem to believe that voters will hold both sides of Congress equally responsible if no additional stimulus money becomes available. It may prove to be a costly mistake for the Republican Party.)

The gold standard evaluation tool for assigning value to financial stimulus is known as the fiscal multiplier, defined as the monetary return to society from each dollar spent by the government. It happens to be consistently higher for liberal causes than it is for conservative causes. For example, the fiscal multiplier for food stamps is roughly 1.75 (meaning every dollar budgeted for food stamps returns $1.75 to the overall economy) whereas the fiscal multiplier for cutting corporate taxes sits at about 0.35. Infrastructure spending at about 1.6, offers a rare source of ideological agreement. Conservatives sometimes get onboard with infrastructure spending because building bridges and schools offers opportunities for businesses to make money. Liberals like the jobs created, not to mention new schools and bridges that won't easily collapse. Not much money is made when poor people use food stamps to purchase inexpensive food items or single moms put their kids into subsidized childcare.

The value of Liberal causes would be more obvious to the public except that when governments move too far to the Left, Liberals have a history of overdoing it. They often invest in many programs that have excessive timeframes, like nuclear fusion and other ambitious basic science research, or in things that have intangible values, such as the arts. No matter how worthy the cause, taxpayers will only fund it if they are educated on its value and the expenditure is not excessive.

Now that we can use our fiscal multiplier *ruler* to assess the quality of financial decisions made by our politicians, we are better positioned to make employment decisions and be the kind of bosses our politicians deserve. When we look at the complete financial picture, it's worth noting that in the past three decades, Democratic presidential administrations have achieved far greater economic prosperity (particularly in the stock market) than Republican administrations.

*   *   *   *   *

Surprising as it sounds, the Trump administration struggled with the successful execution of disbursing funds from the first stimulus package. Though money was quickly delivered to the wealthy and large corporations, millions of checks for individuals were delayed by months.

While some small businesses applied for Paycheck Protection Program (PPP) funds, many did not submit the meticulous paperwork early enough and got frozen out of the program. This cost jobs for businesses that had no available cash to pay employees. Meanwhile, larger businesses with other avenues to capital received large sums from PPP that they didn't need. It was ugly, at least from a PR perspective, and numerous larger businesses had to return money to the government to minimize embarrassment.

As of early July, no follow-up money has been budgeted. There are a limited number of congressional working days left before the election, so unless there is *another* substantial economic jolt, the next round of stimulus funds may wait until the economic pain becomes more apparent to these lawmakers.

The school issue, though, will have to be decided shortly. This may encompass the most consequential decisions of the entire crisis. The push for school reopenings goes beyond deciding between our children's wellbeing versus the expected increase in disease spread. There are many households where school is the only viable childcare option. Without school, some parents will be unable to return to work, which will put an additional drain on the economy. School-supplied food is essential for many children's nutritional needs.

Unfortunately, kids can catch and spread COVID-19, perhaps even beyond the transmissibility of adults. And while it's true that kids don't die from COVID-19 at the same rate , a comparable percentage of kids are hospitalized. In Florida alone, as of July 9, we have lost two 11-year-olds to COVID, and there have been over 11,000 children infected. Who knows how many of those kids will suffer permanent afflictions?

Politicians should start talking with each other and coming up with return-to-school plans that are flexible and work well for as many people as possible. Most of these decisions should be made at local levels. The president doesn't have the authority, nor is he in a position to dictate these school policy decisions. Even governors will be best served by not standing in the way of local school district plans. Ideally, local districts should develop plans based upon epidemiological guidance from the CDC, but that organization has destroyed its own credibility by consistently yielding to political pressure. In destroying that credibility, the CDC has left many subordinate governmental entities, including schools to fend for themselves in making accurate information-based decisions.

The majority of the nation's school-children may be able to return to school, if, and this is a big IF, their respective communities can get their viral spread under control. In much of the South and Southern California, it is hard to envision that the rate of viral infection spread will be low enough to permit in-class attendance by the start of the school season.

Some communities run the risk of seeing true explosions in infection. In situations where school kids return to school with poorly enforced social distancing and slow testing, while simultaneously, parents return to office environments, a frightening percentage of a local population could become quickly infected. Self-correcting factors such as teachers calling out sick or parents not sending their kids to class may be insufficient to prevent huge flare-ups.

Few accomplishments would help the president's reelection chances more than a successful vaccine, which is oddly ironic, since Trump had made zero contributions to vaccine development. Given his disregard for the truth, I expect that as the election nears, we will hear more and more good news about an ensuing vaccine. We can anticipate that these statements will be independent of reality, with one exception: there is every reason to be hopeful that an effective vaccine will become available to essential workers, maybe even as early as Election Day. (Edit: August 4, 2020. The timeline for a vaccine continues to accelerate. Essential workers may have a vaccine available mid October. The effectiveness of the first few early vaccines may be disappointingly low—perhaps in the vicinity of 50%. Combined with a low adoption rate by the general public, it will take time for immunity levels to reach even 50% (perhaps around March 2021), let alone the 70% that would be required to drop infection rates near zero (with luck, by Summer 2021). As immunity builds, infection rates and commensurate deaths will drop. Communities will have to be wary of relaxing mask usage and social distancing too early, though, as flare-ups will continue to be possible until we achieve herd immunity. It's important to note that if Trump is reelected, vaccination rates will likely be lower as trust in safety will be lower.)

The introduction of a vaccine will bring further questions. How many people (in the US – not the rest of the world, because vaccination paranoia in the First World is primarily an American problem) will get the vaccine, and how long will that take? In what order will vaccinations become available? Will people know with certainty when they are no longer susceptible to catching COVID-19? How effective/what percentage of people who are vaccinated will catch the virus? Will people be willing to increase their participation in the economy if that number is not miniscule? Will it be safe to get a more reliable vaccine later, if you receive an early vaccine that is not highly effective?

Once the vaccine arrives, we will not see a "V" shaped economic recovery to nearly the extent that we would want, particularly if the virus is still running rampant. At this point, the Vegas betting odds for the presidency, which are surprisingly accurate, puts Biden at roughly 60% to Trump's 40%. With a Biden win, and the likely expectation that Trump would leave office by the inauguration, I think we could expect substantially tighter controls over behavior; however, the US may maintain a higher level of the disease than the rest of the First World, due to continued noncompliance with social distancing. At best, I would imagine the economy won't be back to the robust metrics of 2019 until 2022. It may be an exceptionally long time before we see unemployment numbers below 4% again.

As far as the vaccine itself, it was clear from the outset of the crisis that it would be worth spending extra money to accelerate any potential COVID-19 vaccination progress. Of course, for an administration that has been winging nearly everything, there was never any true financial analysis – just the obvious intuitive notion that we need a solution soon. If such an analysis had been undertaken, I think it would point to a ridiculously high fiscal multiplier of somewhere between 200 – 1,500. It's hard to pin it down exactly, because I don't have access to necessary data, most notably the likelihood of delays. But if you just rough wag some numbers, with a 2020 GDP of $22 trillion, a conservative estimate of 15% GDP reduction would amount to $275 billion lost every month due to the virus. Could vaccinations become available a month earlier for a billion dollars? That would be a multiplier of 275. It's possible a "meager" investment of $200 million could get us vaccinated a month earlier, resulting in an amazing 1375 multiplier.

Do you see where I'm going? We can't throw enough money at this problem. Instead of states bidding against each other for ventilators because the president, for some inexplicable reason, is unwilling to make sufficient use of the defense production act, we should have vaccine companies bidding against each other for the brightest scientists. While not ideal, bidding wars for scientists would be a sign that we are at least approaching appropriate spending for this problem. It's July, and it's being reported that there aren't even syringes purchased for vaccine administration. You can't build a syringe factory overnight.

In today's dollars, the Manhattan Project cost about $23 billion. It was clear by mid-1944 that the Allies would prevail. The Manhattan Project began only at the end of 1942, and Hiroshima wasn't bombed until August 1945. It's likely at least $10 billion of the project was expended after the fate of the war became obvious. My point is that when being faced with a comparable loss of life and the loss of our way of life, our government should be similarly motivated to protect its citizens. For obvious reasons, the Manhattan Project was conducted in total secrecy. Without that limitation, it's easy to imagine even greater expenditures.

The only person I've heard discussing COVID-19 in similar pragmatism is Bill Gates. Somehow though, one of the brightest minds in the country, the epitome of a thought leader and an advocate for the ethical application of science, has become the boogeyman of the hard Right. One has to wonder about the motivation of this segment of our society. Do they truly want America to succeed?

Ironically, Gates is everything that Trump supporters have been fooled into believing of Donald Trump. Gates is a billionaire genius who rose from humble beginnings to become the wealthiest man in the world, strictly on his business and technical acumen. We should have no illusion that Gates is a perfect angel. As a businessman, he's been ruthless. But following his resignation from the leadership of Microsoft, Gates and his wife Belinda have spent decades of time and billions of dollars helping to make the world a better place. Gates and Warren Buffet joined forces to create the Giving Pledge which has so far committed over $1 trillion dollars from the wealthiest people in the world toward philanthropic causes. If you were to argue with God for why he should not smite the lot of us for our ignorance, selfishness, and inhumanity, Bill Gates might be the first argument against God's anger. He may not have the soul of Mother Teresa, but he has likely exceeded even her impact. And even with that lofty praise, I would not be eager to have him as president. It's just asking for trouble to consolidate so much power in the hands of someone of great wealth. To be clear though, I would sacrifice a few fingers, if I could exchange Bill Gates for Trump.

We have at the helm of the great disaster of our time, a man of limited intelligence, whose wealth derives not from hard work and talent but primarily from inheritance, misrepresentation, and in all likelihood, fraud. A man whose greed might only be exceeded by misplaced arrogance. Gates has given away over $45.5 billion of his own money! Trump was found guilty of stealing from his own charities! Something is frighteningly wrong with a society where some 40% of its citizens see Trump as our savior and Gates as evil.

I can't stress enough that the metaphor of being on a rudderless ship is not exaggeration but understatement. To say that we are on a rudderless country has no meaning; the United States of America is not a ship. I just don't have the words to convey the magnitude of the problem. If we had today as our president, Dobby – not the Harry Potter character for whom my dog was named, but my dog himself, we would have far fewer deaths and far fewer COVID-19 infections. Dobby would not be undermining scientists. Dobby would not have encouraged governors to lift quarantine restrictions too early. Dobby would not have held rallies in infection hotspots, trying to gather as many people as possible into as tight a space as possible, while encouraging them to scream and shout at the top of their lungs with no masks on. Dobby is smarter than that, although in full disclosure, Dobby is a particularly intelligent dog.

Being a particularly amenable dog, I imagine that I could even get Dobby's paw print on some orders to triple or quadruple our investment in a COVID-19 vaccine. Some might argue that there are only a limited number of ways to attempt to tackle the problem, and that may be true, but what if, and I know this is just an insane notion because America is unquestionably the epitome of competence at the moment, but what if some of the vaccine companies' chief scientists make some bad calls? What if they accidentally contaminate some samples without realizing it?

Ordinarily, these problems get fixed eventually through the peer review process, but that takes time that we don't have. We should have several companies independently employing each strategy. Fortunately, we do have some of that, particularly when factoring in the vast amount of science being conducted outside the US, but our country needs a vaccine more than any other. We should be investing in greater redundancy.

We need to invest in more engineering to rapidly produce and deploy the vaccine, once it becomes available. There are 2.86 million nurses in the US. We could have each of them work an extra eight-hour shift for just one day, where they each vaccinate 100 people. With 15 vaccinations per hour – 1 every 4 minutes, that's sufficient for these nurses to take a long lunch break and several smoke breaks. I suspect few nurses smoke, but they could take it up for the day, if they wanted. Just one day to vaccinate our entire nation, if we wanted. The vaccines could be delivered in advance and administered following final approval.

Anyone think we could pull it off in a day? A month? Six months? Not if we get stuck with the current administration come January 2021, I can tell you that.

If "health" is the *product* that the government wishes to purchase, a vaccine is only one of several potential ways to buy it. Though only a vaccine can offer an eventual end to the crisis, other *products* for improving our health would be extremely beneficial and offer commensurately large fiscal multipliers. We should be investing more in testing and contact tracing to be sure. An accurate, rapid, and inexpensive test would be a game-changer. Therapeutics, such as monoclonal antibodies, which might end up being highly effective at reducing hospital stays and mortality rates, should be targeted for increased investment. Anything that can save lives and/or reduce hospital stays should be a target for stimulus money.

June 26, 2020

Vice President Pence conducted the first COVID-19 press briefing in two months, and it was extremely telling; there is just so much to unpack. Notably absent was one Donald J Trump, which was probably wise as the president is currently focusing the majority of his energy and time on saving our Confederate statues. He also seems intent on attaining herd immunity for at least red states, by Election Day.

Strategically, it's the best time to hold a briefing because the death rate is currently at the minimum of the crisis. It will soon be much higher, and the administration knows it. Trump's supporters don't understand that there will soon be a rise in infections and many new hospitalizations will quickly follow. The doctors have gotten a lot better at saving lives, but there is still some percentage of COVID patients who will die, so a rising mortality rate is also in our immediate future. We have been doing more testing. Politicians on the Right are falsely claiming that this is the reason for the rise in infection rates. As medical experts have indicated, the positivity rate is also rising, which is indicative of greater overall levels of infection.

The Oklahoma rally was six days ago, too early to see the coming spike. In Arizona and all the other places Trump plans to hold public events, the virus is certain to take off. Trump is playing the role of the Four Horsemen of the Apocalypse, who in the Book of Revelation brings Plague, Famine, War, and Conquest. Which brings me to my own recent *revelation*. It's too simple to say that so many American citizens reject mask-wearing as a tribal practice. Certainly, it's true for some, but historically, when division between people was truly at a maximum, it was caused by religion. Only when people are truly entrenched by dogma will they zealously fight and even sacrifice their own lives for a cause that is morally wrong. Religion has that power over people, like few other things. The role of religion in America has often been to reject all attempts to interfere with anything viewed as an *act of God*.

The war on science is an age-old problem which first peaked, centuries ago, during the Renaissance. What was so threatening about understanding the motions of the planets? To many, this was knowledge that only God should have. Several religions reject all medical intervention whereas some reject specific therapeutics such as vaccines. This notion of not interfering in God's will even plays a role in current political debates: *climate change cannot possibly be a result of human action because God controls the weather.*

When you believe that God is all-knowing and all-powerful, I have to ask, on whose watch did the COVID-19 pandemic occur? Perhaps the more zealous among us believe that disease was brought to smite the unworthy? If you believe that's God's will, well.... *We certainly wouldn't want to interfere with that plan. Put those masks away!* No doubt, the religious South took comfort in the notion that the virus had come first with a vengeance to the Communists of China, the Socialists of Europe, and the *Wicked* of New York City. *Surely, the devout would be spared.*

I'm not saying that everyone or even most people in red states were thinking these things on a conscious level. That's not how religion works. It seeps into the subconscious, affecting thoughts and actions with little to no trace of its influence. After seven long years in Abilene, Texas, I recognize the intrusive hand of religion when I see it.

Clearly for some, there are other reasons to not wear a mask. Some don't like the discomfort, some have been brainwashed so strongly to hate government that they outright reject anything their government asks of them. Again, tribalism plays a role. For most, there is almost certainly an intersection of many of these influences, but I would assert that the influence of religion is dominant. It is a frightening notion that many people, cognitively, have put little to no distance between themselves and the ignorance that dominated the earliest days of the sixteenth century war on science. Which brings us back to Mike Pence's briefing. Though the daily mortality figure is currently a little over 200, lower than it's been since March, the infection rate is exploding. Pence fails to mention that greater mortality is in our immediate future.

Meanwhile, in this 90-minute briefing, Pence cannot bring himself to say the word, "mask." It may be the most childish act of an adult I have ever observed in my life. He danced around the word like a prima ballerina. He tells people in the states where COVID is spreading to "do their part … to follow CDC guidelines" (which emphasizes the wearing of masks). He quickly glosses over the importance of using "protective equipment," (with a noticeable increase in cadence and decrease in the volume of these words, as though he did not want to say them at all). And he tells everyone to "continue to pray." I was praying he would just use the word, "mask."

It's clear to the entire country that there is a new divergence in the spread of the virus, currently hitting the red states (and California) hard. Pence emphasizes the Federal Government is ready to surge supplies for *these* states. Such support did not come so easily to the Northeast in their time of need.

After some time, Pence let the remainder of his team speak. Of note, CDC Director, Dr. Redfield references the country's earlier losses of "twenty-five thousand" people a day. The actual number should have been twenty-five hundred. He never corrects his mistake. This slip of a decimal point would appear as surely a meaningless gaffe to some. It wasn't. I'm a numbers person. My careers have been based on numbers, as should the person in charge of the CDC.

I don't fly at an approach speed of 14 or 1,400 knots, I fly at 140 knots. As an engineer, I know with the certainty of my home address, that 6061 aluminum has a yield strength of approximately 40,000 psi. Not 4,000, not 400,000. There is a whole multitude of numbers that need to be regularly examined when handling an epidemiological crisis.

Mortality figures are a top priority, particularly in communications with the public. That Dr. Redfield could so easily mistake the mortality figure of 2,500 for 25,000 tells me that this is a number that he was not looking at daily as he should have been. In all likelihood, not even weekly. And if by chance he was, then he is surely not the man for the job. I felt at that moment like a patient about to have knee replacement surgery hearing my surgeon discussing prosthetic legs and medicine available for phantom pain associated with amputation. I was horrified.

Leadership abhors a vacuum

There's a saying, "Nature abhors a vacuum." I've often adapted this to read, *Leadership abhors a vacuum*, which is to mean, when adequate leadership is not apparent, more adept leaders step in. This has been the case from early in this crisis. Businesses understanding, well... business, were among the first proactive entities. Many international tech firms in Europe started directing employees to work at home in February. In early March, as the first known COVID-19 deaths in the USA were being recorded, well before any government mandates, numerous large American tech firms started sending employees home. Granted, work on the computer lends itself well to electronic commuting, but this was still a bold move.

Then on March 9, there was a godsend. My alma mater, MIT, along with Harvard, Cornell, and a few other Ivics, announced that they would be sending all undergraduate students home within a week, likely for the entire remainder of the semester. Trump was still making light of the crisis as something inconsequential—a media and Democrat hoax. To have the nation's most respected learning institutions take this unprecedented step became a wake-up call that the virus did indeed pose a threat to the country. Two days later, for those disinterested in the thoughts of the nation's intellectual elite, the NBA canceled its season, and Tom Hanks announced that he and his wife both tested positive for COVID-19.

The nation's politicians, Democrats included, failed to communicate the severity of the crisis, but thanks to the leadership of others, people started paying attention in a way they hadn't before. Could you imagine the earful that the presidents of those universities, not to mention the NBA commissioner, must have been subjected to? They modeled the courage that our politicians would need when they finally began telling their citizens to quarantine.

Leadership was evident in many corners and frequently forced responses from the government. One might recall when airline pilots quit flying to China. Many bar and restaurant owners were out ahead, shutting their doors even before their customers started staying away. They understood both the economic and medical realities. And by March 11, the Dow was down 20%, a clear signal from investors to politicians that the country had a wide-ranging problem.

There were adverse effects related to the leadership vacuum. With minimal information in the public domain, social media "experts" spread misinformation about the value of hydroxychloroquine and how wearing a mask would be useless and possibly make you sick. A vacuum is a poor arbiter for quality. It sucks in everything.

Lightning Strikes Thrice

As my wife and I sometimes remind ourselves, many families face unbearable tragedies. John's ailments have been awful, and I would not wish them on anyone. But he is still alive. He still brings himself and Lisa and me joy. That did not keep us from feeling the resentment of having him first struck by cerebral palsy and brain damage by some very rare blood transfusion event, and then struck again with the truly awful condition of autoimmune encephalitis, which is rare enough that we had never heard of it before. Lightning had struck twice.

In early December 2019, John began acting strangely again. For a time, we would give him simple allergy medication which was just strong enough to keep his immune system from attacking his own brain cells, and he would be normal the next day. But slowly, he wasn't himself, and there didn't seem to be anything we could do to change it. By New Year's, he was experiencing some minimal level of encephalitis again, which in his case amounted to minor symptoms such as reverting to the strange vocabulary he had used previously when he was sick, some minor anxiety, and a diminished ability to express himself. Over-the-counter meds were keeping the more severe symptoms at bay, but if we skipped doses, he would become significantly irritable and far more anxious. Fortunately, it was nothing like the extreme behavior of early 2019.

Our medical options were limited. We took him back to his ENT to see if anything like the growth in his sinus had returned, but his sinuses were clean. His neurologist had been unable to cure him with the typical first-line defense, and the next level of treatment would be more invasive. John had been stable, so we waited. In early February 2020, he started getting worse. He wasn't sleeping, and he was having angry outbursts. We called the neurologist, but she was on vacation. So we had his psychiatrist put him back on a low dose of the same meds that had helped him before. After some tweaking of his meds, he was mostly stable.

In early March, Mary and Jim came home for break. COVID was starting to take hold, and I told the kids there was a decent chance they wouldn't be returning to class. Then MIT sent their undergraduates home, and I told my kids that they should start making plans that their universities would do the same, which they did a few days later. Now I had two anxious kids home, along with the one who was a wreck unless medicated, and a wife who was really nervous about me bringing home the bug from a flight and giving it to John, which we feared could send him into pure insanity if it didn't simply kill him as he already had some level of immune dysfunction.

On the other hand, everything else was okay. I had just made a fair amount in the stock market by forecasting the drop, there were good indications that the federal government was going to prop up the airline system, and I had all my kids home. Jim and Mary would have much preferred being back at school in normal times, but I always miss them when they're away, and I selfishly enjoyed their company.

As I observed my government's incompetence in dealing with the coronavirus, I felt drawn to action. My first thought was that I should write about it. When I started, it was more an act of catharsis than a serious start to a meaningful project. I got about 15 pages down, but John kept coming into my room and interrupting. Although medically, his inability to entertain himself and his desire instead to seek my full-time company was a minor symptom, it was a major annoyance. And although I liked my first 15 pages and I felt content with my circumstances, the state of the rest of my family, my friends, and my country still triggered anxiety. I just couldn't deal with trying to be creative at the keyboard while John impaled me with repeated dissertations on the various functionalities of the Windows operating system, or the iCarly sitcom, his two favorite topics of conversation. AE caused John to speak tirelessly for hours on his favorite topics. Yes, it's an actual neurological symptom known as pressured speech. No, I don't think your precocious five-year-old has it. I put the book idea aside and worked instead on repairing a major deficiency in our medical system that was severely hampering conventional medicine's ability to meet the challenge of COVID-19.

The problem was that all kinds of valuable medical information exist, but physicians can't access it. I aspired to create a radical new system for IT processing. The dozen Individual physicians I spoke with loved the concept, but to put in place what I had in mind would require high level political support, in addition to a fair amount of capital. It took only a few days to realize that it would take too long to scrape together the minimum needed money and support.

Ten days later, I was back to my book, which meant contending with John's incessant interruptions and need for attention. Pilots are natural experts at compartmentalization and have better than average focus skills. That ability to ignore undesirable stimuli has understandable limitations. Every one of John's interruptions was not merely a nuisance, but a reminder of a medical condition that was not getting better. Achieving focus became a steep uphill battle.

By March I realized that if for some reason the neurologist in Miami couldn't help my son, the next best option was to get on a plane to Philadelphia, Boston, or New York. But if we waited to the point where we needed that help badly, John's behavior would not accommodate an airplane flight.

I called Philadelphia and began the process of getting John seen by one of the nation's few specialists. Then John had a really good week. He started getting much better, such that his symptoms would only be recognizable to family. So taking an airplane to Philadelphia, risking exposure to COVID, did not seem a good decision.

Then, sometime in April, he took a turn for the worse. He was having angry outbursts and was frequently disoriented. By now, the hospitals were only taking emergency level patients. His symptoms were not emergent, and I knew that they could be subdued with an increase in his meds, but our inability to see a path to a full cure made us feel like being stuck inside a Halloween maze with no exit. We upped his meds. The chaos subsided, but he was no less sick.

John's condition wasn't the only stress in my life. In February, I had slipped in the snow. People had told me how awful the pain of a broken rib is, and I wasn't feeling that bad, so I figured the area was just bruised. I went about my typical routine, which is fairly physical. After a couple of weeks of the pain getting better, it got worse, though oddly only in bed. In the day I was fully functional and didn't feel anything, but at night, I had awful pains which kept me awake all night. I began to travel from my bed to the living room and its chairs and couches, searching all night, every night, for a comfortable position.

I finally went to an orthopedist, who was having a particularly busy day, so I saw his PA instead. I told her I didn't think my rib was broken. I found symptoms on the web regarding a condition called "slipped rib" that I thought was a better fit for my symptoms. The PA took x-rays anyway and confirmed it wasn't broken. She said it could be a slipped rib but that their office didn't perform the type of nerve block treatment I had asked them about when I first made the appointment. The PA referred me to a chiropractor. Several days later, said chiropractor put quite a hurt on me, supposedly in the name of treatment. I'm a big advocate of chiropractic medicine, but this was more a military interrogation, the kind you'd receive after being shot down behind enemy lines. Somehow, I managed to drive home. Then I iced the area, downed a handful of ibuprofen, and did my best to forget about the whole mess. Fortunately, I wasn't flying by this point.

As a pilot, you learn to deal with interrupted rest. I can get by without that much sleep, so my nightly laps around the house searching for some comfort was at first, just another annoyance, much less resonant to me than the pandemic, and in particular, the dreadful way in which the federal government was still handling it. After a while, I started feeling a bit like a ghost in my own home, haunting about all night long.

Eventually, fatigue started to build, but once I reached a certain level, I'd manage to sleep 30-45 minutes before waking up in pain and then moving on to my next haunting spot. I tolerated this for about a month before seeing another orthopedist who did do nerve blocks.

The doc was a nice guy and sharp as a tack. I was rather assertive in not wanting more x-rays because I get plenty of radiation in my job, and I had already taken x-rays which showed no breaks. Plus, I felt quite sure about this slipped rib thing – it all fit. We mutually agreed upon an ultrasound, which showed quite clearly that I had indeed broken my rib. I felt embarrassed as well as disappointed because I knew what the treatment for a broken rib is. Nothing. Unless you call tolerating the pain and discomfort until it just heals, *treatment*. I asked what he could do for me anyway. Pilots always cover the bases.

Time would show that my rib was not healing properly. I didn't have a single decent night's rest from February until July. Through the stress and strain of the pandemic, the family's various stresses, and my inability to capture sleep night after night, I somehow took comfort in the journey of this book.

In some other universe where my ribs (I learned later I had broken two) had healed quickly, and I was able to properly sleep, I would have more aggressively pursued my ideas at improving healthcare, but I just didn't have the inordinate amount of energy required to pursue that goal.

I still did what I could to help where I could. Somewhere in mid-February, I told close relatives to start stocking up on supplies, and of course, Lisa and I did the same. I told my elderly aunt to buy some N-95 masks. I started donating to local food banks and had the kids select charities that I donated to as well. I don't think I saw a fundraiser for several months that I did not donate to. Yes, I was scared for the future of the airline industry. As a veteran, I didn't have too many qualms about sealing my life up tightly away from the rest of the world, and I knew many others would do the same. I recognized that if something wasn't done to combat the immense loss of business, the economy would be in even greater peril. Any *stimulus* I could offer my local economy would be badly needed. We had quit eating out in early March. It took a while to get over the fear of infection as I remained concerned for John's health, but in early April, we decided that it was especially important to support the local restaurants. My research gave me confidence we could keep the risk sufficiently low, so we started ordering takeout.

Local quarantine guidance and enforcement was noncommittal. The constraints I established for the family were more exact, but they did not protest against a single restriction. I made sure we took limited opportunities to release steam and emotionally decompress. For the most part, though, we have had extremely limited contact with even close friends or family because it just hasn't been worth the risk, particularly with the ability to video call anyone at any time. I've been grateful that the Maurer household, at least, avoided insurrection.

This was how the majority of my personal COVID-19 journey transpired. What about you?

In many ways, despite what went wrong, I already have fond memories. Remember that Kennedy speech, "Ask not what your country...." How did President Trump inspire us though this time of challenge? I have tried to make it innate within my kids, when you see challenge, think opportunity. 2020 could have been a year of inspiration and unity unlike any in our lifetime. Where were the calls for neighbors to help neighbors? Who dared you to make or even envision something that could help ease suffering or somehow make another's day better?

If you asked my kids about their most valuable resource, they'd better tell you it's time, as much as I've drummed that into their heads. Those fortunate enough to not be in need have realized that COVID-19, for all that it has taken, has given this incredible gift. For those worried about health or the ability to care for their family, time seems much less a blessing, but it still can be. This crisis could have been our country's finest hour. It truly could have. We could have collectively taken this gift of time and done something incredible.

When historical perspective arrives to pass judgment, it will look kindly upon some. If you participated in peaceful protests in support of your fellow human beings, I hope history reflects that you built a legacy of transforming challenge into opportunity. If you found ways to help those in need, I suspect you'll be able to point to some fond memories of 2020. But of those who used their time to inspire fear and hate, to sow division, or to offer endless complaints with no solutions, they are likely to find mostly darkness and despair when they recall the events of this year.

Politicians are an odd lot. In spite of the way they drive us to frustration, most of them are intelligent and knowledgeable. Inside most of them, there is narcissism and aspiration, yearning for greatness. Only a psychopath would enter office hoping for a major crisis, but to those who have had disaster thrust upon them, I imagine they had some level of appreciation for the opportunity. The best American presidents are remembered for having led our nation through some seemingly insurmountable challenge. Today, though, we have in the Oval Office a very square peg that will never fit into this very round-holed pandemic. Trump will be remembered as the leader who was never meant to be.

As for John, after more waxing and waning, he got worse in late-June. For the first time in his life, I didn't know what to do.

July 2, 2020: A Tale of Two States

I'm pretty sure I said earlier, I did not intend for this book to be a journal. It's just the slow-motion train-wreck nature of our nation's handling of this crisis demands some sort of chronicling of the missteps and the madness. Despite the success of the remainder of the Western World in driving infections down to a trickle, American infections have ballooned to new highs exceeding 50,000 per day. Several days ago, Dr. Fauci declared that we were headed to 100,000 a day, if we didn't make significant changes, and I'm hard-pressed to make a case against him.

Currently, the peaks of epidemiological dysfunction are centered within Florida, where I live, and Texas, where I just had to travel for my annual flight training. It's been an unsurprising reflection of my "luck" such as it is. These two states have been battling back and forth for the lead title of worst handled reopening. Both states have Republican governors. Ron DeSantis of Florida is a Trump sycophant. He refuses to take statewide action, even for something so simple as mask-wearing. Various local governments, some run by Republican politicians such as Miami mayor Francis Suarez, have been doing the heavy lifting again, shutting down businesses, mandating masks, and otherwise mandating social distancing.

The same is happening with local politicians in Texas, but now with slightly more support from Governor Abbot, who has frequently appeared with a mask in recent days. He has been more aggressive than DeSantis in statewide mandates and has attempted to tailor the responses to the varied levels of infection in disparate communities throughout Texas. Nonetheless, Texas Lieutenant Governor Dan Patrick is playing some sort of right-wing good-cop/bad-cop game, doing his best to deny science like he's just fled the seventeenth century Vatican. Abbot seems to have gotten the last word for now, and in a move that must have surprised some, he mandated mask usage statewide today. It's of particular surprise as it was roughly a week ago that Abbot had made it illegal for any local municipality to mandate masks. Apparently, the rapid rise of infections in Texas has helped Governor Abbot "see the light." I would love to be a fly on the wall during the next sit-down between Governor Abbot and his science-denying lieutenant governor. Anything seems possible—maybe a full-fledged shouting match, or perhaps mutual praise for their respective good cop/bad cop roles.

The less decentralized Texas strategy may be showing slight signs of success. After battling for the lead for several days, the rate of new infections for Texas might be starting to peak somewhere below 8,000. This is nothing to celebrate, unless they compare themselves to Florida, where the daily infection total just exceeded 10,000. My state of Florida has roughly the same infection rate as New York at its peak. DeSantis, who has always fashioned himself as a mini-Trump, is playing his role perfectly, with expected results. The mortality figure today in Florida is highest in the nation, and what may be even worse, hospitals in hard-hit areas, in several states, are rationing health care. This is what critics of Obamacare most feared, but it is happening now, solely because of Republican mishandling of this pandemic at numerous levels. Hospitals are running out of the successful drug, Remdesivir. Some are out of ICU beds and ventilators as well as numerous other important resources. If we're learning about this on the news, there's a good chance that doctors are having to make a lot of difficult rationing decisions. Patients who should be getting certain drugs and therapies simply aren't. The result is more pain and death.

* * * * *

At some point, I fear that we may run low on healthcare providers. Doctors, nurses, and respiratory therapists are fighting a war, except this war is being fought without the support of their countrymen. One of my son's friends, a physician, has said that his hospital wasn't providing interns with any PCP at all! Nurses and doctors have become COVID-19 statistics, and some have even taken their own lives. Historically doctors commit suicide at a rate exceeding the general population, but today, our physicians are needed as much as ever. Generally, people who feel needed are less prone to suicide. But after the crisis, in the moments of remembering and reliving, when the adrenaline is long gone and it feels like the appreciation is gone, and the let down of not being needed feels more real than all of the earlier expressions of appreciation, I fear we will lose some who should never have been lost. There is not much I can write about that is as forward-looking as this.

There are a lot of smart people in healthcare. I know I'm not saying anything they don't already know, but I still want to emphasize this. Once the pandemic finally subsides, you will be exhausted. Some hospitals will give the PTSD issue lip service. It is human nature to want to put disaster behind us as soon as possible, and the thought of therapy after going through hell is understandably unpalatable to many. *Please, though, if you have anything to do with obtaining the emotional care of healthcare professionals, particularly in the aftermath; if you're a healthcare professional yourself, please give this the consideration and high priority it deserves. Do everything you can to ensure there are no regrets over what might have or could have been done. Make sure those heroes who need help get help.*

* * * * *

Not to be left out of the discussion for terribly run states, Oklahoma and Arizona infections are exploding, a week after their Trump rallies. But in many other locations where racial injustice protests have taken place, there appears to only be a minor spread of infection. Meanwhile, few states have done the hard work of applying rigidity and discipline to their opening plans. There is minimal evidence that more than a handful of states have made substantial investments into contact tracing. Infections, hospitalizations, and deaths are all going up in more states than they are going down.

There are clear reasons for this. First, the opening of previously shuttered businesses, by its very definition, will cause a rise in the infection rate curve. All communities will perform worse after they open.

Epidemiology dictates that without aggressive mitigation, the infection rate doesn't come down. It goes up geometrically if there is little to no restrictions on social contact—and not just in a straight-line rise; unchecked, the line curves upwards until it points straight up to infinity. We don't have an infinite number of citizens, but if we don't change something, a good percentage of our 330 million will become infected soon, and too many of those will die. Of those that don't die, far too many may be permanently affected. The good news for the well-disciplined among us is that mathematical models suggest that roughly 30% who best protect themselves will remain healthy as herd immunity eventually takes hold. So there's that.

Herd immunity feels like where we're headed, at least in some red states. Certainly, it seems that way here in Florida. It should be noted that even the wildest estimates put the percentage of prior infection at 7-10%, which is not yet remotely close to a level of herd immunity. But with the virus so poorly contained, it's easier to place faith in a vaccine or herd immunity than in our government's ability to decelerate the current community spread. I can only hope that once enough people fear that things have gotten out of control, they will change behavior. Unfortunately, just as there is a lag in observed infections following moments of public stupidity, there is also a lag in any corrections, to include new government's restrictions to slow the spread. That is why it is so important for governments to act quickly once increased spread is noticed. Florida has been particularly slow to impose restrictions, and we Floridians are likely to pay for this.

The children of alcoholics and addicts might feel a certain sense of familiarity. At some point, addicts lose interest or the ability to supervise their children. In a family that might have once been governed by conventional rules and norms, a new power structure and system of governance will emerge. Often, the older and stronger children assume control and responsibility. In most cases, human instinct ensures a certain level of normalcy, but families where there is substantial dysfunction often encounter abuse and neglect. In Florida, today, it feels too much like this.

Some may see the infection growth charts shown on the nightly news as appearing bad nearly everywhere. However, in a small state like Wyoming, where the number of infections goes from 8 to 12, well, that's a 50% increase. That's huge! Except really, it's not. It's an increase of 4 people. That's all it takes to turn a state dark red in some of those charts. It's far better than going from 8,000 to 10,000 in Florida, which would be *only* a 25% increase. Still, the charts do have their uses, and they show that for the most part, the United States of America has become the world's scariest slow-moving train wreck. *Woot-woot, all aboard.*

CLIMATE CONSIDERATIONS -- HOW TO SAVE THOUSANDS!!!

On first glance, charts show the South doing badly. One might believe this is a sign of red-state foolishness, and it certainly is, but there also might be a climate component. Those paying close attention may have noticed that California has been contending for the lead of the most daily cases.

Math and science tell a different story from the news. California dwarfs the rest of our states in population. On a per capita basis, the infection count remains in the healthier half of US states. Of note, infection rates in Northern CA remain particularly low. Any hot spots appear bounded to Los Angeles and surrounding counties.

Why there? It's not immediately clear. The mayor of LA, Eric Garcetti, is a bright and articulate politician. He fully supports the wearing of masks and other social distancing guidelines. With California governance somewhat consistent from south to north, and many more infections to the south, climate emerges as a possible culprit.

When it gets hot outside, people head inside. Indoors with a high density of people who are not wearing masks is the most likely place to catch the virus. You absolutely do not want to be eating indoors, because *you can't eat without taking off your mask*!! Without very high-quality filtration, any virus particles inside a restaurant or any indoor facility are just going to be recirculated by air conditioning. This is the closest thing to a petri dish that you can find, short of a petri dish.

God bless our restaurant owners. We need them; we love them. Let them set up widely spaced outdoor tables where they can, and let them work on their takeout business, but people need to understand that indoor dining and drinking, for most of us, is the activity most likely to result in a COVID-19 positive diagnosis.

There is an odd overlap between Republican governance and the warmer Southern states. When COVID took off in early summer in the South, it was easy to label the problem as a red-blue policy issue, and certainly, that was part of it. California stands as a glaring outlier, but only Southern California.

It's a complex problem. Scientists must account for differences in policy, socioeconomic status, political affiliation, culture, customs, and population density, just to name some of the influencing factors. Climate doesn't immediately emerge from the data as a disease driver.

Epidemiologists are scientists, and most scientists are not systems engineers, which is to say, they think linearly and direct their focus toward highly specialized tasks. Systems engineers, such as myself, think holistically, appreciating the big picture. Scientists rarely rely upon common sense because science is often counterintuitive. Occasionally, though, common sense is our best tool available. We *know* that uncomfortably hot weather forces people indoors. We *know* that COVID-19 spreads more easily indoors. Ipso facto, hot weather increases COVID-19 spread. The data will eventually validate this, but as with other considerations, time is not on our side. We can and should use this information now. So how?

Stay outdoors, especially in the presence of those outside your household. At restaurants, work, social gatherings, and everywhere you can, stay outdoors. Easy. Fortunately, as schools open up and the kids head indoors and increase spread, the rest of us can head outdoors, somewhat moderating the spread. Teachers, when you can, take those kids outdoors!

When it gets wetter and colder, though, and we head back indoors, we are likely to see a resurgence.

Keeping windows and/or doors open will cost us in higher heating bills, but will be more than worth it. In many cases of viral shedding, where sneezing and coughing are not involved, the virus depends on the air being still. Recirculating heating and cooling systems that move air around without maximum possible filtration only exacerbate the problem. Virions build up to become even more hazardous than they might be in still air. Creating airflow diminishes the viral load sufficiently to reduce spread. If you have to be indoors with those outside your household, accept a higher heating bill, put on a sweater and warmer socks if you must, but open the windows and doors.

July 5, 2020

Young (and I don't know of the specific age group, but presumably college age) people in Atlanta have been holding contagion parties. For reasons, I've yet to be interested enough to discover, these kids are attempting to catch the virus and are rewarding each other with cash prizes if they do.

Those old enough might recall the films about hiding under your school desks if and when the nukes started dropping. By the time I'd been born, the world had narrowly escaped nuclear Armageddon a handful of times. Growing up, I figured such restraint couldn't be depended upon forever. It was only a matter of time. It never occurred to me that the true danger would come from sheer unadulterated stupidity. Statistically, some of these idiots will die. I would return to my previous suggestion that we actively infect young volunteers to better understand the virus. At least in that case, they would get better medical supervision and be hailed as heroes. They would likely end up with a much better outcome than the Covidiots, as some are calling them, who infected themselves for fun.

Which brings me to the final news of the day. Herman Cain attended Mr. Trump's Tulsa rally and did not happen to wear a mask. Two days ago, he was admitted to the hospital with a diagnosis of COVID-19. Perhaps there is some cause and effect to this data? I do expect he will survive. One wouldn't be confident in the disposition of a person of his demographic, except for this: money may not be able to buy you happiness, but it sure as heck can buy you great healthcare. As bad as this disease is, there are some adequate medical intervention strategies. If the hospital that admitted Herman Cain has no Remdesivir, he certainly has the resources to send someone in a car or a jet airplane to get some elsewhere. The same goes for convalescent plasma or anything else Mr. Cain's doctors might prescribe.

Numerous famous people were dying from the virus early on, but as the medical understanding has advanced, it doesn't seem like the virus has taken too many people of wealth lately.

(Edit: August 4, 2020. Yeah, I was wrong. Herman Cain died last week. Wealth in his case proved an insufficient defense after all. There's no way to be certain that he caught the bug at the Tulsa event, but wearing a mask that night would have likely saved his life. Who might have guessed that several dollars invested in a mask would turn out to be more valuable than millions of dollars in the bank? Me. I would have. You too, if you've read to this point.)

July 8, 2020

I thought I had written the last of what I've come to see as journal entries, but current events continue to be stubbornly meaningful, and not in a good way. My aunt tested positive for COVID three days ago, and she is not doing well. She's the last living relative of my parent's generation, the type of person that writers love to write about. There's just so much depth to her persona. She's always had shocking red hair, which even at 81, looks natural despite being dyed regularly. She only began revealing her age a year or two ago. I don't recall knowing before then. Friends and relatives say that she barely looks 60. I have friends she met once 35 years ago who've told me they remember her vividly. It wasn't just her good looks. She possesses a unique combination of charm and force of personality. With my aunt, everyone always knows where they stand. As she is generous to a fault when you are in her good graces and mean as a rattlesnake when you're not, people generally aim to make her happy, which I suppose is by design.

She has no children of her own, so my sister and I are her next of kin. She still intimidates family members who (like everyone else) see her as larger than life. As a result, both her mistakes and her good deeds are blown out of proportion. I've never been intimidated by her, which I suppose accounts for our strong bond. We have a running joke about which one of us is the *true* black sheep of the family.

My sister and I tell each other that this woman is far too strong to be hurt by this disease, and I believe what we're saying, in spite of what I know. I have lived COVID-19 for the last several months or so I thought, but when someone close to you is affected, all the things you thought you understood hit you on an entirely new level.

Three days ago, she and her boyfriend were visiting friends in Central Florida, obviously against advice. My aunt called and told me she had gone to the ER because she was feeling hot and cold, and she hit me with her COVID diagnosis. She sounded okay, and her vitals were fine, so there wasn't any immediate concern. Still, at her age, she should have been more careful.

I'd previously experienced my parents' normal geriatric progression—the slow miserable reversal of capability that is the opposite of what parents experience with offspring. You notice they are no longer able to drive safely, then no longer able to take care of certain needs. Eventually, they're no longer able to take care of most needs, personal or otherwise. Each step backward is a battle between generations. The inescapable end for both parents was the mirror image of their birth.

It seems a silly march when you're younger. I still have some inkling of being a teen and saying, "Someone should just kill me when I reach 40." At 56, I recognize the march to the endgame as just another part of life, and I'm hard-pressed to argue that it is any less meaningful than any other sacrament. I can imagine when it's me marching to that final ending that I won't be in such a hurry to take that last breath. So it's hard to even describe the emotional revulsion that I feel when I've seen so many younger people declare that we need to accept an immense loss of (primarily older and sicker) life as a casualty in the need to "get back to normal."

My sister and I discussed months ago that it was somewhat a blessing that our parents did not survive into the COVID era. They were not particularly careful people in their prime, and they would have been a source of constant worry. We suspect they would have caught the virus quickly. Both of them had comorbidities and might have met awful ends. I miss them both terribly, but given the power, I would not have brought them back for such a possible outcome. My aunt was a bit different – a meticulous woman with healthy habits and a need for rigid orderliness and cleanliness. Even at 81, her hair is always done, her clothes are always in fashion, and her make-up is always meticulous. It is a palpable burden to the remaining females in my family who are held to her high standards. I've generally been let off easy if my clothes are clean, but my kids are still intimidated to walk into her sparkling Miami high-rise.

Although she has had more than her fair share of minor medical issues of late, she had yet to suffer any meaningful decline. The first battle over independence and autonomy was still in our future. My aunt had been a businesswoman in her prime, a numbers person. I explained to her on several occasions that every time she risks exposure, however innocent it seems, she plays the odds, and that eventually, if she continues even taking small risks, the odds would catch up with her. She seemed to understand these concepts on the phone. I gave her my best advice, but I was probably in denial thinking there was even a chance that my words would rule the day over the influences of her peers—again bearing witness to that sense of impotence that is often the strange dualistic perspective of the sandwich generation. Somehow, it's easier to understand when your kids insist on making their own mistakes. They don't have the experience to know better. Of relevance, she is politically Right of center, and her social circle, to include her boyfriend, are well Right of her.

I expected the hospital would hold her there, but she called later to tell me she had been released. The next day, her boyfriend was experiencing unusual fatigue. My aunt told me he was having a bad headache and was achy all over. They decided, against more advice, to make the drive back home to southern Florida. Fortunately, they were in a new car with all the new safety features like lane-keeping, et al. There are so many ways now, in which financial status determines well-being. They made it back home, probably with the help of the new car's safety features. Later that evening, her boyfriend went to the ER.

The next day (yesterday), after numerous attempts to contacting her at home, my sister and I finally got my aunt on the phone. She was coughing, and it was immediately clear that she was mentally disorientated. The internet is a source of much that is wrong in this world, but it's also pretty good to have at your fingertips a list of COVID-19 symptoms that should make you want to seek immediate medical help. I already knew that mental disorientation was a serious red flag. We told her she needed to go to the ER. She didn't want to and didn't even understand why we wanted her to go-not a huge surprise for a mentally disoriented octogenarian. Though her apartment is only a 40-minute drive, the nature of this disease is that it steals away our ability to support each other. It would have been a substantial risk for me to go pick her up to drive her to the hospital. Meanwhile, she would not have been safe to drive herself, and she was entirely unwilling to get in an ambulance. Her *friends*, who she had been running around town with, were now worried over their own health. Putting aside the irony, they weren't going to take her, nor should they have, as it would not have been any safer for them.

* * * * *

I'm chronicling aunt's story because, God willing, not every family in America will have to experience this disease firsthand, and I think it's important to understand the nuances. It's not July 8 anymore. It's oddly difficult to write when you're phone is ringing and texting off the hook. Also, it's funny. I don't much care for hospitals, having spent months of my life within their confines, attending to the needs of my kids, particularly John. But there's something oddly unsatisfying about driving 40 minutes to the hospital to drop off supplies for a loved one and then heading home without even catching a glimpse of that person—even if you know that an in-person visit would involve hours of listening to whining and kvetching, not to mention having to explain the same thing over and over again to a mind that is even on a good day, in minor decline, all while trying to get past those uncomfortable moments witnessing too much of the indignities that are defining attributes of hospital care—even all that seems preferable to the donning of your mini hazmat suit so you can stand in a line with numerous sick people outside the door of the ER to drop off a care package and then leave without a glimpse of your relative. First world problems, I suppose. If you have loved ones, though, alone on the other side of that virus firewall, confused and afraid for their lives and feeling totally alone and uncared for as their doctors and nurses are busy like they have never been before, the whole thing is enough to make any heart ache.

This is a disease like nothing humanity has ever known. Not the absolute worst. There are a few maladies that make COVID-19 look not so bad. But it's not a cold or the fucking flu. I can tell you with technical knowledge and the sincerity of experience that it is closer to Ebola than it is to a cold or even a mild case of the flu. The next days will involve errands and hospital trips and phone calls with doctors and relatives and my aunt. Dealing with this disease will consume my time, and though I write this as though it is the 8th, it is now past that date.

In that phone call, my aunt was showing signs of what was looking like it might turn into a serious case of COVID-19. We had to get her to the hospital as soon as possible. Uber/Lyft was our remaining option. My sister and I didn't like it on moral grounds. We didn't like the notion of her possibly infecting anyone else. On the other hand, if some driver in South Florida on July 8, 2020. was willing to drive an elderly person from her apartment to a hospital, they should have known perfectly well what they were getting into. I was torn, wondering if I should have insisted on an ambulance, but concerned she might refuse it. Such are the moral dilemmas that so many Americans have been facing these last few months. My sister and I settled on the path of least resistance, expecting that no driver would be interested.

My aunt hung up and requested a car. I was surprised that someone quickly took the fare. We put our moral qualms aside and directed her to gather her necessary belongings, knowing full well that we wouldn't be entering her apartment anytime soon. She was understandably scared, stewing in some awful combination of confusion, guilt, and the notion that her life was for the first time ever truly in peril. My sister and I told her that we would stay on the line as long as she needed, but she wanted to call her boyfriend.

She made it to the ER, and they got her situated at a patient station quickly. There she would remain for several days, as the hospital had no available hospital rooms. As time passed, the confusion would intensify.

We are extremely fortunate to live in a time of cell phones and video calling. This pandemic would otherwise be more burdensome and deadly. Even on a good day, in a better year, hospital care can get confusing. Doctors make themselves available for questions only a few minutes a day per patient. In the days of COVID, one can only imagine the extra hours. I learned recently of a doctor who hadn't had a single day off in 100 days. This is more like a war than most of us understand.

My sister and I were to have regular conference calls with hospital staff over speakerphone so that nobody has to touch a phone and our aunt could listen in. As we were updated on our aunt's condition, the ER alarms and announcements sounded off in the background. It's a sobering reality to hear "code blue" multiple times in the background. I only hoped they were going unnoticed by my aunt. Add the strong Hispanic accents of some of the staff and the imperfect technology of speakerphones, and at times, it felt like we had regressed by 75 years in communication technology.

When it was just the three of us with the speakerphone off, my sister and I could hear our aunt perfectly well, but we had to discount anything she said in her state of confusion. The doctors and nurses were extraordinarily patient. They were going through similar conversations dozens of times per day, while administering life-saving treatments and therapies, all behind their own substantial protective equipment which I know from friends on the front lines, only partly eased personal anxieties over safety. Add to that my aunt's demanding nature, and I'm just saying, some of these people ought to be in the running for sainthood.

Then there were also some cranky staff who without a doubt, needed to take a long vacation. I say this as someone who has moved around the country and has had direct encounters with numerous hospitals: you or a loved one have to be an advocate for patient care. Don't get me wrong—everyone gets a basic level of care at a minimum. But staff are just too overworked to go beyond the basics without an advocate's regular needling.

For example, alarms for an empty IV bag are permitted to sound off for 30 minutes or more. These systems were not built with pilots in mind. Alarms in my world require immediate attention. They must be quickly silenced, so that if something else goes wrong, as can and does happen in an airborne emergency, the pilot is aware of each new condition. As a personal policy of a kid who has spent more days in a hospital than I can fit people inside a 737, when an alarm goes off, I will alert the nurses immediately. After a couple of slow responses, I just turn the alarm off myself. I am not encouraging this behavior mind you, but for many nurses, it makes them just a little nervous to have a patient's dad playing with their toys, and subsequently, they tend to respond more quickly to John's alarms. Beyond alarms, it's everything from making sure the patient gets fed to reminders for medication or testing that seem to happen more reliably with the input of an advocate. Yes, the staff gets around to these tasks eventually, but being in the hospital is miserable enough without having to do it hungry or in pain.

So, my sister and I did everything we could to advocate for our aunt, but we were limited to the few things we could say over the phone. Knowing how demanding our aunt could be, my sister and I made sure that we were all carrot and no stick with the staff. Often we would call and there would be no answer. We'd hang up after a certain number of rings, knowing full well that on the other side of the ringing phone there might be one more code blue or other dire emergency.

The morning following our aunt's first night in the hospital, she was less confused but struggled harder to breathe. It's a scary progression of the disease. They put her on a nasal cannula and four liters of oxygen per minute. At some point that evening, they started her on a vitamin regiment. Medically speaking, this fell under the category of *couldn't hurt*. It at least gave them something to tell a scared patient who wanted to be cured immediately. The next day, a chest x-ray and CT-scan revealed clear indications of COVID-19 pneumonia, with telltale signs of what the radiologists refer to as ground-glass opacities. After hearing the dry cough over the phone, and with the positive PCR (swab) test, I already knew what the chest scans would show. I've been studying the disease for several months. There is not much that the doctors or nurses could explain that I didn't already know. Unfortunately, this says more about how much is not known by the medical community, than how much I understand.

My aunt's nurse tells me that the physicians consider the CT scans a more reliable indication of diagnosis than the PCR tests. This makes sense, even though I'd read six weeks earlier that that was not the case. Science and medicine are learning about this virus only a few news cycles ahead of the public. This new paradigm has become a source of confusion, making fodder for science-deniers.

* * * * *

As to what else is happening July 8, the virus has gone crazy in the South. There are more intelligent ways of describing the problem, but at the moment they seem insufficient. With all due respect to my more intelligent conservative friends, the virus seems to love the combination of stupid governance and stupid citizens that appear to be plentiful in red states. Meanwhile, I feel certain that all governance is being severely hampered by the slow reaction time to policy changes.

Imagine driving a car in some strange dream with new rules. When you see a hazard, it takes you 10 days to realize you need to stop. Then when you step on the brake, the vehicle continues to accelerate for the next 8 days. Then you coast at high speed for 7 - 10 more days, and finally, after about a month, the car starts slowing down. By the time you reach five weeks, you're only back to the speed you were at when you first stepped on the brake. It takes close to two months to bring your car to a stop—the metaphorical equivalent of bringing new infections close to zero. This is with everything working well. That's the reality of using reactionary leadership to set public policy in the time of COVID.

So, how do you get your car to stop more quickly?

Anticipate.

The situation calls for proactive leadership, but we don't have that. Even without being entirely proactive, with a little planning, leaders could develop triggers so that instead of 10 days to recognize a problem, it takes as little as one. Leaders can institute guidelines for remediation that are not driven by local political pressures but can be put in place quickly when triggered. This "car" will never stop on a dime, but we can do much better than what we've been doing.

Until we have immunity, mandatory mask usage should go without saying. In locations where the virus is growing, the bars have to close. Restaurants should be limited to outside dining, with maximum table spacing. Unfortunately, public officials are ill-equipped, especially after the initial widespread quarantine, to shut down economic activity for people in real economic pain. As before, the federal government could have been providing cover to local politicians, but of course, the president and his most ardent protégés are doing the exact opposite.

In a perfect (nothing like what we currently have) world, we'd have a federal government discouraging local governments from permitting the virus to spread unchecked. Instead, we have to rely on the next level, state governments, to override the stupidity of the federal government, but that's just not happening in red states where the local governors are more interested in pleasing Trump and placating their constituencies of science-deniers than in saving lives. Confusion and absurdity rule the day.

This is what is happening in Texas now, where one day things are improving and the next they're back out of control. Are people complying with orders immediately, or is there a multi-day lag between mask orders and some cohesion of compliance? Local public health officials should have a better picture, but if they do, it's not being shared with the public. TV analysts debate the problem with no clear determinations.

You almost have to have a notion of time travel to understand the problem. When you wear a mask today, you are helping to reduce deaths a month or more from now. That's just one more explanation that is not getting out. In this age of immediate gratification, some people will never understand without immediate feedback. China was smart to deploy drones to yell at anyone not in a mask. I'm thinking this country might need robot nuns to smack the mask *sinners* with electrically charged rulers.

Trump realizes he can't maintain the attention he craves by repeating the same stupid stunts every day. He is regularly mixing it up, ramping it up. His aides finally got him to put on a mask at Walter Reed, but then, of course, he later said that he only wore the mask because he was around injured soldiers. We all understand how important injured soldiers are to Donald Trump. Just ask John McCain, whose extraordinary heroism he dishonored, or the Goldstar families he insulted, or the families of the soldiers who were killed in Russia's campaign to pay the Taliban to kill Americans.

A leak came out of the White House that they were developing a strategy to get Americans to accept and forget the high level of death and mayhem. Apparently, part of the plan involves an inordinate amount of attention given to saving Confederate statutes. Also Confederate statues.

We are in a really strange moment in history. One of the very few areas of agreement about Trump from the Left and the Right seems to be this notion that he is crazy...like a fox, when it comes to how to win a political campaign. Very few people saw his 2016 win coming, even the night before the election, let alone the start of that year's Republican primary. Somehow, though, he carried all the red states and then managed to squeak by in all the swing states by small margins. It was easy to suspect some kind of genius at play.

Thought leaders on the Left are more apt to attribute dumb luck, plus a lot of help from the Kremlin, but regardless, they have adopted a "fool me once...fool me twice..." strategy concerning the upcoming election. Still, the incessant bad decisions, the continual return to his hate playbook, and a total disregard for the public's disgusted reactions have many people scratching their heads. Trump has been asked several times if he *really* wants to win the 2020 election. He emphatically replies, 100% yes. Then the commentators somehow leave it at that because the one thing we know about this president is that his answers are always 100% truthful.

Suffice to say, President Trump's approval continues to slide with each misstep. Being a contrarian, I was hoping to point to something that he has correctly accomplished recently—just to say, "See! I'm not out to impugn the president! All I want is to get to the bottom of our problems." The thing is, at the bottom of nearly every problem, I find the footprints of Donald Trump. I can't point to a single intelligent decision he has made since he had Pence brief the American people without him—before the death rates took off again.

Donald J. Trump vs. the Paper Bag

It's time to serve some meat and potatoes—to take the deep dive into President Trump's leadership throughout the pandemic. Except I'm not going to do that. Not entirely. When I began this investigation, I was eager, for lack of a better word, to talk about the rampant ignorance, wanton disregard for life, and utter absurdity that has been President Trump's consistent policy. Several months later, with over 130,000 dead Americans, I am mentally exhausted. He has done so many stupid things for which we would look down upon an intelligent sixth grader. Pointing out the majority of his ignorant statements (and it is predominantly statements because he has set almost no actual policy) would only serve to be boring and depressing. Suffice to say, the president could not lead his way out of a paper bag. But the reasons are not simple ineptitude. There is clinical psychological dysfunction. It's time for me to roll up my sleeves.

The arrival of Mary Trump's book, *Too much and Never Enough...*, was delayed due to unprecedented demand, which is understandable because the president's niece details a level of ineptitude and emotional dysfunction that makes clear Trump's unsuitability and lack of skillset for public office. Ms. Trump traces the president's many inadequacies back to his youth. She's certainly better qualified than me in every respect to psychoanalyze her uncle, but sometimes when you're too close to a problem, particularly when there is trauma involved, you miss something.

Donald Trump is famously known to have never drunk alcohol or taken drugs, one of the more intelligent moves of his life, but there are many kinds of addictions. Those who suffer from the effects of addiction almost always suffer from mental health or behavioral dysfunction. This is referred to as *dual diagnosis*, meaning the addiction does not exist in a vacuum. The converse is often true, that when certain mental health problems are present, particularly with genetic predispositions toward addiction, addiction is frequently present as well.

My wife occasionally refers to herself as a grateful alcoholic. This expression is a reference, not only to an alcoholic being in a sober state of recovery. It is also generally a reference to a journey of self-exploration, insight, and enlightenment that leads to a greater state of psychological fitness and well-being than had existed even before the beginnings of addiction.

Far less typically, I call myself a grateful spouse of a recovered alcoholic. Me being...me, when my wife's alcoholism began to threaten both her well-being and that of our family, I embarked upon an immersive exploration of the disease to better understand what my wife was going through, and if possible, offer some level of help. This path of study led to personal enlightenment as well as a better understanding of human psychology. In the process, I came to understand alcoholics and addicts well.

When I read Mary Trump's book, it became obvious to me that the president behaves like what some people would call a dry drunk. This phrase refers to an alcoholic or an addict who isn't using but still suffers from the same emotional frailties of someone in the throes of addiction. While there aren't any indications that Trump is chemically addicted to anything beyond diet coke, the signs of addiction are unmistakable. As his addictive issues are so glaring, I surmised the addiction itself would be hiding in plain sight and likely manifesting in self-destructive behavior. Sex and tweeting immediately came to mind. Overeating was also a possibility, and we would certainly have to consider lying, although from a clinical perspective, his lying is likely a coping mechanism related to some other primary dysfunction.

Let's Climb Inside the President's Brain

Addiction is a disease of neurotransmitters and brain chemistry. Mind-altering drugs modify the behavior of brain chemicals like serotonin and dopamine in different ways. Typically, these drugs cause a flood of these pleasure-related neurochemicals offering the addict their high. Repeated drug and alcohol use rewires the brain to expect and need the drug of choice. For some emotionally fragile individuals, various other activities can cause a flood of neurotransmitters. Gambling, sex, porn, overeating, and social media have all been shown to elicit neurochemical surges. These repeated activities rewire the brain to be dependent on whatever is driving the surges. The result, as it is with mind-altering chemicals, is addiction.

Could Trump be addicted to tweeting? Twelve-step programs have been used successfully to fight addiction by tens of millions of people. There is a tool sometimes used in these programs to help demonstrate to members that certain aspects of their recovery may not be properly working. This tool offers an ironic reflection of the member's failures in achieving the objectives set forth by the twelve steps. In other words, "If this sounds like you, your recovery still needs work."

It is called, "The 12 Steps in Reverse." The list has been made and redone numerous times by multiple individuals. I'm simply using the first one I found online at:
https://www.erikbohlin.net/handouts/12_steps_in_reverse.htm.

I substituted *tweeting* where *drinking* appears and was immediately impressed by the results. I think nearly anyone will quickly recognize the following behaviors and attitudes in one particular orange-faced politician:

1. I declare my complete control over (Twitter) and everything else; and further declare that my life is in perfect order.

2. I recognize no power as great as I am; nor any person as smart as I am, and if you don't like it come outside.

3. I made a decision to run my life and everyone else's life to suit only me - and I pity those who get in my way.

4. I make a searching and (thorough) inventory of everyone other than myself - and find them woefully lacking in all respects; and I never hesitate to tell them so.

5. I admitted to no one, including God and Myself, that there could possibly be anything wrong with me, or my actions.

6. I went to extreme efforts to protect and increase my defects of character-and did a little tweeting besides.

7. I continued my obnoxious arrogant air of asking no one for anything-my Big Eye was for telling, not asking.

8. I kept a complete list of all persons who had harmed me, either real or imaginary, and swore to get even with them all.

9. I got even where possible, except when to do so might injure me.

10. I continued to bitch and whine about everything to everyone and, when I was right, promptly reminded them.

11. I sought through scheming and conniving to materially improve myself - at the expense of my fellow man. I (never) hesitate, when the opportunity presents itself, to bring disaster and misery to anyone who happens to cross my path.

12. Having had a complete moral, physical, financial and spiritual breakdown, all of my remaining effort was directed toward dragging those near me - and dear to me - down to these same depths of despair; And I did a little tweeting too.

---from The Grapevine

Again, other than changing alcoholic references to tweeting and correcting a few typos, I made no other changes. This passage describes Donald Trump to the letter. If you have ever had an addict or alcoholic in your life, and many of us have, you understand that they are the original "gas-lighters." They make the codependents in their lives doubt reality because they are so convincing; they are so convincing because they reject reality, choosing to believe only what enables their behavior. They are masters of manipulation who frequently turn families upside down, facilitating narratives in which every other member of the family feels trapped by the addict's addiction. In yielding to these anxieties, codependents become powerless to stop the addiction or its ill effects. Every resource of the family becomes relegated to the needs of the addiction.

Donald Trump sees America and all its governmental resources as personal assets, here to serve at his pleasure, which ultimately means here to serve his addiction. In its least appalling incarnation, America is to

Donald Trump a vessel in which to fill an empty void created by his dysfunctional upbringing. Meanwhile, his supporters play the perfect codependents, and the rest of us are just along for the ride.

When highlighted, Trump's addictions may be apparent, but meeting clinical criteria would be impossible. It would take a personal interview with the president *and* his honest answers to verify addiction to the high standards of the DSM 5 clinician's manual. Something else was bothering me. There was too much going on with Donald Trump's personality to say his issues are governed by addiction, even if you include dual diagnoses of narcissistic or antisocial personality disorder. I hadn't painted the complete picture. I knew I would have to identify some sort of syndrome.

After a bit more exploration, I finally had the answer—the missing piece of the puzzle! Our president suffers from a condition called histrionic personality disorder (HPD). The American Psychiatric Association defines HPD as "a personality disorder characterized by a pattern of excessive attention-seeking behaviors, usually beginning in early adulthood, including inappropriate seduction and an excessive need for approval."

According to Wikipedia, "People with HPD have a high need for attention, make loud and inappropriate appearances, exaggerate their behaviors and emotions, and crave stimulation. They may exhibit sexually provocative behavior, express strong emotions with an impressionistic style, and can be easily influenced by others. Associated features include egocentrism, self-indulgence, continuous longing for appreciation, and persistent manipulative behavior to achieve their own needs."

HPD is a predominantly female disorder. Numerous starlets whose sex tapes and other antics lead to frequent appearances in the tabloids are believed to have HPD. On first blush, one can understand why even trained psychologists wouldn't have an answer to, "What do Kim Kardashian and Donald Trump have in common?"

Because of gender differences, males with HPD present somewhat differently from females. If I asked you instead what Kanye West (who is presumed by some psychologists to have HPD) and Donald Trump have in common, it's easier to see how Trump could have HPD (particularly when you factor in that Donald Trump is about as far from being a young black man as you can get).

When you examine all of the DSM 5 criteria for HPD, it reads like Trump's resume. The following behavior should be present for a firm diagnosis:

A pervasive pattern of excessive emotionality and attention-seeking, beginning by early adulthood and present in a variety of contexts, as indicated by five (or more) of the following:

* is uncomfortable in situations in which he or she is not the center of attention
* interaction with others is often characterized by inappropriate sexually seductive or provocative behavior
* displays rapidly shifting and shallow expression of emotions
* consistently draws attention to physical appearance
* has a style of speech that is excessively impressionistic and lacking in detail
* shows self-dramatization, theatricality, and exaggerated expression of emotion
* is suggestible, i.e., easily influenced by others or circumstances considers relationships to be more intimate than they actually are

Those with HPD are frequently impulsive, demanding, manipulative, energetic, charming, and emotional. People with this condition can function at high levels and are often successful socially and professionally. They tend to do better with creative tasks and are generally incapable of deep analytical thought. Those with HPD have more frequent divorces and are often diagnosed with narcissistic personality disorder as well as other personality disorders. Though females might dress and act seductively, in males the behavior is more likely to manifest in acts such as making wildly inappropriate and reputation-damaging sexual comments, making aggressive sexual overtures that can be perceived as sexual assault, and even getting "caught" having sex with high-profile porn stars. Once again, we see that for Donald Trump, his vulgarity is to him, not a flaw but a feature. If he did not thrive on the attention that these antics deliver, why would a person of even average intelligence repeat these mistakes again and again?

The exact causes of HPD are unclear, but those with the condition have often been raised by parents that tend to ignore both positive and negative behavior. Parental attention when given tends to be unpredictable. In Mary Trump's book about her uncle, she makes clear that the president's mother suffered medical issues and was unable to care for her children well, while his father, Fred, was consumed by business ambitions and had almost no interest in rearing young children. Fred started to give Donald more attention only after he was sent to military school for his naughtiness. This type of parental feedback leads to confusion as to what is appropriate behavior. With HPD, we have a diagnosis as clear as the "+" on an EPT. DSM 5 also requires behavior consistent with what is referred to as general personality disorder criteria, which the president's behavior undeniably displays.

You might ask, what about antisocial personality disorder and/or narcissistic personality disorder? Trump does meet the criteria for those conditions, but at the root of his emotional problems is this more encompassing condition of histrionic personality disorder. The HPD drives behaviors that present as other disorders. Unlike plain-vanilla narcissists, who only seek positive attention, Trump's history contains a long list of outlandishness for seeking both positive and negative attention. Likewise, those with true antisocial personalities generally experience a more abusive childhood than what Trump is understood to have known. Those with antisocial personality disorder tend to have a history of blatant disregard for social rules and laws. Trump has a remarkable ability to understand exactly how much he can get away with, and tread right up to that line, but no further. HPD appears to be overriding.

So then, what about addiction?

We discussed earlier, the notion that certain behaviors in psychologically dysfunctional individuals can activate inappropriate levels of neurochemicals. In other words, these habitual behaviors stimulate his brain similarly to drugs that are abused by addicts. Neuroscientists have only in the last couple of decades, discovered that dopamine released in the nucleus accumbens, considered the pleasure center of the brain, is one of the driving forces of addiction.

The accepted theory is that as dopamine surges in the brain, the accompanying responses caused by certain activities such as watching porn or gambling, are almost identical to how the brain experiences addictive drugs. It is currently believed that dopamine interacts with another neurotransmitter, glutamate, and the dopamine surge and associated activity is then registered as a learned activity within the hippocampus. Repeated exposure to this learned reward activity rewires the brain to express inappropriately high levels of desire for whatever caused the dopamine surge.

Unfortunately, over time, the brain develops a tolerance that drives the person to seek out higher levels of drugs or more intense experiences. With Donald Trump, attention-seeking behavior driven by HPD has become his drug of choice. Trump's lust for the limelight has been so consistent and frequent that neuro-chemically, it is extremely likely that the president's need for public attention has become a clinically defined addiction.

Why, though, is it important to see Donald Trump as an addict? Why is all this neuropsychology *really*, important to understand and *really, really* SCARY? Because addiction is a *progressive* disease that gets worse over time. Trump's antics, the crazy things he does to gain our attention, are not abating. They are getting worse. Four years ago, Trump was telling us that Mexico was going to pay for a wall, and he was insulting John McCain for getting shot down in a war that he was too afraid to fight in. Both of those positions were preposterous and insulting, but relatively harmless.

In the last several months, Trump has called for public insurrection and has either held or endorsed public rallies without masks that scientists have said led to disease and death. Just look to Herman Cain. Trump's condition is getting worse. We now have to ask ourselves, what heights of insanity will the president achieve if he's left in office for another four years?

Trump supporters may argue in the face of this evidence that if the president were truly an addict, he'd exhibit more "destructive" behavior. To that I respond, how many hundreds of thousands of people have to die before behavior should be considered destructive? When we add the series of divorces and failed familial relationships, coupled with six bankruptcies, if all of that doesn't establish a history of destructive behavior, I'm not sure what does.

If we are gong to use his professional failures against him, it's important to understand, if the president has been such a poor businessman, how is it that this fact isn't more widely understood?

Decades ago, Donald Trump was able to leverage his wealth along with his one skill of self-promotion to convince banks to start making billions of dollars' worth of ill-conceived loans. These business deals encompassed to various degrees, the Trump brand as collateral. This was a huge mistake for the banks because once Trump proved unable to service the debt of these loans, were the banks to foreclose in a manner that damaged the Trump brand, the banks would lose even more money by devaluing their underlying collateral. I've got to hand it to him. Even Trump's many lenders found themselves as codependents, not being able to take him to task because doing so would cost them financially. Very few people could pull off such a feat. It is remarkable he was able to snooker as many financial institutions as he did.

Keeping with previous business practices, it's likely some of Mr. Trump's loans were obtained in a less than scrupulous manner, but that's someone else's investigation. The bottom line is, to loosely paraphrase Mary Trump, in his entire life, Donald Trump never accomplished anything meaningful on his own.

There are two notable exceptions: The first was his show, "The Apprentice." He built a fictional construct of a businessman (again, assisted by his father's wealth) but then leveraged that into a successful television show. He used that further enhancement of his brand to win the Republican nomination for president. One could argue that none of the above would have been possible without Fred Trump's wealth, but still, Donald's ability to promote his own image should not be underestimated.

Donald Trump's psychological profile suggests that had he been born into a poor or middle-class family, it's possible he would have ended up in jail or even dead to substance abuse. Most of the rest of us could not continue unabated if we were being sued by 3,000 people, but with daddy's money, many things were possible. Trump's enablers accomplished through vast resources what a typical codependent enabler hopes but is rarely able to achieve with the addict in their life. Trump was protected from his many failures in every way.

Many addicts and alcoholics are (in a sense) addicted to anger. It's a coping mechanism and their go-to emotion. This is consistent with Donald Trump's observable behavior. One could even make a case that Trump is addicted to bad deals. His entire life he has portrayed himself as a "dealmaker." His ghost-written book, *The Art of the Deal,* was an effort to showcase the image, and he obviously revels in this false persona. But after six bankruptcies, it is clear that his actual deals have been mostly bad.

His record as presidential dealmaker has been little better, with the American citizens ending up as the ultimate victims. Trump's negotiations with North Korea have given Kim Jong-un all the credibility he had lusted for without delivering anything meaningful in return. In cancelling the Iran deal, Trump has put Iran closer to a nuclear bomb and heightened tensions between our countries at the cost of American military casualties and destroyed American weaponry that brought us to the brink of war. In abandoning the trans pacific partnership (TPP), we have lost influence among a trade group representing the fastest growing economies in the world, not to mention damaging our negotiations leverage with China. And speaking of China, Trump's intransigence and poor strategies have led to a trade war that has reduced revenue for a variety of American businesses while driving up American farm bankruptcies by 30%, all while costing American consumers billions in higher taxes due to tariffs.

Theoretically, Trump has achieved some marginal improvements over NAFTA that have yet to materialize, and he managed to squeeze more money out of our allies toward NATO costs, but that money came at the cost of a reduced standing among our allies. In sum, Trump's "deal-making" has cost America dearly.

Unfortunately, the Republican Party continues to enable the president's deficits. So, as much as Trump is working to destroy his political career, his enablers are working equally as hard to prevent that from happening. When someone returns to self-destructive behavior again and again (even if that behavior does not succeed in self-destruction), this is a hallmark of addiction. America, we elected an addict to be President. "I don't know it for a fact… I just know it's true."

* * * * *

In what follows, I am taking Trump and his supporters' lead in disregarding existing norms. I have concluded that the president's deceased mother was an alcoholic. There's not a lot of supporting evidence, but we know that alcoholism is a family disease. There are typically both genetic and environmental factors at play. The genetic link is not always there, but it's common for it to be.

We know that Donald's older brother Freddy suffered from alcoholism. Donald's father, Fred, was known to never drink. That's somewhat unusual for a businessman of that time who was not particularly religious. We know that Fred's father died at an early age, reportedly from the flu, after being sick for a day. Fred's father ran saloons and whore houses. There's a good chance that he was a frequent drinker, and it's plausible he died primarily from the effects of alcoholism, which could explain Fred's life-long rigid abstinence.

Donald's mother, Mary, despite being a woman of wealth, lived in emotional torment according to the Mary Trump book. Medical issues in early adulthood caused a lifetime of stress and discomfort. Fred was the definition of an overbearing and unsupportive husband, and she had at least, one child, Donald, who had severe behavioral issues from an early age.

Fred did not allow alcohol in the house, but he did allow baking. In Mary Trump's book, Ms. Trump mentions on at least two occasions that her namesake grandmother smelled of vanilla. To my recollection, it's the only smell she mentions in that book. This is possibly a coincidence, but I suspect that Ms. Trump understands that vanilla extract is required by the FDA to contain a minimum of 35% alcohol. In other words, it's a minimum of 70 proof. There's not a lot of vanillaholics out there because it's a fairly expensive and I would imagine unpleasant way to get drunk. But for the wife of a billionaire, who's not allowed liquor but suffers 24/7 from physical and emotional pain? It's quite conceivable.

On page 158 In *Too Much and Never Enough*, Mary Trump writes of her grandmother, "She sometimes smelled strongly of vanilla even when she hadn't been baking. Other times, I would see her out of the corner of my eye surreptitiously slide her hand into her purse and put something into her mouth." This passage appears in the context of describing how miserable the family matriarch's existence had become. What

241

explanation, other than vanillaholic, could there be? Ms. Trump leaves the dots unconnected, perhaps waiting for someone else to do it for her because a direct accusation might be "Too Much."

Is this proof? *I don't know if for a fact*.... But if Donald Trump was raised by an overbearing, abusive father and an alcoholic mother, it puts the president's psychological dysfunction in a new, frightening context.

Now We Understand

Donald Trump's mental deficits make perfect sense when he's viewed as an untreated addict. Sending a tweet or holding a rally can flood the brain with serotonin as easily as taking a shot of whisky. To some degree, the president's addiction explains how well he connects with his base. There may be a strong correlation between Trump supporters and people with addictions or addictive behavior. There is a strong correlation between alcoholics and those with a dark view of the world. Trump's habits of lying and bullying as well as his utter absence of empathy are likely less offensive to other addicts. It fits together well.

I am not suggesting that Republican politicians are all alcoholics and addicts. To many of his supporters, politicians and voters alike, Trump is simply a means to an end. Where most of the world saw in that Access Hollywood tape a flaw, a segment of the Republican Party came to understand they had found an amazing feature. Imagine the grin on the face of his more deviant early enablers when they realized that far from a political liability, Trump's absence of a moral compass was a *sigil of quid pro quo Infinitum*! –A license to pursue any morally corrupt economic or political agenda of their choosing, just as long as they did not interfere with the man's much narrower agenda of personal aggrandizement. Trump was to play the role of neglectful alcoholic father, letting his kids rule the roost without repercussions. The world sees on grand display, codependency at its worst.

* * * * *

Xenophobe or not, history has shown that to rally a population through a crisis, a leader needs to be able to bring his/her people together. In demonizing immigrants, Trump quickly alienated large swaths of the population before the first primary ballot was even cast. Once his misogyny was on full display, that made him *persona non grata* among millions more. Let's not forget his insults of John McCain, which should have driven Independent voters against him in greater numbers but for this: ever since the tag team of Newt Gingrich and Rush Limbaugh, the stink on the Clinton brand continued in a downward slide all the way to Death Valley.

If only my great-grandchildren could get a dollar for each time a student in the future will ask, "Wait, I don't understand. Bill cheated on Hillary, and then somehow Hillary Clinton paid the price in 2016?" The Republican misbranding machine has truly been a work of art. War hero John Kerry somehow got labeled an unpatriotic *swift boat* commander during his political battle against a man who had joined the Air National Guard strictly to avoid the Vietnam draft; Obama was successfully labeled Muslim and foreign-born despite incontrovertible evidence to the contrary.

Joe Biden was one of the most conservative Democratic senators alive. The Conservative Union rates senators, and in the last 50 years, Alaska's Mike Gravel, who left the Senate in 1981, was the only Democrat with a more conservative voting record than Biden. Does that sound like someone who will pull the country to the left? In numerous ways, Trump is ideologically far Left of Biden. Trade protectionism, particularly tariffs and trade wars, pulling out of trade and other international agreements including NATO and the WHO, and consistent blurring of the lines between industry and government are all extreme leftist policies. Add to that his cozying up to North Korea and if not literally, figuratively crawling right up Putin's ass, and anyone should see that we've never had a president from either party this far left since Karl Marx first learned to read. Trump's desire to limit free speech, particularly a free press, his affinity for propaganda, and his manipulation of public media to project

244

propaganda may all be practices that have been observed in fascist regimes, but they were adopted most enthusiastically by the Soviet Communist Party. One thing you can count on: If the Republicans are complaining about a Democratic pickpocket, check your pocket for a Republican hand. They are consistently blaming their opposition for their own crimes. That tactic will never get old for them.

To be clear, Trump's thirst for power easily falls within the realm of fascist doctrine, but I would argue that this thirst, such that it is, does not stem from ideological aspiration. He appears to desire certain powers because he believes that the President of the United States should have these powers. Like many of his adherents, he simply has an immature understanding of the functions of government. He equates the role of president as being *the boss*, and to his understanding, the boss calls all the shots—particularly when the boss is heir to a vast real estate fortune who has rarely been told that he can't have what he wants.

In taking a deeper dive, Trump's aspirations for power more closely resemble that of a sixth grade mean girl rather than a fascist dictator wannabee. As evidence, I point to his presidential record in which he has failed in nearly every courtroom challenge. If he had true ideological aspirations, he would have better positioned himself legally.

In fairness, Trump has delivered consistent results on one single front: the appointment of conservative judges. It's not so much a matter of quantity, as some Republicans brag about and some Democrats fear. In December 2016, there were 105 vacancies for federal judgeships. In December 2019, there were 78. Trump has though, nominated judges, on average, ten years younger than Obama's nominations. These judges will preside longer with the net effect of moving the judiciary to the Right, but the age of Trump appointees has not been out of line historically. As significant as they are, the Right further inflates their relevance because they have so few other genuine accomplishments to point to. The picks have been fiscally and socially conservative, fulfilling most of the aspirations of Trump's coalition, such that it is. Liberals would have more reason to be concerned if Trump's administration had been winning more battles in court, but as of July 2019, in cases against state attorneys general, the administration prevailed only 11% of the time.

That Mitch McConnell approved almost no court nominations in Obama's last two years in office (with Merrick Garland only one of many slights) is far more problematic. Trump's court picks come from McConnell and ultimately from Republican financial backers. There are reasons almost nothing happens in DC without McConnell's approval. His public power-grab is eclipsed only by the power he's been consolidating behind the scenes. Democracy is being stress-tested.

Trump has accomplished almost nothing of meaning legislatively. Most of his executive actions have been symbolic. Only five new miles of his promised wall have been built to date. He's leveraged the loyalty of his base to intimidate Republicans into obedience, but he has done little with this power other than to preserve his political standing and keep himself out of jail. He is the ultimate mean girl.

Americans didn't elect a leader with a platform and an ideology. They elected an addict, disguised as a crafted character—a troubled man with a thirst for attention and division whose only ideology is governed by a psychological condition known as Histrionic Personality Disorder. It shouldn't have been a surprise. Trump has led the country exactly as we might have expected he would, following the release of the Access Hollywood tape. He showed himself in that moment to be clumsy, bombastic, arrogant, and only out for himself.

The country faces some kind of crisis in nearly every presidency, and we had all been hoping that Trump's crisis would be minor. We should have hoped harder. The Obama administration encountered Ebola, SARS, and MERS epidemics. Although deadlier, those viruses were not as virulent as SARS-Cov-2. Understand though that as of June 2020, every other First World country is quickly getting back to something resembling normalcy.

I think that many of us can imagine that an Obama or Clinton administration would have had a much more functional relationship with China than Trump. With certainty, they would not have removed CDC assets from China that existed for the expressed purpose of interrupting another Chinese pandemic before the virus left China. It's crystal clear that scientists under a Democratic (and nearly any other Republican) president would have tracked and traced whatever cases did get out. It's possible a pandemic could have been avoided entirely, or certainly resulted in far fewer cases, particularly in the US.

Though it's difficult to prove such would've/could've hypotheticals, we can certainly be informed by looking to other countries as benchmarks. The major East Asian nations– South Korea, Japan, Taiwan, Singapore, Viet Nam, Thailand, Cambodia, China, and even the Philippines all suffered far fewer cases and deaths than the US, despite having mostly higher population densities. In Western Europe, where the virus first emerges in large numbers outside of China, following a poor initial response, caseloads were brought down to an order of magnitude less than the US, despite having a higher total population, higher population density, and similar culture. Australia and New Zealand put us to shame—our death and caseloads are thousands of times greater. Australasia has the benefit of being remote, but it also had a healthy flow of people between China and Europe. In trailing the world in the success of the American pandemic response, any reasonable analysis will conclude that had we adopted measures similar to the rest of the world, to include more universal mask-wearing and stricter social distancing, we would have fared far better, and ultimately suffered far fewer casualties.

If you imagine for a moment, the United States scientific and medical communities firing on all engines, CDC assets in place in China, scientists and politicians acting proactively at the first sign of trouble in Wuhan, close coordination with WHO—you know, the way it was done with SARS, MERS, and Ebola— it's easy to imagine a very different scenario where infection spread was far lower throughout the world, particularly in the US. Imagine how many fewer cases there would be in

South America and Mexico if the US had a small fraction of its actual caseload. Can you picture, as I can, our economy being returned to normal or near-normal months ago?

Reality instead was that in Florida alone, where we are governed by Ron DeSantis, a man who couldn't dig his way any further up Donald Trump's toosh if he had power tools, our infection rate has been consistently greater than all the countries in the world but three: Brazil, India, and of course, the USA. Just Florida alone! You have to have some serious A-level incompetence to reach these heights and yet still be unwilling to change course!

How We Got Here...The Beginning

We can reasonably conclude that when SARS-CoV-2 was first identified in late 2019 in Wuhan, China as a potentially lethal novel coronavirus, it surely would have been mentioned in a President's Daily Brief (PDB). This is where our leaders learn about, among other things, the threats the nation faces. Remember when protecting the American people was the president's greatest responsibility? You can't protect the American people unless you understand the potential dangers, and that begins with attendance *and* attention at the PDB's. In those times when Trump does attend, it's widely reported that he only pays attention when the concepts are simple and ideally are in some way about him.

There's no reason to believe that SARS-COV-2 captured the president's attention before his first public mention of it on January 22, following the first confirmed case in the USA. While it is true that Trump was impeached by the House in December, and he had a trial that took place from January 16 to February 5, it does not take substantial time, knowledge, or energy to ask the CDC Director to develop a plan to tackle worst-case virus scenarios. It would have been his only meaningful presidential responsibility during that time. If the PDB indicated a potential cost of millions of American lives as some predictions did, it might have been nice to have grabbed somebody or anybody in a suit in the White House and to have told them they were responsible for not letting millions of Americans die. Seriously anyone. Even Jared, though ideally not him.

What is clear is that Trump tasked no person to manage a virus response in the first two months of the year. I know—you can Google "labradoodle covid" and the name of a dog breeder will appear and you can read about how HHS Secretary Azar deputized dog breeder Brian

Harrison to save the country from a novel coronavirus. I think hindsight makes it readily apparent that Azar could have tasked one of the Labradoodles instead, and we would be no worse off today. I guess it sounds kinda funny when you type it out and put in on paper, but these are just the facts.

Ideally, Mr. Harrison ought to have been briefing the president regularly such that the full power of the American government could have been aimed at our virus response. Of course, that was never going to happen because, as the entire White House staff understands, Trump is incapable of managing subordinates. That's how we ended up with Mike Pence leading the COVID-19 task force. Pence understands no more biology and medicine than a tenth grade C-student, but he has a much more important skill. All Trump has to say to him is, "Mike, do this," and Pence knows that his only real objectives are to give Trump credit for anything good that happens, deny the administration's role in anything bad, and every time he talks publicly, look in the camera and pretend he knows exactly what he is doing, despite all evidence to the contrary. That's it. No responsibility for actual results because Trump has only achieved such lofty goals in his life by pure accident. It's not clear that he even understands the concept of true responsibility.

A crime family has higher standards. The only good news is that this is why Trump is incapable of leading a successful fascist revolution (though we must remain guarded as it's not inconceivable that he could inspire one in people with greater capabilities). The only real precedence for his level of incompetence and disregard for performance has been in some of the failed Communist states of Eastern Europe and South America where cronyism, corruption, and reign by fear have been the guiding principles of government.

Trump's inability to delegate, as previously mentioned, is his greatest weakness as a leader—besides his lack of morality, uncontained narcissism, lack of empathy, and nonexistent emotional intelligence. But his emotional fragility with respect to his ego has made it impossible, probably throughout his entire life, to be able to effectively delegate. He has to exert direct control in everything he touches. When a subordinate appears to be successfully doing a good job, Trump feels compelled to undercut that success so that he, Donald Trump, is seen as superior to all others. Someone needs to tell the president that if he can't fill that emotional hole with the tears of the families of 130,000 dead, he might want to try another way.

Generally, there are stabilizing forces that should have kept the country safe from reaching the precipice on which we now stand. The Peter Principle, in which a person presumably rises to a level where they are poorly equipped to do their job but no higher, predicts that incompetent people do not reach dangerous heights of power. The Peter Principle is a reliable theory, but Trump was born into money, and wealth can be even more reliable.

The Peter Principle generally works for politicians. Wealthy individuals have historically run for positions "no higher" than governor or senator in their first election. It's obvious Trump would have been a dreadful governor as he is unable to govern. He would have similarly failed as a senator as that position requires you to understand basic principles of government as well as be able to lead a staff, skills of which Trump has shown no aptitude. Without experience in these "entry" level positions, it's difficult to garner enough party support to win a presidential primary. Trump was able to leverage social media, primarily by stirring controversy on Twitter, to amplify that one true skill of self-promotion.

Although his fortune was the only "qualification" he offered in the election process to validate the legitimacy of his candidacy, he convinced people that he was a gifted businessman. The seeds had been sown years before with the only real success of his life—his role in *The Apprentice*. His presidential run was in many respects a sequel to the TV show, with him continuing his role as all-knowing boss. That so many people bought this false persona is evidence enough of the amazing power of branding.

Trump's business failures, punctuated by six bankruptcies, should have prevented him from rising higher. Certainly, his performance record never justified any executive position unrelated to his only demonstrated talent of marketing.

Where wealthy businesspeople had failed, Trump's cult of (*addictive*) personality shtick connected with a sufficiently large enough segment of voters to time and again propel him to the next level of presidential election success. Trump has been so often criticized for his lack of empathy for those in pain, but analysts fail to note his remarkable ability to connect with those consumed by anger. It's a talent better suited to the role of antichrist than president, but still a remarkable talent.

The final safeguard that Trump defeated was the media. Because he was so outrageous, consistently destroying norms and becoming increasingly preposterous with each passing day, the news media couldn't get enough. Few people who understood politics took him seriously, but his large number of supporters made him consistently relevant. The result was an unprecedented level of free press that validated his candidacy in a way that no paid advertising could. Trump's ability to suck up every last bit of news oxygen has made him the most covered person of all time. So, despite the revulsion I feel every time I see a news clip of him at a rally, berating the press to a level that endangers the First Amendment, a little part of me has to laugh. I have to think Trump is not so far gone that he doesn't fully realize those people with the cameras are the very ones who put him where he is today.

Of course, he would never have become that media darling if not for that third of the electorate, those people who devour every drop of negative energy that he offers, that are now seen as his base. The dark message these people connect with is a toxic mix of xenophobia, racial prejudice, anti-liberalism, and anti-intellectualism. One commonality amongst all of these character flaws is a lack of emotional intelligence—further support of the concept that there are a plethora of addicts and alcoholics among the Trump base.

In fairness to a large block of Trump's supporters, the world has left many of them behind. The digital economy, where borders have lost their economic significance, has reorganized wealth throughout the world, with the American middle class having been neglected to the point of frustration. A few clever pundits noticed how strongly Trump's message reverberated with this segment of American society and how that resonance pointed to a 2016 upset. These poor souls are now the neglected children of an addicted father who promised toys and all manner of appropriate care but delivered primarily beatings. Few people understand why they maintain their loyalty. Though Trump is in some ways just a vessel for various, yes, deplorable notions, the man stands unique in his superior ability to leverage his negative message while being entirely incapable of accomplishing anything else.

It would be erroneous to compare Trump to some random drunk screaming on a street corner. He has achieved a certain kind of self-promotion greatness that should elevate him to the likes of Stalin, Castro, and Idi Amin, though Trump may most closely resemble the inept Benito Mussolini.

Mussolini's father, who the "dictator to be" adored, was an unemployed alcoholic. Though Benito did not appear to have a problem with alcoholism, being close to his father may have made him better able to connect to the marginalized elements of society that are most ripe for fascist rule. It must also be said that the aforementioned dictators had experience and skill in governance and leadership where Donald Trump has none.

It's apparent that before he became president, he never supervised more than a few dozen people, and they were typically assistants, secretaries, accountants, and lawyers. It doesn't appear that he had anyone junior to him making substantial real estate deals, so he never supervised anyone in his supposed area of knowledge, except perhaps his children. He does appear to have micromanaged his legal strategies over the years, and he probably viewed the roles of accountant and secretary as too vulgar to require his attention. Trump famously pretended to be his own publicist on several occasions. Was he too poor to be able to afford a publicist or just felt that he could do the job better than anyone else? And of course, we all know that he wrote his own doctor's note declaring his physical fitness. He is simply paralyzed with the ridiculous notion that he can do absolutely everything better than everyone else.

Unlike any election win in modern history, Trump had considered almost no one for his senior staff or Cabinet by the time he won. This is unusual on several fronts, most notably, that presidential candidates want advisors (many who are eventually appointed to those senior positions) to help them through the election process. Typically, these advisors create intelligent strategies and platforms that they hope become policy. Trump was never, even today, concerned with "strategies" and "platforms;" he was not interested in the opinions of others—expert or otherwise, unless they mimicked his own. There was also that issue, if you believe the reports, that he didn't think he would win. As it was reported that he did not have a circle of friends (particularly personal contacts with national policy experience) anywhere near as wide as a typical politician, Trump faced a steep uphill battle to build a successful Cabinet after his election win.

When he became the surprise President-elect, he had to quickly form a Cabinet from nothing. Despite his unsuitability for office, he had his pick of a large number of qualified aspirants. Of course, Trump's ability in this most important of presidential tasks was primarily informed by his experience on *The Apprentice*. It should have come as no surprise that Trump made Cabinet selections a far more public process than ever before.

This was the beginning of the Trump-Fox-voter-base closed feedback loop. Many of Trump's decisions and comments seemed to have no logical basis, other than that they should benefit his interests or appeal to his voters' emotional aspirations. With Fox News acting as a "free market" of conservative ideas where the viewers' beliefs and desires, rather than facts, drive the news, Trump would discover the pulse of his base from TV and then create policy out of that.

On the surface, that isn't entirely awful to have public policy reflective of public desire. The problem comes when this echo-chamber approach locks out all other input. That's when you end up with leaders that fail to encourage mask usage when every single bona fide expert tells us masks save lives.

Trump's lack of experience with direct supervision, combined with his low emotional intelligence, could have been responsible for his failure to understand that people applying for jobs tend to be more deferential during the application process than when they actually take the job. Trump did select a few reasonable Cabinet members, but those with any intelligence or moral compass didn't last. It's possible even Trump didn't realize until later that the only real quality he values in a subordinate is blind loyalty, with an ability and willingness to pay homage to the brand *Trump* at every possible opportunity. That is how we end up with the Cabinet of sycophants.

Ben Carson is one of only a few Cabinet members remaining from Trump's initial cadre, and he may be the least sycophantic of the lot. Carson understands little of his job at the HUD (as implied to me by one of his subordinates on an airplane one day), so he takes minimal action and rarely makes big news. On those occasions when he does, I suspect Trump's view is that it is *black stuff*, and he likely ignores it. Worthy of note, with race relations very much in the news, Carson, probably at Trump's direction, has tried to take a bigger public role, and not all of Dr. Carson's comments have been supportive of the president. So although I don't expect it, I wouldn't be shocked to see Carson gone before the election, as Trump has been running out of ways to shock us, and firing the only black person in his Cabinet in the middle of a crisis in race relations would probably do the trick.

We have in this presidency, a government that would have to be substantially spackled before it could be considered merely "hallowed out." Cabinet members must continuously kiss Trump's booty to maintain their jobs. They are terrified of taking a stand against him, either publicly or privately. Thousands of government positions have gone unfulfilled because Trump has failed to staff them. This is not because he doesn't have the time or support of Congress. Certainly, judicial appointments that tangibly advance Republican interests get filled as quickly as possible, but other federal positions that do the important jobs of government have gone neglected, and that has not been by accident. As previously mentioned, the last thing Republicans want is to have someone say, "I'm here from the government, and I'm here to help." And then actually help.

So although it would be a nice little luxury to have had federal officials making plans to fight pandemics and then executing those plans; to have had people maintaining our emergency stockpile of ventilators and PPE, and when faced with a crisis, doing whatever it takes to ramp up those supplies; to have had the CDC staffed with personnel who were capable of successfully managing the creation of a diagnostic test for a novel virus and then interfacing with industry and universities to ensure enough tests became available to adequately respond to a pandemic – although those little luxuries would have been nice, Trump's failure to adequately staff the government ensured that we were not prepared. It's important to note that before the first bat from Wuhan ever pooped COVID-19 on someone's sandwich, the seeds for failure had long been sowed.

Lest one believe that it was just a few "bad apples" of leadership that made us unlucky, it's important to understand that Trump's failure of a Cabinet is a band of misfits that have made a disaster of nearly every challenge they've faced:

Treasury: Have you seen our budget deficit this year? (Hint: largest in history)

Attorney Gen:	Thousands of the nation's government lawyers have publicly admonished him for unethical and unconstitutional behavior.
Agriculture:	Have you seen the videos of millions of tons of food being plowed back into the ground because no one in, say the Agriculture Department, could figure out how to distribute food to the millions out of work?
Labor:	Highest unemployment since the Great Depression.
HUD:	I'm not going to pick on Dr. Carson anymore.
Energy:	Remember Rick Perry and … energy? LOL. If you don't, Google it. Secretary Perry is another rare violator of the Peter Principle.
Veterans:	A white supremacist who worships the Confederate Army and lied about this in his Senate hearings.
State:	The US is no longer respected by allies or enemies. International relations are so bad as to be considered irreparable by some.
Defense:	Declining morale and readiness, mismanaged acquisitions.
Interior:	First Secretary released federal lands to oil and gas exploration mocking global warming concerns, then he resigned following ethics violations; the current guy is an oil lobbyist.
Commerce:	Failed to negotiate a China agreement; failed to make any meaningful gains in international trade.
HHS:	Have you seen the COVID-19 statistics? Well, if you reached this point… Good luck if you need a COVID-19 test.
Transportation:	Have you been on a 737 MAX lately? 16 months after being grounded, they're still not flying at a cost to the industry of billions of dollars.

Education:	The Education Secretary without an education; currently doing her best to create an explosion of viral spread by sending kids back to schools with no plan or federal support to mitigate the loss of life or illness or any of the problems this stupidity would cause.
Homeland Sec.:	How secure do you feel? Not so much? You mean putting all of those kids in cages at the border hasn't made us safe from COVID-19?

And the Cabinet-level officials?

Chief of Staff:	Lol, on like number 26 or so. The first 25 (okay it might have been a few less) couldn't tolerate Trump and/or stay in his good graces for long.
Intelligence:	Well, Trump doesn't listen to his intel agencies – publicly disavows our entire intelligence community in favor of Putin's lies. I'm surprised no one has felt the earth move each time every single deceased American who fought 20th century Communism rolled over in their graves.
EPA:	Former pollution industry lobbyist tasked to protect the environment; last pollution lobbyist resigned amid widespread scandals. But please, Mr. President, tell us how that swamp draining operation is going.
SBA:	At best, a source of mediocrity.
US Trade Rep:	No meaningful accomplishments to his name since taking office. The new trade deals have yet to demonstrate tangible benefits.
CIA:	Gina Haspel, seemingly the only competent and ethical government leader – either an oversight by Trump or I missed something. Trump doesn't listen to her anyway.

These aren't the senior leaders of government. This is a Saturday Night Live skit. As the Shakespearean cast of fools above makes clear, Donald Trump did not become the absolute worst president in history on his own. He had some help. Don't get me wrong, he did the heavy lifting, but with corruption and incompetence as defining characteristics of the Trump Cabinet, it's sometimes surprising that we muddled along as well as we have up until 2020—I guess if you consider a slew of indictments and resignations, a bunch of failed legislation and executive actions overturned by the courts, and an impeachment "muddling along."

But now, as our country faces multiple crises and the failing of our most important institutions, the federal government seems impotent in its ability to accomplish anything meaningful in helping the American public. And yes, I did say, "the failure of our most important institutions." Hospitals and all levels of healthcare, police, K-12 schools, universities, and state and local governments are all under stress and strain unlike anything ever experienced before. It is a testament to the strength of our society up until 2016 that the country has not entirely imploded.

As the virus was taking hold in America, in the first ten weeks of the year, none of the members of the aforementioned clown-car Cabinet were doing anything meaningful to mitigate the disaster rushing toward us. And with apologies to my dog as I wouldn't want the job, but Dobby would have done far less damage as president in permitting the virus to overwhelm the country. He would not have laid the seeds to where even today, after 130,000 deaths and 3 million cases, with the virus growing out of control, we still have a large swath of people who have been led to believe this disaster is a hoax. The absolute, galling absurdity!

Dobby wouldn't have encouraged his followers to disregard wearing masks, social distancing, and quarantine, and call for the reduction of testing—the only limited tools we have to fight the spread of this disease. He would not have made every effort in the world to dominate the news cycle, thereby hiding the realities of the pandemic from even those who might change their behavior for the better if only they were exposed to correct information. And Dobby would not have explicitly silenced those in his administration, particularly Anthony Fauci and Rick Bright, who have been willing and able to arm the American public with the most accurate information and recommendations of the moment, rather than the drivel that we are fed every time Trump held a "task force" briefing. And perhaps most telling of all, Dobby would not have created an environment where right-wing extremists feel emboldened enough to intimidate public health officials all over the country into resigning because to once again channel Nicholson's character, these extremists "can't handle the truth."

Instead, the American people were on the receiving end of ... let's just say we all now know how it feels to be a bedpan. Trump first ignored the virus; then he said it was nothing; then he said it would soon be nothing; then he said it was a hoax, and it had always been nothing. After ten weeks of that, he decided to declare a public health emergency, and he started closing borders, only after the virus had arrived on our shores in strength. Then, he claimed to have saved millions even though he had taken no tangible actions. When asked what he had been doing in the first ten weeks of the year to avoid a catastrophe, he continually pointed to his shutdown of air traffic to China, which as I earlier detailed, was not his doing but was instead driven by the airlines. By this point, he had permitted the CDC to start releasing recommendations limiting gatherings of at first, to no more than 250 people. They soon ramped that number down to no more than 10. As the CDC's guidelines were not directives nor anything firmer than suggestions, state and local governments made their own decisions and set limits from as low as 10 to as high as 1,000.

Meanwhile, Trump continued to downplay the danger and effects of the virus, which cost many lives. I suppose his comments about ingesting antiseptics and sodomizing oneself with a black light will make the history books, along with some of his other greatest hits, such as telling everyone throughout the pandemic that the virus is going to just disappear, because ironically, yes, we all know it will eventually disappear. However, adults understand that, like the Spanish flu and smallpox and polio, these dangerous diseases kill and disable a lot of people first. I think, though, the very worst of his leadership failures was to encourage what could arguably be considered insurrection with his tweets of "LIBERATE MINNESOTA," "LIBERATE MICHIGAN," and "LIBERATE VIRGINIA."

With the breaching of each long-established norm since Trump's escalator descent, we know that we are all becoming increasingly desensitized. It's just... this was the President of the United States. It is illegal for ANYONE to call for insurrection. To be clear, this is not protected in the First Amendment. That the president of the United States should call for open insurrection against state governments that are acting in the safety, welfare, and best interests of its citizens.... This is genuinely worse than standing on the corner of Fifth Avenue and shooting someone. By a long shot.

Trump tried to pass off his call for insurrection as some sort of deranged joke, and media outlets only had so much airtime and in-print real estate to offer before they were on to the next act of insanity. I just have to ask, could George Washington or Thomas Jefferson or even for that matter, Herbert Camacho (of Idiocracy fame) fathom such an action by an American President? No. I know none of them are alive, but I feel pretty comfortable speaking for them. No.

Those tweets had real consequences. Armed protestors took to the streets with greater zeal; some even occupied the state capitol of Michigan forcing Governor Wittner to abandon the building, fearing for her safety. How many times has something like that happened in the USA since the Civil War? Maybe zero? Many of the more extreme of Trump's followers thought he was calling for civil war, odd as that seems, as the person they revere was already in power (at least for the moment). Again,

I struggle to look back to the beginning of 2020 and find a single presidential decision or even a few statements that I can fully endorse.

Of course, the lies, which have been a staple of possibly every single public appearance of Donald Trump as president, continue in force. This work could not possibly be complete without mentioning the most egregious, which for me have been the lies about how the USA has handled the COVID pandemic better than any country in the world. It hurt my hands to type that last line, it is such an awful, so easily disproven lie. We are arguably the worst, but from even the most generous of perspectives, we are somewhere in the bottom five. Out of 215. We certainly do have the greatest number of infections and the greatest number of deaths throughout the world. A few months ago, I thought that would change. It still might, I suppose, with countries like Brazil.

Let me rephrase that, regarding COVID, there are no other countries like Brazil—other than us. I fear for India, with its incredibly dense population living in extreme poverty. India certainly bore the brunt of the deaths during the Spanish flu. It's a reasonable assumption their case count is grossly underreported (as is Brazil's), and the true death count is likely higher, but for now at least, the infection spread has not been reported as a conflagration.

The only reason that the American per capita death count isn't the absolute worst in the world is because the average age of our infected citizens is lower than the rest of the world, and the majority of our cases occurred later, at a time when doctors could better treat COVID-19. For God's sake, Florida alone with our population of 21 million currently has *three times* the number of new daily cases than the entire EU, with its population of over 440 million! And Florida's positivity rate is far higher, meaning we're in reality doing worse than reported! No, Donald J. Trump, we are nowhere within a universe of handling this pandemic well.

As for calling for *less* testing, I just can't. There's little of use that I can say to anyone who doesn't already understand what's wrong with that.

This analysis would be sorely lacking if I didn't mention the fact that if Trump had simply listened to his science advisors, the country and his political future would have been in much better shape. Yes, he is inherently a science denier as are his followers. Adopting the guidance of experts might have cost him some of his base. But if he were anywhere near as intelligent as he or even some of his critics believe that he is, he would have realized the potential danger of COVID-19 and how detrimental it could be to his election chances. Trump doesn't seem to have the capability to understand the basic science, and what's worse, he genuinely believes he knows better than his medical staff. COVID-19 will likely ensure an election loss, and when that happens, it will have been very much a self-inflicted wound. If by some combination of election fraud, foreign interference, and mass insanity Trump is reelected, Lord help us.

For years, I've felt that the president's narcissism has turned him into a circus clown, performing more and more ridiculous antics just to hold our attention—not too dissimilar to the proverbial drunk at a party with a lampshade on his head. *Look at me and fill up my emptiness and insecurities with your attention*! Perhaps if all of his critics had just ignored him, he'd have eventually realized that he was not deriving anything of value from his dreadful behavior, and he may have just gone away. That ship of course has sailed.

The remainder of this book will concern what might and should have been. Suffice to say, COVID-19 will not be the last major challenge of the century; or the half-century; or perhaps even the decade. The forces of populism aren't going away. The temptation to bend to mob rule may continue to dominate political discourse. It is critical that we learn to identify and reward markers of good leadership.

But First: The Rest of the Story

I am grateful to still be able to draw on the expertise and experience of my cousin Steven and my dear friend Roger. I've been speaking with both of them since the beginning of the pandemic, and they have continued to inform me in my understanding of COVID-19 as well as John's continued autoimmune dysfunction.

John was getting worse. His frustrations were more common, his vocabulary more divergent. His symptoms were increasing my anxiety more than COVID and at times even more than the stupidity in Washington. Never change a winning game, always change a losing game. We had to change something. The Philadelphia hospital had not yet offered an appointment, so we got more aggressive and insistent, knowing if John's condition progressed much further, we would not be able to take him on a plane. We started him on steroids, which had been effective in the past, and concurrently we returned to treating the only potential source of infection that I could fathom might be toxically reprogramming his immune system—a toenail that had a longtime fungal infection. To be clear, such fungal nails are harmless to just about anyone. Of course, John isn't anyone.

It wasn't conjectured. In discussing John's condition with the parent of another kid with autoimmune encephalitis, I had brought up the toenail, and he had confirmed through discussions with his daughter's specialists that this was potentially hazardous. After removing the nasal polyp last year, John recovered completely without us addressing the stubborn toenail issue, but I hadn't forgotten.

When his symptoms returned, we found a specialist who treated toenail fungus with a series of monthly laser treatments. Initially, it didn't seem to have much effect, except that on the day of his treatments, he got worse. Medically speaking, I viewed this as a confirmatory sign that the toenail was likely causing John's problems. Unfortunately, when the COVID restrictions hit, we had to discontinue the treatments for a few months.

When John's condition worsened, it was truly a blow. I could take COVID-19 with all of its life-altering restrictions and economic implications; I could take the broken ribs and the ensuing months of bad to nonexistent sleep; I had even learned to take John's crazy 2019 on top of his rough start leading to a lifetime of other-abilityness. And of course, I had to take 3+ years watching the country I love devolve into a humiliating mess that I never would have recognized a few short years ago. But when John got sicker, I started wondering if I could take much more.

As soon as we could, Lisa took John back to the podiatrist specialist to complete the laser treatments. It was in a discussion related to this treatment that I realized that she had been skipping his home fungal medicine applications on days that he didn't shower; I explained to Lisa that I didn't think that was a good idea. To be entirely fair to my wonderful wife, she does almost all of his hands-on care, freeing me up to play at my word processor and do the other things I do. Lisa definitely has the tougher job. Caring full time for a handicapped child exhibiting schizophrenic behavior while locked in a house in the middle of a worldwide pandemic? Like they say, *I don't remember seeing that in any of the brochures.*

Neither are there guidebooks for John's disease, kind of like another disease I've heard about that's going around, except with COVID-19, there's probably too much information on line—with autoimmune encephalitis, not nearly enough. After restarting the laser treatments, and between the steroids and the more aggressive antifungal care, along with a resumption of the neurologic treatment that was successful in 2019, John finally started getting better.

Slowly, we weaned him off of all of his prescribed neurologic meds until he was only on the toenail medicine and the smaller list of homeopathic anti-inflammatory medicines we had found to be effective. Then came my aunt's dramatic illness, and the family's attention focused on her. Lisa and I forgot about all of John's treatment for two days, and that's all it took for his encephalitis to flare up again. We restarted the steroids, the strongest tool we have, but it must be used judiciously as it can cause problems if used for too long. Steroids are also immunosuppressant. It doesn't take a lot of medical knowledge to understand the concern there. It will take another six months to complete his laser treatments. Like COVID patients who have been through the gauntlet and come out the other side, my family will have to hone our skills in patience.

* * * * *

So far, ours has not been the hardest luck story of 2020. I'm at that stage in my life where I've had to bury too many relations in the last decade, and right now, I'm just feeling numb, which supposedly is not a stage of grief at all, but it is for me. Maybe it's a privilege thing. I know I can sit here and type and pay my bills. My job is not under immediate threat. I live in a gated community where I rarely see strangers drive by my house. Many people in the upper-middle-class neighborhood where I reside seem to understand little of the challenges of those less fortunate. I grew up with a mother on welfare and food stamps, which may not give me complete understanding, but I have had enough peeks behind the socioeconomic curtain to have seen the larger picture. I know at this moment people are struggling with dying loved ones while they simultaneously handle economic hardship, a lack of food in their fridge, and maybe a few other issues too gruesome to mention.

Meanwhile, Donald Trump, at least for the moment, has a nice house to live in, a wife whose beauty he believes reflects well on him, and as of this writing, remains gainfully employed. How dare he say, as he did and as his disgraceful supporters have also argued, that his response to SARS-Cov-2 was hampered because of impeachment. How dare he. How dare any of them. Trump wanted the job. He took an oath to do the fucking job. And he didn't. And now the rest of us are living through a nightmare.

July 22, 2020:

My aunt passed away. In case you were wondering how things went dark in the last few paragraphs. It's been a shock to the family. She was 81, but she was healthy with no known comorbidities. To the end, she'd been a strong and willful woman. Even two days before she died, I couldn't fathom her not surviving. I'm not sure what day it happened, probably about five days ago.

I'm numb, which suits me fine for now. I haven't written for a week. I just couldn't. Now I have to write. It's therapy, but even more, it's a message in desperate need of being heard. Now that my aunt is gone, I've gained an understanding and perspective that no one wants. This invisible virus that is out there, nearly everywhere—is a serial killer the likes of which few can fathom.

I'm the first to admit that early on, I thought there could be an advantage to catching "the bug" and having it over and done with. My age and health seemed, in the initial understanding of the disease, to put me in a low-risk category. With time, we've grown an understanding that this is often not the case, but even so, when I first heard about my aunt being COVID positive, I actually told her, "You lucky dog. You've got it now, and you're going to get through it and not have anything more to worry about."

I knew this line of thinking was patently false, but she had already caught it. She was scared, and I figured, may as well spin the best story possible.

You'll find very few people being cavalier once they've been personally touched by this monster. Not the symptomless version, of course. That just seems to be a little joke that God or fate or the virus itself can laugh about—how most COVID-19 positive individuals barely notice a problem. To them, a hangnail is a greater problem. For some 20% though….

Imagine the edge of a cliff, where people are lined up peering into the canyon below. Imagine how close you'd want to get to the edge after you see the ground there give way as someone close to you falls into the abyss. That's how the pandemic feels to me right now. Meanwhile, a large percentage of our population wants to put as many of us as they can right up to that edge, starting with our kids and their teachers. This is madness.

Things aren't slowing down, they're speeding up. We've reached over 70,000 cases a day approaching Dr. Fauci's warning of 100,000 daily. Our testing system is entirely broken. Trump has said, correctly (for a change) that we have tested more than any other country. He fails to mention that we have more cases than any other country, and he fails to acknowledge that it takes too long for test results to be returned. The two reasons to test are to confirm a diagnosis so that doctors can prescribe the correct treatment, and to contact trace so that infectious individuals can quarantine. Because test results are taking too long, doctors have to use cat scans and other markers to diagnose COVID.

Since results are taking a week or longer, they're useless for contact tracing. After a week, you're either sick, and perhaps in the hospital, or you're home well and should (in most cases) no longer be contagious. Even two days to get results is not optimal.

Whoever believes they might have the virus enough to go for a test needs to know as soon as possible, so they *know* they have to social distance. We're getting close to a million tests a day at a cost of at least $100 per test. Nearly $100 million a day in testing and it's all medically useless, other than to reveal how dreadful we're doing. $36 billion on an annualized basis, for nearly nothing! Some of that money is coming from the government but most is being paid by the insurance companies. Either way, you and I will be picking up that tab.

Meanwhile, the president seems to have devoted the majority of his time the past few weeks to protecting Confederate statues. If this book somehow survives far into the future, no you didn't miss a page or any words. A pandemic is killing 1,000 people daily, and the president is more concerned about the statues of American traitors. He has deployed federal law enforcement, for now to Oregon but potentially elsewhere, to "protect" federal buildings.

I don't quite know how to…. I don't know what to type next. Anyone without a notion of how entirely fucked up this is, I can only see as irredeemable. For anyone else, I just have nothing. No way to parody this, no silver lining. Nothing I can say will help put this in perspective. November 3rd, vote like your life depends upon it. It does.

Oh, and the president wore a mask in public and tweeted nice things about masks this week, so … yippee. And he held his first COVID briefing since Lysolgate. Reading from prepared statements, he said the bare minimum to be considered not crazy. We've been down this road before, so we know it won't last. Untreated addicts always return to their old ways.

Nearly half of the country's infections continue to occur inside the Three COVID Amigos – Florida, Texas, and California. Everybody understands what's wrong in Florida, except Governor DeSantis. Meanwhile, Texas Governor Abbot has been consistently inconsistent. He's trying to appease both sides, which must be a challenge as these "sides" are mutually exclusive. Meanwhile, cable news is looking to Florida trying to get DeSantis to explain how he snatched defeat out of the hands of victory because up until mid-June, Florida had been doing well.

In California, there are no easy answers. It's by far our biggest state by population, and they were the first to quarantine. Their numbers on a per capita basis are not nearly as bad as the raw numbers suggest. The brunt of the infections is in the LA basin, and climate is most likely the culprit. Poverty may also play a role, and race has been discussed as a factor, but wealth has to be parsed away from those numbers. Unhealthy eating, often a byproduct of poverty, can lead to weight gain and diabetes. Wealthy people wear N95 masks and can often work at home and have numerous other tools to protect themselves from infection. Poor people are using bandannas for masks, which are probably the least protective, and well, you get the picture. There are a lot of related risk factors.

Texas Gov. Abbot knows he screwed up because he warned everyone correctly that Texas' numbers would go up. So, we know he has public health officials advising him, and he isn't disputing their guidance. He just lacks either the political will or the clout to fix the problem. Texas has one foot on the gas, one foot on the brake, and it's hard to say what's going on when it takes at least a couple of weeks to see the effects of each policy change. As there are numerous local policy inputs throughout the state, it will be challenging to tie any decision in Texas to any particular result. The gross COVID numbers are similar to Florida, but Texas has 30% more people, so it's doing better than Florida per capita. Texas's downward trajectory started a bit earlier and looks more decisive for the moment.

Florida, my home state…it's just *crazy town* in Tallahassee, where DeSantis must be playing the song, "Everything is Awesome" throughout the halls of the state capital 24/7. Disneyworld is open; Universal Studios is open; just about everything is open. And we have the highest per capita infection rates and COVID-19 deaths in the country for the past 10 days. If this were a movie…strike that; when this becomes a movie, the writers are going to have to change the DeSantis character into a smarter version of himself because reality is just a bridge too far.

The entirety of COVID-19 infection transmittal analysis involves predicting human behavior. Good luck, right? Actually, in aggregate, it's not so tough to build a model of what people will do when faced with certain circumstances, but as analysts attempt to look further into the future and make estimations on the circumstances people will face, accurate modeling becomes increasingly challenging.

A Tour of Crazy Town

Many of the flawed arguments amount to rationalization—flawed arguments with predetermined conclusions designed to appear logical. "Well, we're opening up so more people might be getting sick. Even if the media reports are true, the people getting sick are just younger and foolish. They're being hospitalized less and dying way less. Meanwhile, things are opening up. We can get back to work! We can go to our favorite restaurants, and bars, and the economy is getting back to normal! It's all good!"

To those desperate to return to "normal," Trump and DeSantis are the perfect authority figures, confirming everything they want to hear. Why believe anything else?

As hospitalizations rise and the death rate follows, people recognize the danger. Nature in its infinite wisdom produces stabilizing forces. In this case, more people are realizing that masks are not only smart but necessary, and other social distancing measures are mandated. Each change means altering or adjusting the models, unless those changes are predicted in advance. One can imagine how complicated a job it is to accurately forecast infection metrics. Frankly, it's a testament to the intelligence of the models and their creators that they can get anywhere close. However, it doesn't seem as impressive to those of us who work with graphs and mathematical functions because with little work at all, one can frequently look at a chart and visually extrapolate a guestimate that can be accurate when conditions are linear and stable. In the real world, though, conditions are rarely linear and stable. Who could predict what day Trump would declare that it is "patriotic to wear a mask?" Not Trump, I would guess.

Jul 24: Fifteen states set new records for COVID hospitalizations. Even as I type, corrective forces are taking hold in those states; citizens and municipal politicians are changing their minds about masks and social distancing, in some cases in direct opposition to the authority figures above them. Those most unable to challenge authority will be the slowest to alter their behaviors, but make no mistake, behavior is changing. A recent poll reported on CNN stated that 75% of Americans believe that there should be mandatory mask orders in place. We've come a long way, even if there is a long way to go.

Unfortunately, citizens react primarily to the mortality numbers, which as discussed, lag behind behavioral changes by a month or more. Some people will alter their behavior, not see an immediate change, and then conclude that none of the "experts" have a clue. The result is something akin to a free market approach to fighting the pandemic. One need only point to any of the other 200 plus countries that have responded much better to COVID-19 with a coordinated, centralized, science-based approach, to fully appreciate the error of our ways. Once again, the free market does not always offer the optimal solution! There are times, such as now, when it is the worst possible approach.

COVID might have first exploded in Washington, New York and the rest of the Northeast, but that was largely the result of a few governors delaying a very difficult decision by a few days. The country has had months now to prepare for, understand, and communicate to its citizens what is needed to successfully defeat this virus. Republican governors have offered platitudes and excuses while downplaying and distorting important knowledge that citizens need to know to defeat the virus, and the result of that foolish policy has been to put the majority of Republican states in the category of worst-performing. To be clear, a few Republican states are among the safest in the country, but these states – Wyoming, Montana, and the Dakotas are only safe because of low population densities.

I've heard many times that the virus doesn't care what political party you belong to. I strongly disagree. If the virus or its components could vote, it would undoubtedly vote Republican. I hate stating this. I do. It's a catch-22 when one political party becomes corrupted. If the problem isn't highlighted, then it doesn't get fixed. But anyone who emphasizes this is viewed as partisan, and their concerns are discarded.

In the Watergate era, Nixon's White House counsel, John Dean, referred to a "growing cancer" within the Nixon Presidency. Just last year he said, "There is very much a cancer growing on this (Trump) presidency."

The thing about cancer is that it spreads. I would argue that this cancer has spread throughout the Republican Party. The only remedy made available by our Founding Fathers to excise this cancer is found at the ballot box, but like a disease that attacks the body's immune system, that remedy is itself very much under attack.

Despite the public's preference for sane social distancing restrictions, the federal government and at least some other Republican politicians continue to push to open up everything, with public schools at the leading edge of this insanity. Fortunately, schools in America are under the direct authority of local school boards. Senior levels of government can hope to influence with recommendations and even threats of withholding funds, but as the federal government has whittled down school funding to such a small percentage, the potential loss of federal funds isn't that much of a threat anymore. Funny enough, probably understanding the problem, the Senate is proposing legislation more than doubling their school funding, just so that more money can be taken away from schools that don't "play ball."

Most school boards appear to be making rational decisions, either opening up with dramatic alterations to enhance safety or simply continuing with online learning until plans are put in place that offer greater guarantees of safety. Just like people aren't going to risk their lives to eat a hamburger in a restaurant, most school boards are not going to approve, or institute plans that don't assure the safety of students and teachers. I fear for those districts where science is simply a disfavored subject.

The return to school that DeSantis is pushing so hard may not happen (at least everywhere) in South Florida—for school-age children. Universities though appear to be full steam ahead. I resigned a faculty position once for a far less threatening reason, but with unemployment around 11%, there may not be a big rush for the doors from the other 89%. Expect to see a lot of PPE bruises on your kids' teachers where schools are open.

* * * * *

I'm near the end of my personal story. The nation's story will continue at least until a new resident occupies the White House. I hope to get the message of this book out first. My schedule must take priority over any desire for meticulousness.

My aunt was a joyful and meaningful part of my life. I didn't imagine when I began this work that it could take this dark personal turn, but now my aunt is gone, and it is unavoidable to believe that had Florida not turned into such a red hot mess, she might never have caught the virus. Even after getting sick, had Remdesivir and/or convalescent plasma been administered right away; had other healthcare assets been made available to her sooner, she might still be with us. The only reason life-saving treatment was delayed was because of the government's mismanagement. My aunt's administration of Remdesivir was delayed for three days due to shortages under the auspices of Trump's favorite governor, Ron DeSantis. I can only imagine the wait has been longer in some blue states, where the federal government has offered less assistance. No one can say with certainty if earlier treatment would have saved my aunt's life, but I can say that statistically speaking, some people have died that otherwise would not have.

My aunt went downhill not nearly as fast as some, but fast enough to shock everyone in her life. Friends of hers were in disbelief. They struggled to wrap their hands around reality, suggesting that she might have been safer staying at home. I rarely bothered to correct them. Her time in the hospital was a miserable thing. No visits by friends or family, my sister and her daughter in grief alone in New Jersey, my family and I alone only minutes away from the Florida hospital. No hugs, just tears over Zoom and Facetime. It's a heart-wrenching thing to have a loved one slip away from life under these circumstances.

I got as deeply involved in understanding her condition as her doctors and nurses had time for, which wasn't that much. It was enough though that I could discuss the best courses of action with my cousins and my friend Roger. My sister and I did whatever we could to be our aunt's best possible advocate. We kept asking about the Remdesivir and the convalescent plasma. I watched DeSantis on the news announce that Florida was receiving a shipment of Remdesivir, and an hour later, her nurse told us that she had finally received it. I never did discover the reason for the delay of the convalescent plasma, but surely there are shortages. Each new prescription required my aunt's consent, but her COVID-induced disorientation and paranoia made every medical discussion a lengthy battle. My sister and cousin and I had to get on the phone with her to explain and convince, multiple times per treatment.

We all made an effort to avoid even saying "ventilator." The nature of military missions inspires a certain callousness. When I finally did use that word, I said it to my aunt as though I had told her to *take the hill,* as in, "Be a good soldier and take that hill." She was only to spend a few hours on the vent, passing late in the middle of the night. My sister and I were conferenced in at that moment, near enough to fully appreciate the anguish, much too far to offer sufficient comfort.

Victims' families can curse the technology for what it can and cannot do, we can curse the physicians and staff and medicine as a whole for the same, we can certainly curse the virus for its cruelty. In the end, a lost loved one is a lost loved one. Once the sanctity of life has been stolen away, the other stuff no longer matters.

The funeral was no easier than the hospitalization or the death. Traditions reaching back millennia have to adapt to this new normal. Zoom burial, Zoom service, my sister and I delivering Zoom eulogies, our kids offering sweet and touching electronic remembrances. It's a lonely tribute, staring back at your own image on a laptop despite the hundred or so in attendance because my Zoom settings were wrong. But I had gotten the final word, I told my aunt and everyone else. "I'm the real black sheep of the family."

The moment ended in a cumbersome sentiment, saying good-byes to friends and relatives without a touch or a thank-you for coming. Not even an elbow bump.

* * * * *

After being as careful as possible with my aunt's personal effects that I had to retrieve from the hospital, John and I are just starting to have some symptoms of a cold. It is an odd thing, as no one in the house has been sick this year, and I've barely been out of the house all week. I am not so concerned about my health as I am too young to be in a high-risk group, but I am not eager to discover how John's abnormal and compromised immune system will respond.

Meanwhile, John has yet to recover from the several days of forgotten medicine. Recovery from illness can be a crooked, jagged line. The Philadelphia hospital finally offered us an appointment, and we decided to take it.

* * * * *

Death is an intimate thing when it gets too close, and it has gotten too close to too many of us. No one in their right mind wants to risk getting on death's radar screen, in exchange for a hamburger or to watch a movie or go to a political rally. What kind of parent will send their kid to school for an education in human mortality? Since my aunt's passing, I find myself incensed by those who fail to take this pandemic seriously.

Politicians that had never made life and death decisions were initially ill-equipped to successfully lead their constituents through this crisis. Well, our politicians have experience now. Some of them have been learning, and their voters are benefitting from this new wisdom with lower infection rates in their respective territories. One can only hope that those politicians who have failed to gain wisdom from the carnage receive a proper education at the polls.

Rebuttal

There are genuinely two sides to every story—even a story as one-sided as this one. Some people have said, "But wha, wha, what about the Democrats? What have they offered?"

This criticism is valid. Although Democrats instituted quarantines ahead of Republicans, they could have saved more lives with even earlier quarantines, as I indicated in my criticism of Governor Cuomo. Trump was ahead of some Democrats on the Chinese travel ban, though again, the ban was happening with or without him. By the time Trump called for the European ban, no Democratic politicians disagreed.

Initially, as quarantines took effect, the Republican inclination to permit local governments to set local restrictions was the correct call. Rigid national restrictions, blind to disparate features such as population density and public transportation profiles, do not make sense. More recently, Republican governors violated that dogma by preventing city and county governments from instituting restrictions in the face of soaring local infection rates.

Criticism by itself, in its purest form, should never be seen in an ill light. It is only when we examine our failures that we can make the greatest improvements. This is the only way to truly become *great*. Problems arise when the criticism comes mixed with partisan smears or any other agenda not related to the success of the Republic. I am not a Democrat. I think the country can only benefit from some measure of intelligent Republican governance. It is not my fault that any place I find mistakes made by Democrats, there are equal or larger mistakes made by Republicans.

My biggest criticism of the Democratic Party concerns its *early* failures to definitively present an opposing and more rational perspective. In a time of national emergency, politicians should take care to only undercut the leadership of those in power when absolutely necessary. As deplorable as the leadership from the president and Republican governors has been, it's been incumbent upon the leaders of the Democratic Party to at least put an oar in the water and try to steer us away from rocky rapids and waterfalls.

In every State of the Union speech and the overwhelming majority of major political moments, the party in opposition to the president presents their rebuttal—their idea of how the country should move forward. Speaker Pelosi and Minority Leader Schumer have been too silent throughout the pandemic for my taste, but in particular, early on they could have and should have been more vocal. Pelosi could have called for a congressional House task force and had briefings from actual scientists, as opposed to the daily shit-show offered by the administration. She could have passed legislation compelling the president to make greater use of the Defense Production Act. She could have passed legislation in the House compelling all government officials to wear masks in public when not social distancing. In short, the Democratic Party leadership should have done more to keep us off the rudderless-ship, hell-ride of the American COVID-19 response.

While legislation would not have been binding without McConnell, at least Pelosi and Schumer would have gotten everyone on record for where they stand. It's also possible that important legislation might have been passed with veto-proof majorities, though we must remember that in an emergency, the executive branch has substantially more power and can be far more nimble than Congress.

As for Joe Biden, he also got off to a slow start. Initially, most Democrats were primarily hoping only for Biden to stay healthy, so in that effort, so far so good. Biden had little to say early in the pandemic, but by June, he was making news with far better and more detailed plans than anything offered by the White House. That seemed to be when Trump's disapproval ratings soared. I would hope that both parties make note of this because for someone such as myself, and I know there are many out there like me. I don't care which party prevails just as long as the American people benefit. How many can genuinely say they are better off after 3.5 years of Trump?

Early in the pandemic, there was scientific uncertainty regarding public health. If Democrats made a bad call, they would have been severely punished. Politically, they concluded it was a better strategy to let Trump fall on his face, and then once the science was clear, they would aggressively punish the president's bad calls. I would argue, even in a strategic sense, it would have been better for Democratic leadership to get publicly vocal earlier. If Trump had through some miracle turned out to be right, then he and the Republicans would probably have won big anyway. I believe Democrats miscalculated the risk/reward calculation in not speaking up earlier.

That said, it would be an error of immense proportion for those who fall under a delusion of false equivalence. Republican murderous malfeasance amounts to mountains, relative to the molehills of Democratic silence.

What Might Have Been

A fundamental tenet of leadership is that good leaders don't divide, they unite. History teaches us that there were Nazi sympathizers in the United States before World War II, and I'd be willing to bet that few of them were FDR voters. Once FDR made his December 8th speech declaring war against Japan, short of the small number of conscientious objectors and devoted pacifists, you will be extremely hard-pressed to find a single American who failed to support our war effort. We won that one, by the way.

Trump campaigned on dividing America, though the roots of today's divisions are planted in the Gingrich era. Responding to Conservative frustration with the rapid pace of societal change, Gingrich initiated a scorched earth strategy of discrediting his political opponents at nearly any cost. Democrats responded with good governance, which ought to have been enough, but wasn't. Democrats face an inherent dilemma in that liberalism is philosophically designed to seek solutions of compromise, whereas Republicans have looked to intransigence for their strategic success. It could accurately be labeled asymmetric warfare. Strategically speaking, Republicans have also been more clever, more aspirational, and more devoted to long-term political success—not by executing winning policies, but by all other means possible. It should be noted that by financial metrics of stock market performance and unemployment, the country has historically performed substantially better under Democratic presidents.

Bill Clinton outsmarted the Republicans by meeting them somewhere close to the middle, racking up political and economic "wins." As president, Clinton had the bully pulpit and was better able to claim these wins as his own. When Obama took office, McConnell was not going to make the same "mistake." He was determined to deprive Obama of any and all wins, no matter the cost to the American people. He executed this strategy openly, furthering his party's agenda of inspiring public frustration with government while simultaneously depriving Obama of political victories.

The Obamacare fight is case in point. McConnell played the role of deal-breaker and successfully branded the new healthcare bill as "partisan" although it was copied almost exactly from Republican Governor Mitt Romney's healthcare program for Massachusetts. Republicans used it successfully as a wedge issue in 2010, and to some degree, the same arguments were successfully deployed in 2016 by the Trump campaign.

And here is where an impartial observer begins to see how democracy is hanging by a thread. Trump's assault on John McCain during the 2016 campaign, declaring he couldn't possibly be a war hero because he was shot down, should have been considered an assault on all military veterans. I cannot begin to explain the absurdity of Trump's comment, but I feel obligated to briefly highlight it because most people don't understand the nature of aerial combat. While it is true that there are better and worse combat pilots, *any* pilot (even the best in the world) can be shot down during combat. There are just too many variables out of a pilot's control.

The accuracy and dependability of equipment used in the sixties in combat aircraft often came down to vacuum tube technology. There is nothing in the public record to suggest that McCain was shot down due to any failure of airmanship. More to the point, once he was captured, he was tortured for months. When the Vietnamese attempted to use McCain for a propaganda win by offering him a chance to go home early because McCain's father was a high-ranking admiral, McCain refused the offer, subjecting himself to years of torture which would leave him permanently disabled. Had he accepted that offer, it would have demoralized American servicemen by demonstrating that treatment in the military was unfairly based upon family contacts. Instead, McCain's incredible personal sacrifice became a source of great inspiration as an example of American ethical and moral leadership. This likely impacted our standing in the world well beyond the footprint of the war. Though I don't care for some of his politics, and he is particularly inept at picking vice-presidential candidates, John McCain is one of the most heroic military figures in all of history. Questioning McCain's heroism is akin to questioning Jefferson's views on democracy.

Meanwhile, as McCain rotted away in a Vietnamese prison cell, Donald Trump was in some club in New York City watching hookers snort cocaine off each other's backsides. If my keyboard contained an indignant emoji, I would fill this page with it.

It appears Trump's insult did not sit well with McCain either. He waited until the best possible opportunity and in the middle of Donald Trump's first year in office, with a single thumb down gesture (though he might have used two if the Vietnamese hadn't crippled his other arm), handed Trump the worst political defeat possible. Had Trump prevailed in repealing Obamacare, there's no telling what political advantage he might have attained with the momentum of such a win. Instead, it stopped Trump in his tracks. And it all happened because Cadet Bone Spurs was ignorant enough to believe that he, the dodger of all responsibility and accountability, was better than McCain.

Biden has a distinct ideological advantage over Trump. It is easier for Democrats to extend olive branches across the political aisle, even to the annoyance of more Liberal Democrats. The result is that Democrats are better equipped to bring the country together in a crisis. As polarizing as she sometimes was, Hillary Clinton would have almost certainly brought the country together against COVID-19 in a way that Trump never could. The value of such cohesion would be a far more unified front in the public's understanding and handling of the pandemic. Greater cohesion would have meant less cover for dissenters. Science deniers would have been seen more as malcontents and conspiracists. Tens of thousands, if not more, would have been saved in just the increased mask usage that greater cohesion would have brought, even if the pandemic had been as badly mismanaged at the start, which it certainly wouldn't have been. Greater national cohesion would also have made it easier for Congress to pass legislation aimed at helping the American people. There would have been more confidence in our economy, resulting in fewer layoffs, and increased opportunities.

Don't get me wrong, it would have been far from *peaches and cream* with Clinton as president. The Right did despise her, after all. But there was civility between the parties in times before Trump that likely would have existed in his absence.

It cannot be emphasized enough that there was no room for the denial of science in our pandemic response. The LBJ administration was rightly blamed for much of the US military's failures in Vietnam because the administration micromanaged the war from the oval office. Rather than co-developing military objectives with military officials, and then delegating senior military leadership the necessary authority to achieve these objectives, LBJ's administration attempted to use the military as an expression of its own policies' needs.

In nearly all cases, getting in the way of experts doing what they are expert at doing is a losing strategy. When the American people put a President in charge, they expect that President to employ bona fide experts in developing relevant policies. Rarely would a senior-level official in any capacity of government or the commercial sector override the recommendations of his experts, and rarer still would this defiance of expert opinion proves to be an intelligent decision. Of course, this was a defining characteristic of Trump's *"I know more about winning a war than the generals" and, "I alone can fix it"* presidency.

Public health policies should have been developed, strange as it sounds, by public health officials. It is then the politicians' job to administer and legislate to support such policies. And though it is ultimately the responsibility of the president that the American people understand the government's policies, a smart President would designate his public health officials to communicate most relevant facts, only speaking directly to the American people on the most important, less technical of issues. Unfortunately, Trump views every single facet of the presidency in terms of how his position can best serve Donald J. Trump. The goal of task force briefings, or any of the president's appearances for that matter, are not to educate and inform the American people, but to enhance the "Trump" brand.

The Trump administration did have at its disposal, from the Obama administration, a pandemic response plan (playbook). It's a 69-page document that is available online, which details how the government should handle a virus-driven pandemic. The playbook does an excellent job explaining the nuts and bolts of what an appropriate public health response to SARS-CoV-2 ought to have been. It's a bit dry, but very educational if you want to understand all of the minutiae that could (and should) have been done but wasn't.

I have yet to see a numerical analysis of how things might have been different had this guide been followed to the letter, though I'm sure there will eventually be numerous such assessments. My view is that if Obama's pandemic response team and the Chinese CDC team had been left in place and the pandemic playbook been followed, we would have had as much as a 10% chance of containing the virus entirely in China. Had that effort not been successful, I believe that in the US, we could have limited total deaths to less than 20,000 and total infections to five hundred thousand. By June 2020, we would have had our economy almost entirely open. Of course, had we been operating in close cooperation with strategic allies, we might have better-shared resources and may have been able to keep infection rates and the death rate even lower.

The thing is, I can hand someone who has never flown an airplane a manual and checklist, but that doesn't mean I would let that person fly my houseplants around. If our task force leader, Mike Pence, had been handed the pandemic playbook, he might have had no more idea of what to do with it than my dog would have been able to fly an airplane with a checklist hanging from his collar. I was not surprised when Trump's attempt to run an airline ended in colossal failure (as did nearly everything else he has ever attempted).

Bring your people together to achieve a common goal, empower your experts, give them the tools they need for success, and create and leverage strategic partnerships to your advantage. This is all leadership 101 stuff, but Trump doesn't seem to understand any of it.

COVID – 19 and SARS-CoV-2

We have had novel viruses in recent years; we've even had novel coronaviruses. What made SARS-CoV-2 different from the beginning was that it can shed (spread) for days before an infected person shows symptoms. The disease that is caused by this virus, COVID-19, has shown itself to be unique in several ways. Although it first appeared to be a disease of the respiratory system, we now understand it to be as much or more a disease of the circulatory system. As such, it can affect any part of the body. Autopsies of COVID-19 victims frequently show tiny blood clots in every internal organ.

There remain peculiarities that we still don't fully understand. Pulmonary dysfunction associated with COVID-19 can drive oxygen saturation (the percentage of oxygen carried in the bloodstream relative to maximum capability) to extremely low levels, but there is often no commensurate respiratory drive. In other words, COVID victims don't feel out of breath when they should. A patient could be close to death due to lack of oxygen delivery, but they are otherwise comfortable and not gasping for breath. We've never seen this in any other disease, and researchers and doctors don't fully understand why we're seeing it now. Our drive to breathe is not caused by lack of oxygen but by increased levels of carbon dioxide in the blood. The problem likely lies in disease-driven dysfunction in the alveolar capillaries.

Also odd for a deadly disease is the large number of people who catch it, have no symptoms at all, and yet still infect others. After six months of discussion and research, it still is not known why or how this is (though there are plausible theories). We still don't know the percentage of asymptomatic carriers or how many people they are infecting. Moreover, there are wide disparities in the severity and lethality of the disease.

Any coordinated response to COVID-19 should have been designed with the disease's unique characteristics in mind. It's a bad time to have a large number of science deniers in our population. As such, the government should have been taking steps to attain the most accurate information possible, and then disseminated this information to the population. We have been doing almost the exact opposite. As it relates to disease spread, having a well-educated population could have dramatically reduced the spread of infections. As for what to do with science deniers, I think I'm going to have to leave that as a challenge to the reader.

As far as available treatment options, it has been less important to keep the public fully educated, but certainly, having the nation's physicians up to speed on the best-known treatments and medicines should have been one of our highest priorities. Unfortunately, existing information channels in the medical community are based upon old paradigms and are not well-suited to current times. From early in the year, it was clear that the medical community needed a central repository of reliable information. Before I started writing this book, I was working on exactly that—trying to create a system that could accumulate all the data on COVID patients and the treatments that were working and failing.

The idea is that any practitioner would be able to access a compiled explanation of this data and view statistically what would be the best treatment option for, say, an 81-year-old woman with no comorbidities, experiencing elevated inflammation markers. Such a database system could be used by physicians to offer tailored, optimized treatment for everyone. Because of the huge number of COVID-19 infections, and the fact that patients were experiencing the disease across such a large spectrum, such a system would rapidly accumulate enough data to be useful. I am certain, even today, that such a system would save many lives throughout the world—not just for COVID-19, but for many other complicated conditions.

In general terms, COVID-19 represents a new paradigm or a "new normal." Our responses should adapt. Centralized political control permitted all other first-world countries to quickly change norms. Masks were mandated, quarantines obeyed. The American (small r) republican system makes the task of changing norms a task akin to herding cats. Before even considering the effects of the Trump presidency, America could be considered culturally and structurally ill-adapted to deal with this crisis. That has to be considered as part of the explanation for our widespread nonsensical behavior.

Paradoxically, America is also the innovation and creativity center of the world. New challenges call for new solutions and these have historically originated in America. At least, these have arisen under the auspices of American leadership. Some of that system is in desperate need of repair, to say the least, but the American creativity machine can still function. We need to attack this "new normal" with a fresh look at the problem.

I've already discussed taking a new approach to medical ethics by lowering safety thresholds for medical research. This is a position being somewhat cast in the light of the upcoming election. It should rather be considered within the context of keeping the greatest number of people healthy and alive. Do you agree?

If we can accept the moral and ethical quandary of sending our young off to die in a foreign land to save American lives at home, would it be no worse to let volunteers at home infect themselves with live virus in the name of medical research? It was not long ago that we conscripted draftees into the military and shipped them away to die.

The medical community has moved the goalposts of medical ethics in the correct direction, permitting several therapies and research programs under aggressive emergency authority, though medical ethicists have objected strongly. Authoritarian countries have been acting even more aggressively. It's easier for countries with a history of subjugating the rights of the individual for the greater good of a nation. China, for example, has already vaccinated their military. I don't think we need to subjugate individual rights. We just need to be a little more flexible in permitting volunteers to endanger themselves for the greater good, which is what young men have done throughout history when waging war and doing other things.

Unfortunately, the president's history of breaking political norms is making the notion of breaking other well-established norms additionally challenging. Typically, the country has dragged out the war metaphor to rally support in favor of a change. The war on drugs brought about new banking restrictions, huge increases in spending for counter-drug operations, and far longer jail sentencing for drug-related offenses. The war on terror brought about huge changes in airport security and a see-something say-something mindset that extends to all public gatherings. Such war cries have come from the Right, so it's a natural inference that the Right side of the electorate responds positively to this line of thinking. It's conceivable that if President Trump had offered this simple message from the start that, "America, is at war against COVID-19. We must all do our patriotic duty to wear masks and maintain social-distance," that the same element of society that now eschews masks would be the first ones out there telling mask offenders to put masks on. Unfortunately, within Donald Trump's *me-centered* mind, he reached the point of saying, "I'm a war-time President," but never managed to extend the metaphor to get anyone besides himself to envision *the country at war*.

With Trump, at absolutely every moment, it is simply always about him. And ironically, because he commands the bully-pulpit (for now) and because he can play the role of broken cog in the machine, inhibiting all normal operations even remotely related to national policy, even the notion of establishing new norms to fight against a novel virus must include Donald Trump in the discussion. Like a hopeless, violent alcoholic father who destroys any possibility of a normal family life, the American family is beholden to his sickness, at least until we are brave enough to vote ourselves free.

Epidemiology

You only have to watch a pandemic horror film to realize that contagious disease will grow exponentially when left unchecked. Without aggressive early action, a novel disease can quickly explode into a full-grown pandemic, so epidemiology focuses first on stopping the disease as early and quickly as possible. That necessitates investments in money and personnel long before the virus is first seen. Then once it is, aggressive action has to be taken as early as possible. We did none of these things and it has cost us dearly.

Nothing happens in a vacuum, so at some level of disease, people begin to self-correct – alter their behavior to reduce contagion. In many cases, these corrections have taken the form of state and local actions where the federal government failed to properly execute its mission. It must be understood that the federal government has scientific, financial, and even structural advantages over the states that make it the logical governmental entity for most of what's been needed in our pandemic response. The federal government's failure to act may eventually be viewed as criminal, but at least, other governmental entities have made an effort to take up the slack.

One problem with COVID-19 has been, how do you alter the behavior of contagious individuals, when no one knows who they are? Skeptics have been saying that this is the first time in history that healthy people have been quarantined. Let's pretend for a moment that this is true. I explained that everyone must presume they have this disease and behave accordingly.

Not enough Americans understand this pandemic in the way they should. This enduring ignorance is a failure of leadership. It is the political leadership's job to learn from the experts and then convey all necessary information to the public, either directly or through proxy. Since the public's cooperation is so important, they simply must be taught what to do. And if we want people to behave appropriately, they need to understand why.

Governor Cuomo took on this challenge to some degree, but he was ultimately preaching to the converted. The message needed to get out to the non-believers. With some Republicans, the message is only now starting to be heard. Unfortunately, pressure from the Republican base will be fighting with full force against certain responsible actions—even though roughly 70% of the country wants the government to proceed responsibly and with caution. If there was ever a good argument to repair the toxicity of the political primary process, this is it. We have institutionalized tyranny by the minority. That at least, we have down to a science.

Epidemiological response is an exercise in logistics as much as anything. The American government has tremendous expertise and resources in logistics, but wc've let many of these resources go idle. Trump wanted to engage tens of thousands of troops in a parade to honor… wait for it…Donald Trump. While we did employ some small number of federal military members to fight COVID-19, those small numbers appear to be only a fraction of that envisioned by Trump for his parade. Kind of puts his priorities in perspective, doesn't it?

The Defense Production Act (DPA) has been the biggest mistake. I've yet to see a sufficient explanation as to why the president has barely employed the DPA (except to obtain some small amount of PPE and ventilators). Perhaps it comes down to that profit-oriented mindset. No one should have to die for the failure to have enough paper PPE or even ventilators. The President believes that expenditures for any amount of equipment beyond what is necessary is wastage. He doesn't understand that is not how medicine is practiced. Medicine calls for safety margins that are by definition wastage. We all want the government to be good stewards of our money, but wastage is necessary for many effective enterprises. None of us eat every bit of food that goes into our refrigerators. Only the most foolish of us would want our doctors giving us chloroquine because somebody failed to purchase enough Remdesivir, but I would bet my car that it was happening in some places.

The President should have been doing everything in his power, DPA or otherwise, to keep our hospitals properly supplied. We have had the opposite, with states having to bid against each other for supplies. The President should have been doing everything possible to keep the hospitals staffed. That has been happening mostly without him, but there are things the government could have been doing, like recruiting more retired healthcare workers in hard-hit areas to assist with low (COVID-19) exposure tasks. Additionally, the US government could assist with temporarily relocating healthcare workers that have been laid off due to COVID restrictions in areas where there is little viral proliferation. With so many non-emergency medical procedures halted due to COVID, too many hospital workers are out of work.

The testing issue has been a failure on all counts. It's just not that complicated, and the fact that HHS has mismanaged this, where other countries have not, is a huge red flag indicating the need for staff changes at the highest levels. If more money needs to get spent to fix the test problem, it needs to get spent. Then testing would drive disease detection which would drive contact tracing—the way it's supposed to work and has worked to great success in other countries. Ultimately, these investments get quickly returned many times over.

Finally, though the president announced an appropriate plan for reopening the economy, politicians needed to be highly disciplined in making sure that if certain statistics were exceeded, reopening activities got scaled back. Governor Cuomo and the Northeastern states appear to have handled this far more appropriately than the rest of the nation.

And of course, let the experts – the epidemiologists – do their jobs. In most circumstances, they should make medical and scientific decisions and be principally involved in educating and briefing the public.

International Considerations

Humans seek out friendships because it's instinctual to do so, but it became instinctual due to evolutionary pressure. Throughout history, friendship has been a necessary component of survival. Countries aren't guided by the same needs as their human components, but friendship is and has been a necessary ingredient of the survival of nations throughout history.

As any wise person knows, the true value of a friend is revealed, not in good times, but in times of crisis. 2020 was a year when we genuinely needed to have cooperation and understanding between nations. In mid-February, the stock market started dropping due to COVID concerns. Businesspeople understood what was happening, but politicians inside and even outside the US were slow to act. Governments should have initiated international discussions and began making plans for a temporary ban on international travel in early February, at the latest. It's true, this would have been challenging. The economic pressures to avoid closing borders were immense, but the more responsible businesspeople would have understood. A strategic short hit to the bottom line is better than a lengthy hit any day. For those businesspeople who didn't understand, we expect from our politicians that they fight for the greater good of their constituents as a whole—not just business interests.

Long before the virus was widespread, governments should have started making plans to smoothly repatriate their citizens with the help of customs, immigration, and other relevant governmental entities. Then as it became clear at the end of February that the virus was crossing borders, governments should have started limiting the "slots" for international air travel. This would have forced the airlines to cancel some flights, accomplishing two things: It would have signaled to tourists that discretionary international travel was a particularly bad idea that might leave travelers stranded. And it would have gotten people traveling home earlier to avoid a "rush" to return home. Instead, we had a hasty end to international travel that drove panic, confusion, and ultimately much more viral spread. And unbelievably, even for the Trump administration, Homeland Security was at that time playing political games by suspending the global entry program to New York residents in retaliation for New York's sanctuary city policies. Global entry is used to rapidly speed international travelers through customs and immigration, but with New Yorkers unable to use the program, inbound customs lines became lengthy, crowded COVID-19 incubators. The DHS shenanigans helped seed the initial outbreak in New York, costing many lives.

Of course, there were many other reasons why we should have increased international cooperation—from the sharing of science to potential coordination of resources to developing creative solutions to limit the impact of travel bans, to planning out the administration of vaccines. Many countries are now contending with simultaneous economic crises and posing unprecedented challenges that can best be faced with the help of worldwide coordination.

Every country has vested interests throughout the globe. Unfortunately, before SARS-CoV-2, we had already partly isolated ourselves from the remainder of the civilized world. Our improved relations with Turkey, Saudi Arabia, and North Korea have hardly been worth the degradation of relations with modern technological countries such as Germany and China, particularly regarding COVID-19.

Finally, concerning the World Health Organization, despite its failings in coping with COVID-19, they provide a real and valuable service to the world's health and continue to aid in the fight against this virus. Particularly in the time of a pandemic, their resources should have been buttressed so that they might have improved their performance. But of course, Trump did the opposite, ordering a complete defunding of the organization.

If you wanted to use a baseball team as a metaphor for our pandemic response, the CDC would have been our pitcher, running the show, with the WHO as shortstop—an integral part of the team. If you have no one to replace him, why would you get rid of your shortstop and leave a major hole in your infield? If he bobbles a few balls, have your second and third baseman back him up better. Make him practice between innings, but don't send him away. And just to extend this metaphor, Trump would be the manager. If the pitcher is retiring batters, there's no reason to see the guy. Even if the pitcher starts throwing crap, and the manager has to pull him, He comes out, hands the new pitcher the ball, and disappears. He doesn't make himself the pitcher.

Economics

It is inconceivable that you could have the economic engine of the United States of America as a resource and not get the job (any job) done. Yet here we are. We beat the Nazis. We went to the moon, invented the computer, the internet, and GPS. Today's failures would not be nearly so striking if we couldn't point to over 200 other countries that have handled COVID better than us. That's the irony and the lesson. Countries far poorer than the US are performing better financially than we are today. The secret, such that it is, for all these other countries, is that they have worked to solve the health problem first.

Just as the economic problem cannot be repaired first, addressing most problems becomes complicated with citizens in impeding or actual personal financial crises. The government has numerous tools to mitigate the adverse economic effects of the virus. State and local governments within the US and abroad have been opening their purse strings and breaking into rainy-day funds. In reality, most of the money has been borrowed, but there's been little other choice. It's been raining. Bigly.

International coordination of central bank policies has become a tenet of successful efforts to reverse worldwide economic downturns. Substantial differences in economic policy between trading partners create systemic imbalances which in the short term might seem to advantage specific countries but in the long term proves to be net negative—reinforcing the need for coordination and cooperation. Capital infusions should be tailored specifically to existing challenges.

Three simultaneous economic crises must be addressed:

1) Citizens are either unemployed or underemployed in numbers unseen since the Great Depression.

2) Specific industries including but not limited to travel, entertainment, and restaurants/bars have all been impacted beyond the rest of the economy.

3) The net effect of the first two crises is a pervasive decrease in economic activity and GDP contraction with secondary effects on all industries and segments of the economy. Without substantial government intervention, businesses and individuals who are faring well today can eventually expect to share in the economic pain.

The first congressional stimulus bill addressed the above economic predicaments well, but was executed poorly and too generous to corporate interests. Individuals were given supplemental unemployment benefits so that many, though certainly not all, have been able to pay for living expenses, at least until the end of July 2020. Adversely affected businesses were also given money to pay their bills, including employee salaries. Congress rightly tied business stimulus to jobs. Companies taking government money have been prohibited from laying off employees before September 30.

As you can see, if you fix the first two crises, the third one is addressed by default. If you assume that the public health problem is temporary, such that consumer demand returns as the health crisis ends, you end up with an economic prognosis that is fairly positive in the medium to long term. Despite incredibly high unemployment that might otherwise be associated with a depression, the US and other stock markets are close to (and in some cases above) all-time highs. We'll be wise to appreciate, though, that investors can sometimes be an overly optimistic lot.

Of course, we don't know if the public health problem is temporary. In the US, we know the pandemic will extend beyond September, but the bigger story could end up being a slower than expected end to the health crisis, if vaccinations become delayed, either to technology or public reluctance. So, if Congress does not extend unemployment benefits beyond July, we will have two brand-new problems:

1) A rapid increase in poverty with all of its accompanying problems of increased crime, worsened health, and increased civil unrest. Combined with the cessation of normal school schedules, the adverse effects on education and health outcomes would be felt for years to come.

2) A significant negative impact on GDP will be spread across all industries due to reduced demand in all sectors.

3) The permanent shuttering of numerous businesses where even in the face of a return to normal demand, the costs to reopen their doors will be too high.

Our political leaders must also understand that there are economic costs tied to each new infection. Hospital and missed work expenses are obvious. More subtle is the fact that as infection numbers rise, people start staying home and spending less. As a medical breakthrough is unlikely before late in the year, the government needs to do absolutely everything in its power to reduce the spread of viral infection. Unsurprisingly, almost every government in the world seems to understand this.

Since the days of Reagan's deficit spending, the markets have been fairly tolerant of new US government debt with minimal adverse effects to the US economy. New government expense must still overcome a certain amount of political inertia. At some point, though, these loans will begin weighing down the economy. Simply servicing the interest on our public debt is beginning to get close to matching the government's entire budget for discretionary programs. Legitimate economic concerns are nevertheless a red herring. If we don't spend the money now, it will cost us even more in the future.

Fiscal realities put new pressure on our politicians to be good stewards of the public coffers. Though the March 2020 congressional stimulus bill achieved its objectives, it did contain serious flaws:

1) The execution of the disbursement of funds was awful. It's not like the government has never disbursed funds before. It should have been better handled. Still, they managed to write a $3 trillion bill in a few weeks, so it could have been mangled worse.
2) The targeting of funds was poor.
   a. Too many people were unable to get their checks on time.
   b. Too many small businesses were not approved.
   c. Too many larger businesses who weren't substantially impacted received funds.
   d. Stimulus was insufficient for some individuals' expenses.
   e. Too much was paid to others such that many employees were dis-incentivized from returning to work (though that was not inherently a bad thing – certain employees who are high-risk for serious complications due to COVID should not be returning to work, if such work involves substantial public contact. They should instead be replaced by lower-risk individuals until the end of the health crisis).

Just as employers and employees were incentivized in certain directions, the government could have incentivized states in the initial bill to reduce the level of infections in their jurisdictions. Of course, we are doing the opposite. Considering the dire importance of public health, the nation's economic engine, which is badly in need of pulling a greater load, should have quickly been unleashed on the medical problem. This brings us back to the DPA, which is an excellent vehicle to compel companies to serve the public in times of crisis. Companies could have been producing PPE, testing supplies, ventilators, and other healthcare commercial goods, which would have required them to hire new workers in some instances. This would have been a quintessential, win-win government success, but it happened at a scale, orders of magnitude too small.

*   *   *   *   *

The novel nature of these simultaneous crises makes clear that the most optimal solutions would be derived by wiping the slate clean of previous paradigms of government intervention and tailoring results to the crises of our times. Of course, this would be a time-consuming process, and the nature of the emergency did not afford governments the luxury of much time; however, there is little evidence that the US government made any effort to develop creative solutions to the problem. It wouldn't have taken much time to consider a few options. For instance:

1) Create a new paradigm of survival mode. What expenses must individuals fulfill?
   a. Mortgage or rent
   b. Food
   c. Utilities
   d. Automotive expenses
   e. Basic entertainment
   f. Other

If the ultimate goal was to minimize foreclosures and food insecurity at the lowest reasonable cost to the government, unemployment insurance could have been better tailored to individual needs. The food stamp programs could have been expanded. Utilities could have received direct grants from the government. Instead, we remained stuck in the old paradigms of our existing social safety net.

2) When restaurants shut their doors, the lost business drove some farmers to literally shovel crops back into the ground. Meanwhile, people had lost incomes and were struggling to put food on their tables when the government's stimulus checks failed to materialize. Farmers could not get the resources to get their wasted food out to the needy, yet there were unemployed truckers and others who could have been put to work. Food that could have been saved would have meant money that could have been contributed to some other segment of the economy. This is the kind of waste indicative of nonexistent leadership.

3) Where possible, the nation's relevant assets should have been inventoried, and our requirements compiled, so that all important needs were met to the maximum extent possible. Capitalism is a great tool for deriving optimized pricing and production. In an emergency, though, for which COVID-19 certainly qualifies, some level of centralized control has clear benefits. We know where many of the bottlenecks and inefficiencies exist and can work around them. The government could have developed public-private partnerships to better leverage stimulus funding and overall public outcomes. Possibilities for such partnerships could have involved:

   a. Getting food to kids (from economically disadvantaged families) who typically receive their food nutrition from school.
   b. Delivering full online education capability to disadvantaged students, to include hardware, software, and internet access.
   c. Delivering online education (and general internet capability) to adults living in remote access areas.

d. IMPROVED TESTING AND CONTACT TRACING!

At least during good times, taxpayers become understandably annoyed when fellow citizens receive government money to sit at home, and businesses receive government money without providing goods or services in exchange. For the existing crisis, such infusion has been necessary to keep the economy on life support as well as minimizing social strife. Fire-bombing the economy with dollars is a blunt and imperfect instrument. It would have been better to expend stimulus funds and receive something tangible for the taxpayers. Even if the suggestions above work poorly or not at all, they would still be no worse than what we did, which was giving away public money for absolutely nothing in return. We simply have this ideological opposition toward permitting the government to take on new roles in participating in the economy.

There is a good reason for that though. Every time the government establishes itself in a commercial enterprise, it sets up a new relationship with new interests. Unfortunately, because of Citizens United, it has become 100,000 times easier to lobby Congress to perpetuate programs well beyond their useful lifespans. Everyone in Washington understands this, so they set the bar high in establishing any new governmental relationships, ignoring the source of the problem. A far better solution would be to fix Citizens United.

Just to reiterate one of the most important recommendations from this book, as we spend trillions of dollars in taxpayer money with no expectation of anything in return, we could stimulate the vaccine industry with some of that "free money." We could *purchase* something incredibly valuable, like an earlier end to the pandemic, in return. We need a Cabinet of intelligent people to be able to present these kinds of solutions to the president and Congress.

Government doesn't have a great track record for arriving at optimal solutions. Few countries throughout history have handled well the problem of reassigning excess capacity to mission-critical economic activity in the face of a crisis. The US during WWII and present-day China stand as notable examples. Structurally, today's American economy is lightyears away from either of the above examples, but it's primarily a lack of imagination and political will (and intelligence and competence) that stands in the way of activating our economy to improve our pandemic response.

In years to come, our economic problem, along with all of the other failures surrounding this pandemic, should be studied in earnest. We can and should do better next time. In this light, such future solutions should be, when possible, developed with buy-in from both political parties. It would be easy to chastise the Obama administration for developing their pandemic playbook independent of Republican input but for the following: *medicine, public health, and science are not, and were not, partisan issues under Obama*!

There may be ideological differences in the level of resources various administrations would devote to address these challenges, but the nature of the problems, and in general terms what should be done to address them, OUGHT NOT BE PARTISAN!

Ultimately, good leaders make the best hands with the cards they're dealt. Donald Trump was handed four aces on Inauguration Day, and he has traded them all away. If he is expert at anything at all beyond self-promotion, it is the ability to trade away a great hand for a poor one. He is, in every way, the worst possible president.

The Future – Why I am a Fan of Friedrich Nietzsche

August 20, 2020: At the beginning of this journey I explained how I was guided by my father's words, "If you can't laugh, you'd have to cry." Well…I can't laugh. Not at this. Not at what we've done and what we are becoming. Humor is survival, especially when everything else has been taken away. Elie Wiesel and other Holocaust survivors told jokes, and they survived. If you ask me, that's pretty damn close to a superpower.

Those of us left behind can't laugh. We can add humor to the list of things stolen away from us in 2020. But humor is not the only means of survival, and there are other forms of power. This November, you and I have the power to repair some of what is broken. What will you do with that power? Whatever you decide, please do it quickly.

The country's addict and even more, his addiction are doing everything they can to run the show. It takes families time to figure out how to extricate the addict's ill effects. Hopefully no more than four years for this family. Addicts are oddly predictable in some ways and entirely unpredictable in others. They will reliably do everything they can to feed their addiction. In Trump's case, the intense levels of attention he has become addicted to are dependent upon him remaining in office. He suspects he will lose a fair election, so we can expect he will do anything possible to prevent one. He will likely fail at cheating to win as history shows he's only occasionally shown himself to be a skilled cheater. We can expect that he will do everything he can to discredit election results in advance of legitimizing his hope to remain in office, even after losing.

He is not a particularly brave person. Addicts usually aren't. They are so beholden to their cravings that they avoid anything that may threaten their addiction, which physical harm and death tend to do. But like a cornered animal, they can attack aggressively if their habit is threatened. I doubt that he has anywhere near enough support at the senior leadership level of the military to successfully execute a coup. I believe Republican Party leaders will eventually make it clear to Trump that he won't be able to have his way.

Regrettably, codependents will go to unexpected lengths to facilitate their addicts' wayward needs. I would not be surprised to see some theatrics in the White House come Inauguration Day. Trump will want to go out with a bang of some sort. He will certainly attempt to negotiate for himself a blanket pardon, and we should all hope he fails. He has broken an extraordinary number of laws and is responsible for an extraordinary level of carnage. President Ford pardoned Nixon to heal the country's wounds and divides. I don't believe that is applicable in Trump's case. The president's supporters will not appreciate Trump in jail, but they will ultimately come to respect that US laws are being enforced.

* * * * *

COVID-19 will not be the last earth-changing crisis we face. Climate scientists have been shouting from the rooftops that a cataclysm is coming, and if nothing is done about climate change soon, the loss of life and wealth due to COVID-19 will seem quaint in comparison. What makes climate change even more dangerous is that it is moving far slower than COVID-19. Instead of a car that takes two months to stop when you step on the brakes, climate change is a car that takes 25 years to stop. Fortunately, polls indicate that a majority of Americans accept the realities of climate change. They believe it when scientists tell us that there is a cliff some 30 years in our future, and we only have a few years to step on the brakes before it's too late. But we will have to find our collective power if we hope to squash the voices of those formidable special interests that stand in the way of a *green* economy.

The challenges to COVID-19 look similar, in terms of the denial of science and the rejection of expert knowledge, tribal forces successfully influencing people to act against their own interests. There are complex problems with simple solutions that are discounted because people have the illusion that they understand the nature of the problem when instead they are ignorant of its realities and unwilling to educate themselves. The optimist within me clings to the possibility that COVID-19 will teach us important lessons. We know it won't kill us. Will it make us stronger?

The overarching story may well be American intransigence against concern for our fellow citizens. This shouldn't come as a shocking revelation. Americans are known for our independence. We are taught to depend upon ourselves beyond all others, to pull ourselves up by our bootstraps, and to successfully make our way in the world. These partly Conservative, red-state values remain popular in Hollywood and other pop culture as defining characteristics of American ideals, enjoying broad acceptance among people from all walks of life. Unfortunately, these qualities, once combined with the me-centered characteristics of today's "selfie" culture, result in an ethos of inhumanity and ultimately a disregard for the sanctity of life.

Anthropologists tell a story that the way they discover the origins of civilizations is by looking for healed human femurs. The femur or thigh bone is the biggest bone in our body. Someone who breaks their femur cannot walk for at least a month. Hopping would cause unbearable pain. Such an injured person cannot get food or water for themselves. They cannot even retreat from their own waste, and they certainly cannot protect themselves from predators.

I was unfortunate enough to have broken my femur at age 15. It took me five weeks in the hospital before I was able to bear weight on that leg, and even then, that was only after the work of nurses, physicians, and physical therapists, not to mention the support of family and friends. Imagine what such convalescence would have required thousands of years before even basic Hippocratic medicine.

Only in a civilized culture where multiple people come together to care for someone so encumbered could a person survive with such an injury. No doubt, people understood the concept of indebtedness, but it's difficult to fathom the implementation of any sort of in-kind repayment. In a time before money, there could be no *loans* to facilitate a transaction that could compensate for the personal sacrifice and selflessness of multiple caregivers.

Humans are a rare breed. Psychological research makes clear we are instinctually predisposed to take pleasure in pleasing others, but we also have the cognition to recognize there can be benefits in doing others harm. In a time before currency, when one of the most valuable acquisitions attainable was the friendship of another in exchange for a favor, our ancestors took care of their own. Long before it was codified in organized religion, they recognized, that when you do unto others as you would want them to do unto you, everyone wins.

As I write this, in America and to be fair in some other countries, there are tens of millions who will not put on a mask, even though there's a small chance that this act may save another's life. Those I know who fall into this category, all the way up to President Trump and VP Pence, are the same people who *preach* we need to put God and prayer back in schools. Now they want to put COVID in schools so that they don't lose any more money. What religion do these people practice? I would argue God and prayer could not have possibly ever left schools, because we carry them in our hearts, not our hallways – at least that's where we should, in this man's view. I'm not Christian. How is it I seem to know more about the New Testament? Jesus went to the temple to overturn the money-changers' tables, not to ask them if the lepers were keeping away business. All I can say is that the next time you see one of these MAGA-hat wearing people with a crucifix and a WWJD bracelet, walking around in public without a mask, you might want to stand clear before something bursts into flames.

312

I tell my kids, it's simple to do the right thing when life is treating you well. It's easy when you have the money and resources for everything you need and most of what you want; when the people around you that you love, love you back; when your future looks bright and nothing in your past haunts you. I *preach* to my kids to seek wisdom in being mindful, respecting, and finding inspiration from those that don't have anything close to what many of us have, and yet day in and day out, manage to do the right things. And in those moments which are sure to come, when life is not treating you well, recall these words and the inspiration you take from others, and always do your best to do what is right. Our country needs every one of us, as much as it ever has before. We all need find our moral compasses and put them to use.

I am not so naïve to believe that we will never again elect a leader of such colossal incompetence, but I do hope, with the help of continued discussion, that we will have many successful years before doing so. Most US Presidents have been tested in ways that would make most of us fail. They have felt enormous stress and pressure to make decisions that were in the interest of our entire country. Despite their high station, they discovered wisdom and learned humility from the humblest among us— people of decency who put country and duty ahead of themselves.

The centers of power will always ebb and flow in every political system. Historically, when power and wealth have found themselves in the hands of the very few, it has led to dissatisfaction, political unrest, and instability—but it is frequently an evolution. We find ourselves in the early moments of just such a potentially harrowing journey. Resistance to such avarice of power is a function of how aggressive the grab for control becomes versus the ensuing dissatisfaction of the masses. It is rational to be fearful for the future of our country, not only from the threat of Donald Trump but of an environment that seems so ripe to welcome the saplings of fascism. The American experiment has consistently offered a robust defense against forces that would derail our journey away from a destination of greater good. To paraphrase Colin Powell, the American voter broke it; now they must fix it.

Donald Trump is everything his predecessors were not, and nothing of what they were. To serve your country in any manner, from being the lowliest private in the army to an elected politician in Washington (including the president), is an honor that also comes with responsibility. Any public servant who is not willing and able to accept the responsibility of their position has an outright obligation to immediately resign. How dare the president continue to occupy this highest office of the land with the lowest of mind, heart, and soul!

The presidency of Donald Trump, despite its many enormous failings and overall ineptitude, is an underappreciated cautionary tale. A person of greater competence and a talent for nurturing relationships with senior military officers could have easily plunged us into the depths of a fascist nightmare. With the hopeful expectation that the election process sends Donald Trump back to whatever hole he decides or is forced to hobble into, we will have to work harder than ever to buttress our defenses against the dangers of populism. In particular, the fight for control of valid information must be won by moderating forces. We need an army of patriots of reason and reasonableness to counterbalance and dare I say educate the segment of the political center that is prone to sway with the wind. J. R. Tolkien may have said it best in the words of the character of Galadriel: "The quest stands upon the edge of a knife. Stray but a little and it will fail to the ruin of all."

At some point, the American voter accepted a cancer into our body politic. Our only hope now is that the American voter has the cure.

Epilogue

October 2, 2020: Around 1 a.m. this morning, the president tweeted that he and the First Lady tested positive for the coronavirus. I belong to several social media groups whose themes involve voting the president out of office. It should not be a huge surprise in the context of today's environment that these groups have hosted smug commentary over the last 12 hours. I candidly confess that I participated in this commentary.

I'm troubled by my moral failings, though only mildly so. It's beyond dispute that the president has reaped what he has sewn. To put it even more bluntly, karma is a bitch. I nevertheless consider the president's new status bad news. It's my assessment that most of the potential outcomes are undesirable:

1) The most likely scenario is that the president and all affected staff have mild to no symptoms and emerge from their quarantines with boisterous *told you so* attitudes trumpeting their standing position that the virus is no big deal.

2) The president gets moderately sick, sending uncertainty into political and financial markets. Anything from attempts to delay the election to questions as to who is actually in charge of the country brings chaos to our government. Russia takes advantage of the situation and ramps up its military shenanigans against American targets. In a patriotic response and an odd offering of sympathy to someone incapable of this emotion, the president ekes out just enough support to win the election.

3) The president passes away. VP Pence is sworn in and immediately enacts admirable changes that the medical community has been begging for. In some combination of patriotism, sympathy for the Trump family, and appreciation for *President* Pence, the Trump/Pence ticket wins the election,

potentially delivering eight years of a Pence administration whereby our federal court system, to include the Supreme Court becomes a toxic 90% Conservative (I would say the same thing about a 90% liberal court system). Even with a Biden win, there's a certain unfairness if Trump were to die before the election. He and the entire world should bear witness to a humiliating Trump defeat at the polls so that it is clear to everyone that America has not entirely lost its moral compass.

4) I admit the most likely scenario is that the public views the incompetence of the Trump administration in a new light and votes them out with an even greater margin for victory. It should be mentioned in this context that four years ago, FBI Director Comey shed doubt on Hillary Clinton's suitability to be president because, in his assessment, she had been careless in her use of a private email server. Today, we bear witness to a president who has been careless with the health and administration of the entire Executive branch of government. Even a molehill/mountain comparison proves inadequate.

Meanwhile, the COVID positive diagnosis has me wondering if the president has any tennis players on his staff. *Never change a winning game, always change a losing game.* Before today, the polls were strongly in Biden's favor. Trump's only apparent plan was to continue with the same losing game. I can't help to wonder if we're now bearing witness to some sort of Hail Mary play. Lisa and I have been watching *Kobra Chai*, a clever Amazon Prime show that examines the present-day lives of several characters from the eighties classic, Karate Kid. Spoiler Alert: Against insurmountable odds, the smaller, weaker, less-experienced, and injured protagonist, Daniel, beats antihero, Johnny, using 'crane technique.'

Daniel's instructor, Mr. Miyagi, teaches him that the crane kick is indefensible. The thing is, the crane kick was ridiculous on all levels. It's not a move practiced by any martial artist; as a practitioner, I can tell you it offers no offensive advantage while leaving the person doing it undefended, and it just looks plain stupid. It failed on all levels, yet it worked for the movie. I only hope the Biden campaign takes nothing for granted. Meanwhile, I also hope that the president doesn't find out the hard way, that as with Herman Cain, a mask might have been more valuable than millions of dollars and more powerful than all other tools available the leader of the free world.

Afterword

Process defines the product as much in writing as anything else. You won't reach your destination on the wrong journey. This book grew organically out of extreme frustration with the failure of Donald Trump's leadership, which in fairness began well ahead of the coronavirus. But as I became witness to unprecedented negligence at the national level, I had to do something.

I was nowhere near alone. Across the nation, as I wrote, tens of millions of you marched and protested. Many of you were threatened, gassed, and beaten, and over 14,000 were arrested. Though the 2020 protest movement was rooted in frustration over racial injustice, how *you got there* was certainly driven by inept presidential leadership. These are confusing and fearful times to be sure, but we should all remember that countless heroes walk among us. In the face of scorn from the political right and small instances of violence that crept into the movement by some combination of misguided frustration and degenerate opportunism, you marched and you protested.

I suppose having been to war qualifies me to speak on the topic of heroism. Peaceful protestors along with the many first responders are all heroes in my book. The doctors, nurses, and paramedics receive the brunt of the praise, but every hospital is a mini-city with its own administrators and janitors, security, food workers, med techs, and dozens of other necessary professionals. Without the many support workers, the doctors and nurses can't save the rest of us. Without the bus drivers and other transportation workers, hospital staff and other essential workers can't even get to their jobs. Without supermarket workers, none of us would eat. Millions of Americans from all walks of life, at great risk and fear of personal peril, have kept the essential cogs and gears of our modern society moving. Heroes all. Despite my many concerns over the direction of our nation, I love it as much as I ever have. We are redeemable, and we are worth fighting for.

Except for a passing reference to George Floyd, I did not discuss the BLM movement, though I hope this afterword makes evident my respect. The 2020 leadership failures in healthcare and the 2020 BLM struggle are both worthy of careful examination. I did not want to dilute one of these stories by what would likely have been an inelegant effort to include the other.

I wanted to capture for posterity some notion of what it's been like to live through this pandemic. As I seem to be living what some would call an outlier's life, I figured seeing the crisis through my eyes would be as interesting as anyone else's, short of your favorite celebrities and athletes. Unfortunately, my experience became more relevant and tragic than I would have wished.

I thought it would also be of value to take the reader through a discovery process. I began writing in March 2020 with no knowledge of what fate had in store. Concerning the biology of the virus and the medicine to treat it, there have been a few meaningful surprises. No one realized at the outset that this virus would prove to be as much or more of a disease of the circulatory system than a respiratory illness. The variability in how this disease presents to different people has also been unexpected. The latest estimate is that 40% are symptomless, but that estimate continues to vary. There is even concern that the virus does hidden damage when no symptoms are apparent. One surprise we really didn't want to hear was that the virus' ill-effects can be awfully long. So we're still trying to nail down exactly what this virus does to its victims.

As far as treatment, I think the inadequacy of convalescent plasma eventually may turn into a bigger story. It should work better than it does. Figuring out why may hold important clues in better understanding the immune system. Monoclonal antibodies have been showing promise for months as the best potential treatment. Unfortunately, existing technology makes it difficult to produce these antibodies quickly. No costs have been announced, but costs for similar treatment can exceed $100,000 per dose. Trump has made out pretty well for $750 in taxes paid. He's also exceedingly lucky that he did not get sick sooner, as the trial for the Regeneron treatment he is taking only recently completed its 275 patient trial.

American intransigence to science and logic was for me the biggest surprise. I knew Trump was a science denier at heart, I knew he wasn't following the guidance of specialists, and I knew the level of devotion he inspires. I should not have been surprised by how all of this manifested. For better or worse, I tend to put too much faith in humanity. As vices go, this one isn't the worst.

Finally, Sweden confused me, and I'm still not certain what is happening there. Caseloads started increasing near the end of September, just as I forecast, but at a rate less than I expected. Given politicians' propensity to lie, my best guess is the Swedish government is understating the level of social distancing voluntarily in practice.

I had no idea, of course, the odd confluence of misfortune that would strike at the personal level. In verbiage that didn't make the final cut, I wrote that we are all part of the story. I also felt as I was writing, that the journey was part of the story. I felt compelled to memorialize an account of how events transpired—the sequence, how decisions and events evolved, and the way in which we all experienced the 2020 shit-show. If I have any regrets, I wish I'd carried the journal format, with dated chapter titles throughout.

French philosopher Blaise Pascal was probably the first to introduce the notion that, *If I had more time, I would have written a shorter letter.* (John Locke, Benjamin Franklin, and Mark Twain have all made the statement in their own words, but Pascal is believed to have said it first.) Being the contrarian that I am, I'm compelled to write that, if I had more time, I would have written a longer book. You may note that I have not included many public quotes, extensive external references, or a bibliography. Attribution requires additional research and time. Being on a tight deadline from the beginning, I wanted to release this book as soon as possible, so I discarded any non-mandatory tasks that would have taken longer.

In that light, unless otherwise noted, all observations and analysis is my own. If I had more time, I'd have gone into more extensive explanations of my analysis and conclusions. As my target is a general audience, I've worked to limit technical jargon and improve readability.

One cost of writing a journal is that it limits the tools available to structure the story for maximum entertainment and impact. Those are limitations of non-fiction in general, though I certainly would not have wanted any additional drama. There are countless more talented writers than me, but I can still write to emotional effect. I consistently tortured myself over how much emotion was appropriate in the accounts of my family. Not enough is boring and misses the point. Too much is tasteless and personally discomforting. I hopefully achieved an appropriate balance.

The political effects of the president's illness are yet to be seen. We might expect little movement from Biden or Trump supporters, as they all seem to be locked into their decisions. Of those few Americans who have yet to make a choice, some may settle upon Trump out of sympathy or what they believe to be patriotism. Others will pick Biden, concluding that if Trump can't take care of himself or the people closest to him, he is ill-suited to protect the country. How many people fall into each camp will soon be revealed.

It brings me no pleasure to deliver such a damning account of presidential malfeasance. America is well on its way to becoming a scattered mass of exposed nerve endings. We are living through a unique moment in history, though we should not fool ourselves into believing it is uniquely special. Our ancestors have lived through the big wars, pandemics, great floods, civil unrest, famines, mass migrations, and well... you get the picture. One hundred years from now, COVID-19 and Donald Trump will gain no more attention from school children than any other notable moments from other decades. But for those of us in the moment, the intensity of 2020 is palpable everywhere.

My one hope for the ending of this story is that science takes its rightful place as the guiding mentality of our decision-makers. I only see that happening in force if we elect Joe Biden to be our next President. And we give him a majority in the senate so that he can actually get things done.

Others have been through far worse than the current pandemic and emerged out the other side better and stronger. We can do the same if we just keep the faith. In science.

Acknowledgments

I'm first and foremost grateful to my wife, Lisa, who has been far more supportive of my many ambitions than I deserve. My kids have been my inspiration and my instructors. *John* continues to teach me about priorities, not to mention the many little-known capabilities of MS Windows. *Jim*, who owns and has read more books than any 21-year-old I can imagine, has been a wonderful sounding board. To my favorite daughter, *Mary*, I am grateful for her ability to bring Lisa back from the brink after I've neglected her for too long. I'm indebted to my dear friend Roger for his boundless education and friendship. I'm fortunate my cousin Steve has on many occasions helped me look smarter than I am. To those who've read for me, particularly Lynn, who gave detailed feedback on my last two books, and Ken, who was kind enough to offer conservative feedback, I am more than thankful. To Ellyn, thanks for helping spread the word. Last but certainly not least, thanks to CommunityAuthors.com for all your assistance. All errors in this document are entirely my own. I welcome corrections and any other feedback sent to dontdenyscience@gmail.com.